CONVERSATIONS with EDUCATIONAL LEADERS

SUNY Series, Frontiers in Education
Philip G. Altbach, editor

The Frontiers in Education Series draws upon a range of disciplines and approaches in the analysis of contemporary educational issues and concerns. Books in the series help to reinterpret established fields of scholarship in education by encouraging the latest synthesis and research. A special focus highlights educational policy issues from a multidisciplinary perspective. The series is published in cooperation with the School of Education, Boston College. A complete listing of the books in this series can be found at the end of this volume.

CONVERSATIONS with EDUCATIONAL LEADERS

Contemporary Viewpoints on Education in America

ANNE TURNBAUGH LOCKWOOD

State University of New York Press

Published by
State University of New York Press, Albany

© 1997 State University of New York

All rights reserved

Printed in the United States of America

For information, address State University of New York Press,
State University Plaza, Albany, NY 12246

Production by Christine Lynch
Marketing by Nancy Farrell

Library of Congress Cataloging-in-Publication Data

Lockwood, Anne Turnbaugh.
    Conversations with educational leaders : contemporary viewpoints
on education in America / Anne Turnbaugh Lockwood.
        p.   cm. — (SUNY series, frontiers in education)
    Includes bibliographical references (p.   ) and index.
    ISBN 0-7914-3287-4 (hc : alk. paper). — ISBN 0-7914-3288-2 (pb :
alk. paper)
        1. Education—Social aspects—United States. 2. Educational
leadership—United States. 3. Educational change—United States.
4. School management and organization—United States. I. Title.
II. Series.
LC191.4.L63 1997
370.19′0973—dc20   96-17472
                                                                              CIP

10 9 8 7 6 5 4 3 2 1

Contents

Acknowledgments

I extend my grateful appreciation to the educational leaders whose comments are included in this book, especially for their willingness to engage in this project, their generosity with their time, and their helpful suggestions for revisions and refinement.

I gratefully acknowledge the North Central Regional Educational Laboratory for granting permission to reprint the segment entitled "Dennis Williams: An Illustration of Reform," which appeared originally in their publication, *New Leaders for Tomorrow's Schools* (Winter 1995), entitled "The School Development Program: West Mecklenburg High School, Charlotte, North Carolina."

David Chawszczewski and I have enjoyed a long-time professional conversation about the topics featured in this book. I appreciate his willingness to engage in an ongoing dialogue with me and the spirit in which he offered his suggestions.

I would like to thank Kent D. Peterson for his original suggestion that I write this book, for his continuous and generous encouragement, and for his mentorship over the years.

Finally, I am indebted to my dear husband, Alan L. Lockwood. His kindness and constancy truly make all things possible for me—including, but not limited to, the writing of this book.

Introduction

This book grew out of nearly nine years of work at two University of Wisconsin—Madison research and development centers: the National Center on Effective Secondary Schools and the National Center for Effective Schools, respectively. My formal role at both centers was to disseminate research findings and news of exemplary practice through prose intended to engage the reader. Specifically, at both centers, I developed an ongoing series of national publications for diverse audiences composed of researchers, practitioners, and policymakers—based on the principle that substantive, yet accessible descriptions of topics sustaining national debate and discussion would aid in cutting through the complex and often bewildering language of educational reform.

As my work evolved, I noticed that frequently the most captivating stories, viewpoints, and opinions came directly from the mouths of researchers and practitioners—those who through their research, publications, and brave, sometimes heroic efforts in schools were furthering new or improved practice. I was not alone in my recognition of the value of these opinions and viewpoints. Reactions from our audiences informed the evolution of these publications. Researchers, policymakers, and practitioners alike reported that they enjoyed reading the answers that key figures in education provided to the questions that I posed to them. Frequently, they told me in letters or phone calls, they were either provoked sufficiently by the content to read further on a topic, or found that reading these conversations gave them a new slant on the person's work. Often, they reported, hearing the practitioner's voice—so often overlooked or neglected in the educational research literature—helped ground in reality theoretical discussions of abstract concepts. In addition, hearing the researcher's voice in a format different from his or her writings and conference presentations provided a more accessible entree into that individual's work.

My preparation for those interviews—and for the conversations in this book—was intensive. Rather than approaching researchers and practitioners in a purely journalistic way, which I felt frequently overlooks the complicated tangle in which current issues are nested, I believed it necessary to thoroughly research each issue, conduct an exhaustive literature search, and then formulate questions for the few key individuals selected.

My work at the School of Education within the University of Wisconsin–Madison provided an ideal place in which to pursue discussions about current educational issues. The National Center on Effective Secondary Schools, funded by the U.S. Department of Education, pursued an ambitious research agenda which brought me into close contact with researchers, practitioners, networks of educators, and professional educational organizations nationwide. In my work there, it was necessary to connect what appeared to be disparate, even lonely themes into an integrated, harmonic whole. In my work at the National Center for Effective Schools, I built upon the foundation established at the previous center, expanding and refining the previous work.

However, although ideal in many ways, I did hold one concern about the environment peculiar to the educational research community: it is a type of hothouse for ideas and proposals for action. This somewhat rarefied environment promotes particular visions for education, visions frequently not shared by practitioners. In an effort to insure that the voices of practitioners were heard and that their reflections on contemporary issues in education received attention, I decided that selected practitioner viewpoints must be included in this volume. I located key practitioners and invited their participation in this project through the recommendations of colleagues, since practitioners frequently do not have a body of publications. I selected researchers for this book on the basis of their writings and other work.

A few principles remained constant, however, and are the backbone for this book:

- It is possible to provide stimulating, substantive discussion of a topic without attempting an exhaustive treatment.
- Hearing the voices of educational leaders in a more informal context than that provided by a perusal or study of their writings or attendance at one of their conference presentations has clear benefit.
- Certain themes in education intersect and overlap, sometimes surprisingly.
- The questions posed to the educational leaders raise more questions than can be answered in the scope of this book.

Why this book? The answer is straightforward. Each publication I wrote for the two national research and development centers focused on a single topic, training multiple lenses on it. Many readers, as well as colleagues in the educational community, suggested that a compilation of topics treated in this fashion in a single volume would be especially useful for the student of education, for the practitioner, and for the researcher who maintains a focus in one area but is interested in other areas of education as well.

By the time I was ready to approach this book, I was determined, however, that it should not be a potpourri of disparate, loosely collected topics. To guard against this, I differentiate between issues and themes—and have organized this book accordingly.

Certain educational issues appear again and again—in the popular media, the research literature, and professional dialogue with colleagues. Cutting across these issues are central themes, which I frame in the following way:

1. The social and political context in which American education occurs, that is, issues raised as problems by national blue-ribbon panels, critics of education, educators themselves, and the educational research community—along with responses advanced to mitigate or solve these "problems." Examples range from the prevalence of violence, the emphasis on teaching values, and the influence of peer culture to the roles of race, language, culture, and ability.
2. The political and practical context in which educators in the schools must function: attitudes towards professionalism and professionalization, the role of teacher unions and organizations, and the significance of leadership.
3. Specific suggestions, proposals, or critiques advanced by leaders of educational reform, including perspectives on the national standards movement, the push to privatize schools, restructuring initiatives and their effects, the quest for "authentic pedagogy" and "authentic assessment," and what lessons, if any, can be learned from the history of educational reform.

Whenever possible, I provide an historical context for these themes, since an examination of current issues yields little without some scrutiny of how we reached the point that these issues and cross-cutting themes are paramount. I also provide an extensive bibliography to guide the reader to the research literature on the themes presented in this volume. Finally, I conclude with an afterword that synthesizes the key issues and questions raised in this volume.

After identifying the individuals to appear in this book, I invited each of them to be interviewed, either by phone or in person. Each interview was tape-recorded; I then worked from a transcript. After each segment was written, I sent it to the person whose remarks it contained, asking that he or she read it and make any suggestions for revision. I did this to ensure that each person would be accurately quoted and characterized. Each person contacted me with suggestions for revision or refinement and those suggestions then were incorporated into the book.

The reader may wonder where I stand on each of the issues discussed in this volume. In each of the conversations, I deliberately maintained a neutral stance, careful not to allow my own opinions to intrude upon those of the interviewee. In that sense, one could argue that these are not true conversations since my own voice is carefully neutral. I believe that the discriminating reader who wants to discover my views will be able to detect my passions and opinions. Yet the ultimate value of the conversations lies in what I have been able to extract from each of the educational leaders through the questions that I asked—free from any overlay of my own opinion. I do not always agree with every leader featured. Sometimes I agree in part and not in toto. However, the views expressed in this volume are significant enough to warrant their inclusion, regardless of whether I agree completely with every statement expressed.

This book is not intended to be—nor can it be—an exhaustive examination of every issue on the national scene. Many more questions could be posed to each of the educational leaders. However, every discussion has a finite point. Within the parameters of this volume, I have tried to ask the questions that would stimulate answers that might provoke the reader to embark upon further reading and study. Finally, this book aims to inform the current educational debate and hopefully create a fresh genre through which the discussion can be extended.

Part I

Troubled Times:
Violence, Values, and Youth Culture

It was the best of times, it was the worst of times, it was the age of wisdom, it was the age of foolishness, it was the epoch of belief, it was the epoch of incredulity, it was the season of Light, it was the season of Darkness, it was the spring of hope, it was the winter of despair, we had everything before us, we had nothing before us, we were all going direct to Heaven, we were all going direct the other way . . .

—Charles Dickens, *A Tale of Two Cities*

Overview of Part I

It often appears that our society is falling apart, that we are poised on the brink of an awful abyss. Numbing accounts of pointless violence and cruelty permeate our newspapers and newscasts; politicians, educators, and national commissions call for the teaching of values to shift the destructive tide into a more constructive direction. Finally, today's youth frequently are viewed as vacant and amoral, without the guidance that families provided in some halcyon past, devoid of values and rudderless—easily influenced by whatever peer group seizes upon them and imprinted far too readily by the media, rock music, computer games, and drugs. In short, we hear a great deal about "alienation" and "at-risk" behaviors.

I call this part "Troubled Times" because that is the timbre of the era through which we currently pass. What role, though, can or should schools play in dealing with violence? Should they attempt to teach values? If so, whose values, and in what way? Is there evidence that inculcation into the values held by "moral" individuals will result in the profound behavioral changes for which its advocates clamor? What about the peer group and other influences on youth? Are adolescents significantly different from their counterparts twenty years ago? If so, in what ways? What can schools do to reach their psyches—and should they try to do so?

These are some of the broad questions I asked the educational leaders featured in this section. Deborah Prothrow-Stith, Assistant Dean for Government and Community Programs at Harvard University's School of Public Health and Professor of Public Health Practice for the Harvard School of Public Health, begins the discussion with her views on our violent society and what schools should do to mitigate its influence on youth. Next, I turn to a scrutiny of values and moral behavior. Kevin Ryan, who directs the Center for the Advancement of Ethics and Character at Boston University, defines good character and advocates a disciplined program of values education in schools, arguing that such a systematic approach will succeed in stemming the antisocial tide with which we are confronted as a society. Thomas Lickona, who directs the Center for the Study of the 4 Rs (Respect and Responsibility) at the State University of New York at Cortland, approaches the teaching of values with a proposal and agenda for teachers and families to follow. Alan L. Lockwood, Professor and former Chair of the Department of Curriculum and Instruction at the University of Wisconsin–Madison, casts an objective eye on the values rhetoric, assessing its underlying logic and overall goals. I end the section with my conversation with B. Bradford Brown, a developmental psychologist, professor, and researcher at the University of Wisconsin–Madison, who tells us who adolescents are as they head into the twenty-first century, how they differ from their peers twenty years ago, and the influences of peer groups and parenting styles on their behavior.

Deborah Prothrow-Stith:
Schools as Safe Havens

Deborah Prothrow-Stith, M.D., traces her interest in adolescent violence to her work as a staff physician at the Boston City Hospital and the Harvard Street Neighborhood Health Center. Currently Assistant Dean for Government and Community Programs at Harvard University's School of Public Health and Professor of Public Health Practice for the Harvard School of Public Health, she was State Commissioner of Public Health in Massachusetts from 1987 to 1989. In the latter capacity, she established the first state office of violence prevention and expanded treatment programs on AIDS, drug rehabilitation, and other urban health issues. Author of the first violence prevention curriculum for schools, she is also the author of Deadly Consequences, *which presents a public health perspective on violence to a mass audience.*

Meanness of character is one powerful reason the United States has become a violent society, Deborah Prothrow-Stith believes, coupled with a synergism of abundant influences steered by the profit motive. Manufacturers prosper from the sales of guns, video games, and movies that are targeted to children and actively promote and celebrate violence. A uniform—and disturbing—image that such manufacturers put forward is that of the hero as a figure who reacts quickly and violently, is deprived of a conscience, and is motivated solely by his own interests,

How have we, as a society, reached the point where children and teachers are afraid to go to school, where violence and crime are no longer solely urban problems? I asked her.

"I use the metaphor of a slot machine to explain our current infatuation with violence," Prothrow-Stith replied. "Unless you get five oranges, you don't hit the jackpot. In the windows of the slot machine, put up the widening gap of poverty we have experienced over the past 12 to 14 years; the crack epidemic, alcohol use and other drugs; the availability of guns; the big money that gun manufacturers have made in this country; the sociocultural issues, which are probably the most devastating; and it is clear that there is no jackpot. Instead, in every window of the slot machine we see how mean we have gotten as a society and how popular it has become to be mean."

The Marketing of Meanness

It is easy to enter the arena of violent behavior, she insists. "Being mean didn't become popular because it was natural," she pointed out. "Meanness has been promoted and sold in a very deliberate fashion; 'mean' as a state of being has been marketed carefully."

In her work on public health and violence prevention, Prothrow-Stith travels widely around the United States, taking painstaking note of ever-increasing tendencies toward violent behavior. Her observations alarm her: the nearly universal admiration for violence that youth display is disquieting at best. "In addition to being able to *give* it— in terms of violent behavior—you have to be able to *take* it," she emphasized. "Since violence and its consequences are no big deal, youth do not display much emotion about it. We don't see pain and empathy and remorse until there are very devastating consequences."

Why is life so devalued among so many youth?, I asked.

"Children have to be valued in order to learn that life is valuable," Prothrow-Stith said. "Obviously, most families do a pretty good job of teaching their children that they are valuable. But this important job can't be left to the family alone. Society has to think that children are valuable, and that belief has to be demonstrated in public policy and in the ethos of the community."

As a society, our commitment to children is woefully inadequate, she believes. Instead, children are exploited as a lucrative and vulnerable market for a plethora of violent, life-diminishing products. "Children are viewed as economically valuable by major corporations who sell them products. Of course, the same corporations are nonchalant about the effects of their sales. As long as children buy their goods, manufacturers can be indifferent to the fact that their products are unneeded *and* unhealthy. We must decide, as a society, that some things really are more important than money."

In what ways, I asked, can public policy effect change? "We're doing more crisis intervention and imprisonment," Prothrow-Stith said evenly, "and spending loads of money being big and mean and bad and tough on crime, but literally ignoring the front end of the problem. We have schools that are housed in horrible buildings, places in which none of us would spend our work day if we had a choice. We have schools with no books; we have schools with no physical education programs. Most communities that I visit have built new jails and have cut needed educational programs in the schools."

She added, "At one level, you get what you pay for."

The School's Role in Violence Prevention

How can the school play a role in mitigating violence in our society?, I asked. Is this truly the school's responsibility?

"The school has a major role," Prothrow-Stith replied firmly. "The socialization process that takes place in the school is an essential part of the educational process. Occasionally I hear teachers say, 'I don't teach how to get along.' But you can't teach math without teaching kids how to get along. While you're teaching math, you're teaching children how to treat each other, how to treat people who are different, how to behave with people who don't understand. Literally, you are teaching children how to get along with others and how to be socialized."

She places responsibility squarely on educators to create a movement that recognizes and promotes the importance of adequate socialization in schools, so that they are environments where children learn the difference between right and wrong. "Those students who do less well in school are often more at risk for being involved in violent behavior," she explained. "Schools could—and should—make a big contribution to this issue by not only teaching everybody how to read and do math, but also how to exist in an environment in which that would take place."

Finally, she believes schools should engage actively in programs aimed at reducing violence. "We need to teach children how to handle conflict and anger, how to solve problems in a very deliberate way. Schools must be safe havens, examples of nonviolence, places where children learn the essentials for functioning in society in addition to learning the basics of reading and writing— in some ways to make up for what the rest of society isn't doing now."

She points to research conducted by the Governor's Alliance Against Drugs in Massachusetts to illustrate how powerful advertising is in promoting self-destructive behavior among youth, citing a pre- and post-survey of children who entered a three-year substance abuse prevention curriculum. "Self-reported behavior around drugs decreased after the three years in every category except alcohol," she said, "where it rose slightly. This was unexplained for a long time because the curriculum dealt with alcohol more than with other drugs."

While casually watching television one evening and viewing an anti-drugs public service spot immediately followed by an alcohol commercial, Prothrow-Stith was struck with a realization: educators possess and transmit the correct prevention messages, but are contradicted by the media—which in turn contradicts its own messages and public service announcements. Commercials for alcohol preceded by anti-drugs messages are too contradictory and confusing for children to absorb, she told me.

Doesn't this suggest, I asked, that the problem of violence is simply too global to be placed upon the shoulders of educators who are held increasingly accountable for the systemic problems of society? What about harnessing a coalition of forces to combat it?

"Schools can't do it alone," she acknowledged in reply, "but obviously they can mitigate and counter some of the things that are going on, just as families always have intervened in the lives of children.

"I challenge educators to do this, because I think classroom teachers ought to be outraged by the lack of priority public policy gives to children and schools. Educators should lead a movement to change that. Instead, most of the teachers' unions debate salary and contract issues, which is disappointing, because there is a larger mission."

Prothrow-Stith quickly added, "I realize that I'm prescribing something for another profession that my own profession of physicians hasn't been able to accomplish in terms of health care reform. Nonetheless, even given the substantial difficulties, I would love to see teachers leading a violence reduction and conflict resolution movement."

I asked if she believes that parents should monitor videos and books that their children choose to ensure they are nonviolent. "Yes," she replied, although she was clear that such monitoring should possess a core of reason rather than blind censorship motivated by fear. "Throughout the education process, one ought to analyze with students *why* they like something, how they have learned to like it, and why people produce whatever it is."

Since the profit motive lies at the core of the production and promotion of violent entertainment and weapons for children, she maintains that the allure of such products will be lessened if children's sophistication about the motives of manufacturers and advertisers is elevated. "There is the need to indicate to youngsters that all these things they watch and see are lies," she said. "Many kids, especially older ones, think they know what is real and what is not, but when they're watching the stories, they get caught up in them to the point that they don't think of alternatives."

Learning Alternatives to Violence and Rage

Alternatives to violence are Prothrow-Stith's main message. "Unless you train yourself, you go right along with the story," she noted. "There are strategies for watching movies and television that should be shared with children, and it is the school's responsibility to do that. After all, the parent may think the school assigned a project and the child should complete it."

What elements comprise a good curriculum against violence?, I asked.

Prothrow-Stith believes the first step in any educative campaign against violence begins with the need to acknowledge the primacy of violence in our society. "We have to realize that violence is the norm," she said sadly, "and that children admire violence. We actively promote and celebrate violence ourselves. In some ways, children are being socialized very actively to have the opinions about violence that they hold."

Acknowledging that violence dominates our society, she believes, sets the right tone for violence reduction programs. "We don't want to make children defensive; it is very helpful to have them understand that people make money from guns and from movies. Nobody worries about the consequences; nobody is liable for the consequences except an individual—but the individual doesn't make money from the products."

Recognizing that anger and conflict are normal human responses to stress is another key educative component, she maintains. "No one is perfect. Conflict and anger can be energizing; they can provide an opportunity for growth and creativity. Most of us, as adults, have learned to use our anger creatively to solve the problem. We also need to focus not just on the kids who fight, but on the whole—the kids who create the fights, who instigate the fights, who pass the rumors, who run to see the fights. If we look at adolescent development and sociocultural issues, a lot of these fights represent peer pressure that accumulates over time. They are carefully choreographed. Often it is more important to deal with the whole class, not just those who have been labeled as fighters."

How has she seen youth respond, I asked, when violence reduction is taught actively to them in the school setting?

In her response, Prothrow-Stith points to the youngsters who are the most fearful as the ones who benefit most obviously from a violence prevention curriculum. "They are the most receptive," she emphasized. "Often it is the suburban, middle-class kids who are callous and playful with violence. Some of my colleagues, who have a very analytical approach and don't feel pressure for things to change, believe that nothing will work.

"The people closest to violence—those who live with it daily—are often the most receptive. They know who is authentic and who is not. Kids know if you are talking from your experience. As another starting place, teachers of violence prevention programs need to deal with their own issues of anger and violence. How do they feel about violence? At what point would anger push them to violence?"

This is especially important, she emphasizes, because the classroom can be a setting in which students challenge the teacher, pushing for limits. "They will ask: 'What if I hit you? What if this or that happened? What if somebody did this to your daughter; what would you do?'

"As a teacher, you must be prepared to respond, not in a trite way, but in an authentic way that means you must know yourself and your own reactions and attitudes toward anger and violence."

Such awareness of one's own tolerance of stressors suggests teachers need considerable inservice of their own before embarking on delivery of a violence prevention program, I said. Is this indeed the case?

"It does require significant thought and energy," Prothrow-Stith responded. "In the curriculum I developed, for instance, there is a way to do the training in a short period of time. However, some teachers are better prepared and better equipped to go ahead with it than others, depending on their level of interaction and how much they challenge themselves on issues."

Violence prevention should not be something special tacked on to teachers' already crowded work lives, she believes, but instead should be an integral part of a school's educative mission. Particularly in high schools, where teachers frequently are locked into teaching only their content area, attention to issues surrounding conflict resolution, the management of anger, and violence prevention is especially appropriate. "Kids in high school are at the peak of their adolescent development," she explained, "and it is very helpful for them to learn to understand their own behavior."

Examples of an Anti-Violence Curriculum

In the past 25 to 30 years, I said, it appears that we, as a society, have slid into a terrible state—into an antisocial situation where we glorify and profit from violence, where human life has lost much of its meaning, where the loss of life seems inconsequential, where people are numbed by news reports of yet another murder or incident of domestic violence. If this continues unchecked, I asked, where does she see us twenty years from now?

"We will be in something very close to the Wild West," Prothrow-Stith said ruefully, "where everybody carries a gun, there are regular shootouts on the street, and killing is the way of solving conflict. In my worst fears, that is something I can envision. We already have lost a certain amount of safety, which is visible when we look at our homicide rates compared to other industrialized countries. Many people feel they must be armed to go out. Ultimately, of course, this attitude contributes to the problem.

"One student in an alternative school said to me: 'What is the big deal? I have a gun. You have a gun. We have a beef. We have a shootout.'

"What else has he experienced?" she asked. "How else has anyone taught him to handle conflict? That is what all the superheroes do on TV. They don't stop to try to solve a conflict. Some of the movies that are marketed directly to children, like *Kindergarten Cop*, show people shooting others in the bathroom at school. If we look at this, we realize our children are sent down a path that says they have no other way to solve problems other than through violent reactions."

Since she is a physician with a background in public health, how did she become interested in violence prevention as an educative mission for schools?, I asked.

"I started looking at violence as a public health problem, so naturally health education came to mind," she replied. "Health education is one of the major strategies within public health. Using the same strategies that have been used to prevent smoking or drunk driving to prevent violence was an irresistible challenge."

Providing information on a consistent basis to children, Prothrow-Stith insists, is the best way to ensure that the future will improve. "We hope that the information we provide becomes part of children's standard knowledge base and is incorporated into their day-to-day activities, their attitudes, and their behavior."

Admitting that children are a "captive audience" in schools, she asked: "Why do you rob a bank? Because the money is there. Why do we think about health education in the schools? Because that is where the kids are. Obviously all kids aren't in school, and that suggests the need for an additional set of strategies. But health education in the classroom is a mainstay of public health."

Prothrow-Stith believes a successful violence prevention program moves in carefully coordinated stages. The curriculum she has developed is divided into ten sessions, offered for forty-five minutes to an hour, depending on the length of the class period.

"The first three sessions set the stage for our work. We talk about violence in America compared with other countries. We talk about friend and family violence, and, in particular, we hone in on violence being a learned behavior that is preventable."

The second stage of the curriculum deals specifically with anger, opening the discussion to questions such as: What makes you angry? What are ways in which you can handle anger in a nonviolent way? "We culminate," Prothrow-Stith explained, "with a cost-benefit analysis of fighting. After listing causes of anger and solutions to anger, the discussion centers around healthy and unhealthy reactions to it, including specific targeting of fighting." At that point, Prothrow-Stith hopes students are primed to prevent fighting.

Finally, the last section of the curriculum engages students in role playing and distinct strategies for handling anger, for preventing violence, and for resolving conflict productively. "If teachers wished to add to the curriculum," she observed, "they could provide additional sessions on conflict resolution, anger management, and issues of dating violence or family violence."

As with many other educative efforts, she believes it is important to target young children—but she also maintains adolescents must not be neglected, since part of their development and peer socialization encourages unhealthy reactions to violence.

"Although it is important to offer this early, we should offer it throughout the educational experience," she said. "Actually, it is something we could teach to parents, or to future parents, so that they could have some sense of child development, of handling anger and emotions within the context of a family."

Adolescents are especially susceptible to violence, and Prothrow-Stith is deeply concerned about their vulnerability. "Some reasons for their vulnerability have to do with peer pressure, with adolescent narcissism, with self-consciousness, and with a certain amount of risk-taking. Even if we have taught good anger management and excellent conflict resolution skills to youngsters, during the adolescent years we have to do something extra."

Part of the "something extra," she told me, has to do with redefining the popular image of the American hero, which has edged closer and closer over the years to one of an anti-social, semi-psychotic figure who acts violently without remorse, conscience, or guilt. "We need to change the peer pressure so that the pressure is not to fight, but to solve the problem without fighting. If we could adjust the social norm among teenagers to one where fighting is considered stupid, then we have made progress."

In order to successfully implement a violence prevention curriculum, what conditions in the school must be present?, I asked.

"Teachers must be interested in teaching these skills," she noted, "and they must have the full support of the administration. They also need dedicated training time and some support as they implement it, so that they aren't helpless when questions come up. In general, the teachers who are the most successful teaching these skills are those who are committed not just to helping their students but to helping this society deal with the issue of violence."

Kevin Ryan:
The Quest for Truth and Justice

Kevin Ryan is Director of the Center for the Advancement of Ethics and Character at Boston University, where he is also a Professor of Education. He explains the mission of the center as one that addresses the needs of schools and teacher education institutions, working to renew interest in character education. The co-author (with Edward Wynne) of Reclaiming Our Schools: A Handbook on Teaching Character, Academics, and Discipline *(Macmillan, 1993), he has written or edited fifteen books as well as over eighty articles. A former high school English teacher, Ryan's primary academic foci are moral education and teacher education. He has received awards from the University of Helsinki, the Association of Colleges for Teacher Education, and the Association of Teacher Educators.*

It is clear that Kevin Ryan is an individual with a diamond-like and pristine vision: Morality and character are scarce commodities in an eroding American society, he believes, and public schools must intervene actively with focused character education programs that will redeem character and thus rescue American youth from an increasingly perilous society.

Ryan likes to refer to a statement made by Fred Close of the Ethics Resource Center, who said that the fundamental problem of U.S. schools is that they are graduating moral savages. What exactly does that mean?, I asked him. Certainly there are education reformers who would not agree with the statement, placing other concerns before those related to morality.

"It's a dramatic way," Ryan said, "of acknowledging that over a four-decade period we have graduated children with lower standards of achievement and increasing problems of social disorder."

Ryan's view is absolute: There is right, there is wrong; good and evil do exist; and good character is nothing less than democratic since it lies within the reach of everyone. But times are dangerous and difficult, he says, pointing to the rise of school vandalism, in-school fighting, violence against teachers, suicide, homicide, and teenage pregnancy. All of these factors, he believes, show "enormous lack of responsibility on the part of both boys and girls."

This lack of responsibility, he says, points to signs of what he terms "moral savagery."

"Our children are achieving less in school by both standards of the past and also relative to the rest of the developed—and in some cases—undeveloped world," he stated.

I asked: To what degree do you draw a correlation between deviant, criminal behavior and a lack of character? To some character educators, there is a distinct correlation; others draw little direct causal relationship between the two, pointing to other factors as roots from which criminal behavior can grow.

Ryan belongs to the first category of character educators. "Clearly there are acts of violence performed by mentally deranged people," he replied, "but most criminal behavior is enormously self-indulgent and shows passions that have never been controlled. Our society has not been very good about communicating what a good person is. We have celebrated deviance, so people are confused about what it means to be a good person or a successful person. Instead they look to financial gain, notoriety, and freedom as the ideal, rather than to a quality such as integrity."

Family Values Defined

There is so much attention currently expended on "family values" as a benchmark of good behavior that I asked Ryan: How do you define family values? What should happen if they conflict with the values taught by the school? Whose values, in that event, should take precedence?

Ryan replied, "When people talk about family values, they really are talking about moral values. The current term is a moral compass that helps people direct their desires to the right things. Values represent where our hearts lead us, what we want in life. Moral values are values that have been acquired through training. Certainly justice is a moral value; integrity is a moral value; wisdom is a moral value. When people talk about family values, they're talking about the problem that families and the whole society is experiencing, which is trying to transmit these values to children at a time when families do not have a lot of direct supervision over their children."

He points to history to buttress his point. "The world has changed very quickly in two generations from a society that was primarily agrarian or focused on work in small family businesses, in which fathers were very present to their families. Children were absorbed very early into the family work; daughters with their mothers, sons with their fathers. Children, by and large, saw their future as becoming what their parents were."

By the end of the nineteenth century, fathers were going out to work in factories or offices, and that was followed more recently—"within the last generation and a half," Ryan noted—by the exodus of women to work outside the home. "There also has been the emergence of a youth culture," Ryan said, "and with the culture has come a certain kind of value system. This value system is very commercial and very pleasure-oriented.

"While in the past," he continued, "families had control and supervision and also a high investment in their children acquiring certain moral values, that has now been deeply eroded. When I hear family values raised as an issue, I hear a plaintive cry on the part of parents. I hear their nervousness when their kids come home with earrings, rings in their noses, condoms they got at school, or pornographic videos. Parents are concerned that their children are growing up with a very different moral compass than the one they had, with different habits than they had.

"They look around for the enemy," he added.

To Ryan, parents are not completely blameless, although he has empathy for their feelings. Perhaps, he contends, they have been slack in their duties as transmitters of moral values. "Perhaps they've given too much time to their own pleasures," he mused, "to the bowling league or their own work—not enough to the primary work of raising children.

"But parents also look at other elements outside their control or that are difficult to control, such as television. They can't do too much about that, but when they hear about the things going on at school, they view school not as a traditional extension of the family, but as something else—something in conflict with their values."

Looking to the school as an extension of the family and not seeing that role enacted, Ryan maintains, may result in an antagonistic relationship between schools and families. "When people talk about family values, they primarily are talking about the values that a child learns in the home, including loyalty, certain kinds of work habits, the sense of duty to one's immediate group, and one's religious values.

"There's also the value of internationalism or concern for people on the far corners of the world, and the value of a real understanding of and reverence for the democratic process. Those tend to be values that the school advances through knowledge. By and large, schools typically have been concerned with teaching family values: the persistence of hard work, concern for the underdog, civility, respect for private property, respect for people's rights. But in latter years, this has declined, and now parents point the finger at the school and say: 'You've let us down.'"

In-Depth Character Education

One of Ryan's key concerns as a character educator is that current emphasis on character and moral education may lead to superficial treatment of serious issues with the implementation of trendy programs that will ultimately fail. I asked: What guidelines for educators does he suggest to ensure that character education will be an integral part of the school's program?

"One, we must recognize the potential for character education to become a superficial effort," he said. "We must promise ourselves that we will give major attention to character education and really make it a priority.

"Two, in order for this to happen, character education needs to be institutionalized."

One way to institutionalize character education, he believes, is to form a strong committee of serious people interested in schools, composed of lay people, an administrator, and core faculty members. Ryan recommends a monthly meeting—kept a priority by the group members—during which attention is paid to development of character education programs throughout the school, including inservice for teachers. "This group ensures that character education will remain a priority," he said.

"Third, the entire faculty ought to have special time away from the school to discuss these issues, such as a week after school closes or before school begins. They need to study and reclaim this whole area."

Areas that demand study, he said, include but are not limited to the formal curriculum. "To what degree is the formal curriculum bringing to young adults the core moral ideas of the culture?" he asked. "To what degree are these young adults learning about the meaning of responsibility? The meaning of friendship? What betrayal is all about? What self-indulgence is?

"This group needs to see that the curriculum which traditionally has been used to pass on a moral heritage to the young is, in fact, really doing that and that the curriculum hasn't slipped away into more utilitarian activities. Once one is sure that the curriculum is there, the next point is to see that teachers are retaught or learn to teach themselves how to engage children in moral and ethical analysis of the curriculum."

Slavery, he said by way of example, is not merely an event: it is a moral lesson. "Students must understand the moral injustice of slavery and its dehumanizing quality. If one reads *Huck Finn*, one needs to see that it conveys important moral ideas about America and how we have lived together. I've seen teachers ignore the moral center of that book to focus on the steamboat as opening the West or the dialect of the Missouri Valley."

The fundamental organizing question for the group, Ryan believes, could be stated as: What are the things that we as elementary or middle school teachers can do to engage our children in the moral ideas that are embedded in the content of the curriculum?

"A fourth way to ensure character education will not be trivialized is to look at the life of a school and examine to what degree the rule system is understood. At the very least, youngsters need to understand why rules are present, so that if there is a rule about running in the hall, kids know that the reason for it is that you can hurt other people if you run in the hall. They need to know that in a good society, we don't cheat because society runs on the fact that we keep our promises."

He added, "If we keep our promises, we don't need a cop on every corner. We can rely on you to tell the truth. We can rely on you not to pick up every spare wallet that you see. The rule system and discipline of the school need to be something that is not heavily imposed upon students, but is part of the teaching effort."

The Importance of Ceremony and Ritual

The ceremonies that form the texture of the school are extremely important, Ryan cautions, and must not be allowed to disintegrate into displays of student rowdiness. Instead, their solemn nature should be maintained. "A fifth way to ensure that character education permeates a school is to make sure that the school continually celebrates what it sees as the ideal. There are people in every community who have done years of community service. They need to be brought together as examples of what we would like our children to be. Those children who achieve things—from becoming an outstanding long distance runner or winning a regional spelling bee—need to have their accomplishments celebrated, so that others can see that excellence is valued in this school."

Ceremonies such as graduation need to have a solemn tone that reflects upon accomplishment and the challenges of the future, "not just release," Ryan noted.

School spirit may be a misnomer, because he maintains that it clearly must transcend pep rallies and football games to encompass a higher moral content. "Children need to feel that they are in a special school, in a special place, that their school is about excellence and not just academics. Excellence is reflected in the quality of the people who are there."

Ryan mentions his affinity for the work of Emile Durkheim, particularly his emphasis on the importance of developing a spirit shared by children so that they take genuine pride in being at their school. Speaking in the collective voice of students, he said: "We're proud of being here because our school does wonderful things. We're the only elementary school in the country that has a band, or a chess team. There is an emphasis on developing a strong sense of specialty in our particular school and in our class. Our teachers try to get us to compete to be the very best, in a healthy way. When we go to the auditorium, our class looks the best. Nobody from our class is going to be reprimanded for yelling out or misbehaving at an assembly.

"We want," Ryan emphasized, "to show how good we are."

A sixth way to ensure that character education deeply permeates the fiber of a school is reflected in what he calls "a level of civility in the school." Vulgarity is eschewed, as is sarcasm and raised voices. "Kids know that embarrassing other kids or being disrespectful to teachers won't happen at *our* school, because we have an ethos of concern for others, particularly those in trouble. That means everyone. It might mean a child who has experienced divorce in the family; in that case there is a natural reaching out to help that child. A deep ethos of concern pervades the school. This is seen immediately when one visits a school and kids come up and ask if they can help you. In other schools, they look at you strangely or you're ridiculed."

Developing Virtue in the School

Finally, Ryan insists that the school must have a vision, an ideal of "the good student."

"To me," he reflected, "a good school is one that defines a good student as someone who develops virtue, who has clearly overcome his or her own selfishness and is ready to help others. A good student is highly self-disciplined; if given an assignment he or she knows how to do it, and do it well and to completion. A good student is not just someone who gets high grades.

"It's a very democratic idea," he continued, "because what we know about genetics suggests that some people, just by the fact of who their parents are, will have more athletic ability or more intellectual skills. As far as I know, there's no gene for kindness and no gene for prudence. All those characteristics are developed. Every child is able to become morally great, to develop a strong character.

"A strong character," he added firmly, "would appear to be within the reach of all of us: handicapped people, people of limited intelligence, people from enormously dysfunctional homes. These people may not win on the ball field, but they can develop strong character."

This is a rather inspiring way to view character education, I commented, but is the superficial approach to character education more tempting because it involves less concerted work on the part of school staff?

Ryan paused. "There is good news and bad news about that," he answered. "One reason we have a very relaxed, disordered school system around the country is because we are not expecting very much of our children, either in terms of how much work they do or the kind of behavior they exhibit. This is a result of an implicit agreement between teachers and students that says, 'I won't hassle you if you won't hassle me. If you don't want to work, just don't bother the rest of us.'"

He sees that bargain as "deadly, very deadly," and insists it must be "rooted out." As part of a comprehensive approach to character education, Ryan insists that teachers must be held to a higher standard, as well as students. "Teachers need to become more diligent themselves. They have to make demands on kids and follow those themselves."

He added, "They are going to have to walk uphill for a bit."

The Benefits of Good Character

The positive news, he says, is that schools that really work on character in a concerted way are much more pleasant workplaces. "Schools that have clear expectations of kids, where good behavior is expected, where good cheer is the order of the day, are much better places to work At the end of the day, you may have worked harder, but you feel that you have taught. You've seen change in kids. You don't spend the day hassling kids, listening to them push the envelope in terms of behavior and language and disrespect to you."

So the results obtained by unified adults, focused on moral development, differ sharply from those obtained by teachers divided philosophically from one another on issues of discipline or values, as in a family where the parents aren't united on discipline? I asked.

"That is exactly the situation," Ryan agreed. "Rules are rules. Some teachers will enforce them, and others won't. That is so tiring. When teachers spend special time together, they clarify what kind of an environment they want, and then are ready to sanction those teachers who get out of line. That is not just the role of the principal, but also the role of teachers. If teaching is ever to become a profession, teachers have to be able to say to those people who are not doing the work: 'We're trying to shape the school up; you are not helping.'"

One of Ryan's persistent themes in his writings is that the religious component of character education cannot be ignored. How, given this, should public school teachers and students deal with religion?

"I'll state the negative first," Ryan said. "If schools cannot find ways to respect and reinforce the religious views and the religious morality of children, then the public schools are doomed. In other words, if the schools can't accommodate what, for most people, consists of a religious base to their morality, then they are betraying their role in our society."

Why is the religious undercurrent so urgent?, I asked him. "People are much more concerned," Ryan said, "with preserving religious freedom and passing on those traditions to their children than they are committed to state-supported public education. If not satisfied, they will find—as they currently are finding—a voice in the choice and voucher programs. This will result in a wholesale removal of support for public education."

He pointed to the number of children currently home-schooled. "One of 88 children is kept at home. Home schooling is a growing movement. Many who move away from public education are people who feel that public education undermines their religious faith. They believe that public schools make kids believe that religion is some sort of a social invention that will go away in an increasingly scientific era."

Ryan shakes his head over what he sees as avoidance and fear of religious issues within public schools. "As a former public school teacher and a parent, I don't understand why public schools are so fearful of celebrating the religious aspects of life, at least in the sense of acknowledging that religion has been a powerful part of human culture. For many, many people, their religious views are the source they go to when solving moral problems."

Religion, rather than psychology, is the foundation on which to place moral conflicts and problems related to a plethora of issues, Ryan maintains, including teen pregnancy, suicide, fights within the family, and other self-destructive or antisocial behaviors.

"As a school community, we have been psychologized to death in the United States," he stated. "We have undermined theology, we have ignored philosophy, we don't teach the history of education, but we make sure that every student who goes through teacher training has Educational Psychology courses and learned what essentially is a psychological view of man.

"Psychology is great," he continued, "except when it gets into issues of ethics, because by the very terms of the discipline of psychology, it can't deal with the rightness or wrongness of things. Those require philosophy or theology or a combination of the two. Psychology, by definition, observes human behavior and tries to categorize it. It cannot say what is right or wrong."

Does he connect the concept of cultural literacy with character education?, I asked. If so, in what way?

"I talk about moral literacy," Ryan replied, "which is a part of cultural literacy. Behind all those factoids that E. D. Hirsch wants people to know lie the moral seeds of our country and our society. We want people to know about George Washington and the cherry tree. We want to know stories about the Pied Piper of Hamlin, just as we want to know about Lincoln's anguish over the Civil War.

"I believe," he concluded, "that when teachers look at their curriculum and examine it in terms of character education, they must make sure that those stories, those ideas, those historical events, and those people who have failed us or contributed to our society are represented. But, most important, they are not there simply for cultural literacy, but because they represent our moral map, our people's moral heritage."

Thomas Lickona:
The Promulgation of Virtue

Thomas Lickona is a developmental psychologist and Professor of Education at the State University of New York at Cortland, where he has done award-winning work in teacher education and currently directs the Center for the 4th and 5th Rs (Respect and Responsibility). He also has been a visiting professor at Boston and Harvard Universities. A past president of the Association for Moral Education, Lickona serves on the board of directors of the newly formed Character Education Partnership, a national coalition working to promote character development in schools and communities. He was a participant in the 1994 White House Conference on Character-Building for a Democratic, Civil Society and was invited to speak at the opening of the Second Annual White House Conference on Character-Building. He is the author of several books, including Educating for Character: How Our Schools Can Teach Respect and Responsibility *and* Sex, Love, and You: Making the Right Decision *(co-authored with his wife Judith Lickona and William Boudreau, M.D.).*

Character education, in Thomas Lickona's view, is not an amorphous, vaguely spiritual entity with ill-defined aims. Rather, it is aggressive, proactive, and sure: it constructs education in the most absolute terms—good or evil, right or wrong—and eschews relativism. Lickona explained, "Character education starts with the philosophical principle that objectively there are important ethical values which constitute the foundation of good character."

Why the current emphasis on character education? I asked. Why now? Why is there such an insistent message, coming from a plethora of sources, that we need a program of character education in our schools?

In his answer, Lickona points to the condition of our society, which he describes as riddled with moral decay. This moral erosion, he maintains, legitimates and necessitates character education as a deliberate enterprise for all social institutions, including public schools. "We need character education everywhere that human beings interact with each other," he said largely, "public schools being just one domain. We need it in our families; we need it in our churches, temples, and other religious institutions. We need it in our neighborhoods, in the media, in our government, and we need it in our schools.

"One can argue that modeling and transmitting the values that constitute human decency is a fundamental part of the human enterprise," he said. "After all, that's the way we sustain a civilization, the way we keep ourselves growing as a culture."

The Role of Schools as Character-Builders

What in particular should be the role of public schools in this moral enterprise?, I asked. First, Lickona believes they need to be active, vital forces encouraging character education—a role he says they have abdicated in recent years. "Kids are in school 12,000 hours from kindergarten to graduation from high school. Schools have countless opportunities to have an effect—for good or for ill—on the developing character of their students.

"If schools don't attempt to do this in a systematic way," he warned, "that sends a message that character is not important."

More largely, if schools are absent from the promulgation of virtue, what Lickona terms "a moral vacuum" can ensue. "The most negative influences then rush in to become the dominant forces in the moral environment of the school, such as the worst parts of youth peer culture. If schools are to be effective, they must be as thoughtful and as intentional about developing character as they are about teaching math, science, reading, and anything else that is important."

He points to three fundamental reasons for an active program of character education: "One, we need to be moral to be fully human. Two, we need character education to create schools that are civil, caring, orderly communities where teaching and learning can occur. Third, we currently face a moral crisis in our culture, where there has been rapid moral decline on many fronts. Schools need to be in the lead in responding to this challenge since so many of the other social institutions have been weakened badly over the past several decades."

He observed, "The school is the institution of last resort. Every child has to go to school. The school is positioned to reach out to other groups, to families and religious institutions, for example, to try to get everybody working together in a common cause.

"Character education doesn't simply wait for teachable moments to arise," he continued. "It creates teachable moments. It creates opportunities to teach, model, promote, and celebrate these core ethical values."

Lickona continued by elaborating on the theme of societal moral breakdown. "There is a growing conviction that our society is in deep moral and spiritual trouble, which can be seen in various youth trends: the rise in youth violence; increasing dishonesty; the growing disrespect for parents, teachers, and other authority figures; increased peer cruelty; an explosion of bigotry and hate crimes; the deterioration of language; the decline of the work ethic; a rise in self-destructive behaviors; growing materialism; a decline in personal and civic responsibility; and what a number of people have called ethical illiteracy."

Perhaps the most alarming, he believes, of this constellation is ethical illiteracy. "The late sociologist Will Herberg," Lickona remarked, "observed that there are two threats to the moral health of any society. One is when lots of people do bad things. The other is when lots of people do bad things and don't have a clue that what they're doing is wrong. There has been growing evidence of this sort of ethical illiteracy, especially among young people—ignorance of moral knowledge as basic as the Golden Rule."

Specific Character-Building Strategies

How might interested practitioners compelled by the case for character education begin to implement moral education in their schools and districts? I asked. In his reply, Lickona refers to his work developing a set of principles and broad strategies that undergird a comprehensive approach to schoolwide character education.

"First, a comprehensive approach calls upon the teacher to act as a caregiver, model, and mentor—treating students with love and respect, supporting prosocial behavior, correcting hurtful actions, and so on. Second, teachers must create a moral community, helping students to know and respect each other, and feel valued in the group as a whole."

Other principles include the practice of moral discipline, the creation of a democratic classroom environment, teaching values through the curriculum, using cooperative learning to develop students' appreciation of others, developing what he calls "the conscience of craft" by fostering students' work ethic, developing the habit of moral reflection, and teaching conflict resolution.

"These principles make full use of the moral life of classrooms," Lickona clarified, "but there are three more strategies that are schoolwide. The first is to foster caring beyond the classroom, using positive role models to inspire altruism and providing opportunities at all grade levels for school and community service.

"The next schoolwide strategy is to create a total moral environment or ethos that supports and amplifies the values taught in classrooms. This makes use of the leadership of the principal, a schoolwide discipline plan, creating a moral community among adults, and simply setting a priority on moral concerns, without which effective moral education is impossible."

Lickona believes that time to reflect on moral concerns that arise in the life of the school is essential, noting that other matters—such as daily crises—too frequently receive the primary attention of school staff. This, in his view, is convoluted logic. "This is one of the main challenges schools face, protecting time to reflect on the quality of the moral life of the school."

Finally, school staff must reach out to parents and communities as full partners in the school's character education program. While this outreach actually may diffuse some parental opposition to the teaching of values in public schools, that is not why he advocates it. "The school needs to let parents know that the school considers them their child's first and most important moral educators. Then the school needs to offer parents specific ways they can teach at home the same values that the school is trying to teach. When the support of the wider community is enlisted, kids then hear the same messages and see the same good models all around."

With such a huge agenda, I said, what would he suggest to educators who might agree with the principles he outlines, but not know how to begin?

In his reply, Lickona offers some comfort. "They should realize that a comprehensive approach doesn't have to be done all at once," he said. "Actually, if school staff analyze what the school is already doing, they will find that they are doing many things that fit into those twelve different strategies. It might sound overwhelming at first hearing, but when staff discover they already are doing some work in conflict resolution, in cooperative learning, and in other areas, they can see the beginnings of a more formalized character education initiative."

Making character education an integral part of school life often means strengthening existing efforts more consistently across grade levels, he points out, or attending to areas where there are unaddressed problems.

"I recommend a leadership group as the first step, a character education task force or council. Next, this task force analyzes what the school is already doing. The third step is to ask: What else can we do? What can we do better? Where are the problems? Is there sexual harassment in the corridors? Food fights in the cafeteria? Terrorism on the school bus? Disrespect and incivility between adults and kids? Peer cruelty?"

Targeting the problem area or areas for special effort at the outset, Lickona noted, helps show observable results which encourage the further growth of a concerted character education effort. Also pointing out that character education is nothing new in the life of schools—although perhaps neglected in recent decades—gives school staff a frame of reference for their engagement in the moral endeavor.

Character's Common Cause

"Schools throughout history have had two basic purposes," Lickona said. "One is to help kids become smart; the other is to help them become good human beings. Developing both intellect and character have been the twin objectives of schooling from the ancient Greeks to the present, although we have lost sight of this during the past two to three decades in American education for a variety of reasons."

These reasons, he believes, range from what he terms "the growth of relativism, privatism, pluralism, personalism, and a number of other 'isms' that have undercut people's confidence that there *is* an objective morality that can be embraced and taught by our public institutions."

"Character education isn't new," he added. "What is new is the failure to teach it and to deliver it in a deliberate way."

The composition of the leadership group in the school and, more broadly, the district helps diverse constituencies pull together for the common cause of character, he says. "Some schools have a district committee, with representatives that include everybody from the school bus driver to the school superintendent to board members, parents, teaching faculty, clergy, and heads of youth organizations. It is wise to represent all groups because the effectiveness of the character education program depends upon everyone being on board.

"The next step is to set up individual building committees, because the building is the key unit."

He added, "In mounting a schoolwide effort, it is also important to avoid ethical schizophrenia where one thing is said in classrooms and another is done in other parts of the school environment such as the corridors, the cafeteria, or the Friday night football game. Consistency is the business of the ethical life."

Overcoming Barriers and Solving Problems

I asked: In his experience working with school staff, what problems block implementation of specific, targeted efforts to teach character in a schoolwide fashion?

Lickona paused, and then said with care, "One of the main challenges the field faces is how to get character education higher on the agenda of the nation's schools. Only a tiny fraction of schools approach this in anything close to the deliberate, systematic way we recommend in the movement."

One reason for this, he believes, is the lack of attention paid to character-building as an integral part of undergraduate teacher education. "Teachers don't have this as part of their mindset from their training."

Most professional educational organizations also have neglected character education as preeminent, he says. "Major educational establishments, with the exception of the Association for Supervision and Curriculum Development, haven't made character education a high priority. It hasn't been elevated to a position of importance equal to that of computer literacy, mathematics, reading, or writing."

The federal government has only recently taken an interest in pushing character education onto the national agenda, he points out. "Until recently there hasn't been strong visible federal leadership. The language of character education is not part of Goals 2000. Only recently has it become part of the rhetoric of the Secretary of Education. The 1994 and 1995 White House Conferences on Character-Building have been the exceptions."

States have been negligent as well, he maintains. "State education departments don't hold schools accountable for character education in the way they hold schools accountable for performance in math, reading, and writing. Typically, they don't ask schools to articulate how they plan to teach the values on which a democratic society rests."

The fear of possible controversy at the local level may inhibit the desire of school boards and school administrators to engage in a forthright, clearly articulated program of character education, he maintains. "Many school boards and administrators still think of anything related to values as a political hot potato, consequently to be avoided. They need lots of examples, lots of success stories that show how schools have been able to approach this in ways that have not been controversial and that have had some measure of success."

Sometimes parents, especially conservative parents, can become entrenched into deep pockets of resistance as well. "There are parents, understandably, who don't trust the schools to do a responsible job in this area. They ask: Aren't these the same people who are teaching our children how to put the condom on the banana? Are we going to turn over our children's moral formation to teachers and give them a green light to do what they want when we can't trust what they're doing in an area like sex education? Parents need to be assured that character education means teaching noncontroversial values—honesty, respect, fairness—in noncontroversial ways. It doesn't mean 'safe sex.'"

Finally, many teachers are reluctant to engage directly in character education because they worry someone will object, Lickona maintains. "Teachers need to have the security of a schoolwide effort that legitimates their efforts and gives them something from which they can draw strength."

Although there are a constellation of obstacles, Lickona points to the growing belief among educators that without the most basic rules of decency, teaching and learning cannot take place. "Principals and teachers everywhere are saying that increasingly kids are coming to school without any foundation in the area of values, without even a minimal sense of right or wrong. Schools know that if they don't do something in the area of character, they will not accomplish much in any other area."

Lickona believes that teachers' comfort level with character education rises once they know that such efforts result in pleasant, orderly environments that enhance teaching and learning. "Jan Gorman, a first-grade teacher in Syracuse, New York, begins the school year by focusing on one value each week. She starts with caring. Gathering the kids in a circle, she asks a series of questions: What is caring? Who can show caring? Where does it take place? How can each of us show caring in our classroom, our school, our neighborhoods, and our families?

"She makes a visual map of all the children's responses and posts it at the front of the room. Then she reads a story that she has selected on the theme of caring and conducts a discussion of the book with the children. Subsequently, she looks for opportunities during the rest of the school day to make connections between the discussion of caring and children's personal behavior. If a child behaves in a caring way, she'll compliment the child. If a child behaves in an uncaring or thoughtless way, she'll privately ask the child if that behavior showed caring. Each day of the week she reads a different story on caring and again has a discussion. By the end of the week, she says that caring has become established as an expectation in her classroom.

"This is just one of many ways to weave core values into the fabric of the classroom," Lickona observed.

Character Education and Religion

Are school staff and parents uneasy about the religious overtones of character education?, I asked Lickona.

"There are people on both sides of that concern," he replied. "Some people are worried that teaching values and character will mean teaching religion and they don't want that to happen. Others worry that teaching values and character will exclude religion from the conversation."

He told an anecdote from his recent experience of a parent who attended a presentation he gave on character education and asked: "If you can't bring the Bible into school discussions of morality, what basis do you have for saying something is right or wrong?"

Lickona responded by pointing to his own Catholic faith, which he said "holds that there is a natural moral law that tells us to be just and caring toward each other. We arrive at that natural law through reason and experience. If we lie, cheat, steal, and kill, human relations and society don't work very well.

"Reason and revelation can be shown to lead to the same moral truths. People of all faiths—and people of no religious faith—can agree that core ethical values are the rational foundation of a civil society and the basis of good personal character.

"Four reasons for these core values can be acknowledged by all," he continued. "Values such as respect, responsibility, honesty, and fairness promote and affirm our human dignity. They promote the development and welfare of the individual person. They certainly serve the common good. We cannot survive as a society without them. They meet the classical ethical test of reversibility: Would you want to be treated in this way? They meet the test of universalizability: Would you want all persons to act this way in a similar situation?

"These values," he added, "can be found in all the great religious traditions. They cut across religious faiths."

But Lickona has another, bolder point to make about religion in schools. "We need to educate students to be religiously literate as part of cultural literacy. Schools ran away from religion after the Supreme Court decision that banned prayer, but the same decision instructed schools never to become hostile toward religion, to have students learn about the role religion has played in their own cultures and histories. That part of the decision wasn't attended to; publishers and educators alike began to avoid even the mention of religion for fear they would be stepping on somebody's toes."

What does it mean to be religiously literate within the secular context of public schooling?, I asked him. "It means three things," Lickona replied. "It means understanding the role of religion in our moral beginnings and moral development as a nation. It means understanding that our country's continuing social reform movements—from the abolition of slavery to the Civil Rights movement to the current effort to secure the right to life before birth—all these movements have been inspired by a religious vision that life is sacred, that we are created equal in the sight of God and are called by God to live in harmony and justice. Finally, it means understanding the role of religious motivation in the lives of individuals, both in history and current events."

Cultural and religious literacy Lickona deems "legitimate" parts of the character education crusade, but he goes beyond both to emphasize that youth need to be provided with opportunities for moral action.

"The action part of character education is the toughest challenge, and character educators should not be glib about promising effects on behavior because that is the hardest part to accomplish. Developing habits of action means that kids need repeated opportunities to practice these virtues. Schools must provide opportunities to practice cooperation through cooperative learning, to practice caring through school service, to practice respect by working out rules that ensure respectful treatment in the classroom through class meetings and by holding people accountable to following those rules."

So he advocates practice in moral arenas, I asked, so that the moral decisions of youth are rooted in more than theory?

"Aristotle emphasized that virtues are not mere thoughts; rather, they are habits we develop by performing virtuous actions. People underestimate the number of experiences that children need before something even begins to be a matter of habit," Lickona answered.

This is a lot of work for school staff, parents, and community members, I commented. As our society has become busier—out of economic necessity—I asked, is that one reason scrupulous monitoring and careful attention to moral habits may have fallen away?

"Absolutely," Lickona agreed. "Character education takes a very definite investment of time and attention. As an adult, you have to have the character quality of persistence if you're going to form good character in kids. It's easy not to make that effort."

Lickona's work emphasizes the importance of enlisting parents in the character education effort. What happens, I asked, if the parents refuse to be engaged? Should the schools forge ahead, independent of their support?

"Schools make a profound mistake," he replied, "if they try to do this alone or even if they try to be the primary agent of children's moral socialization. As families go, so goes the nation. We know that no culture through history has been able to survive the massive disintegration of its families. We need a twenty-year plan for rebuilding the American family. The character education movement has to be very thoughtful about how to develop a full active partnership between schools and families.

"Schools will become discouraged if they feel that parents are indifferent and not holding up their end. They'll have a sense that something is wrong with this picture, that the school is stepping in and becoming the surrogate family, taking over what is properly the role and responsibility of the parents."

For that reason, Lickona recommends strongly that schools develop strategies to achieve the active involvement of parents, ranging from parent representation on the character education committee to forming a second committee composed entirely of parents. "The latter have the main mission of informing other parents about the character effort, getting them to support it in the life of the family by doing things that reinforce what goes on in school, and actively support what the school is doing so that the school feels it has the backing of parents.

"There are lots of ways for schools to strengthen this partnership," he said, sounding another note of optimism. "If you can't get parents to come to the school to talk about raising good kids, you find ways to send the program to the parents via the child. Children can report on a values project they did in the classroom, or they can interview their parents about their attitudes toward drugs and drinking. A number of successful sex education programs have sent parents copies of what was discussed that day in school so that there's an opportunity for parents to continue the conversation with their child and add their own perspectives on what the school has taught."

He concluded, "The greatest danger facing character education, as educational researchers David and Cheryl Aspy have observed, is that severe social problems will be met with only weak educational efforts. When weak efforts fail to ameliorate the problems significantly, people will say, 'We tried character education, and it failed.' The scale of our character education efforts must therefore be commensurate with the seriousness of the moral problems that confront us. In the long run, this means that all groups that touch the values and character of the young must work together. As we seek to secure a future for our children in the next century, educating for character is a moral imperative for us all."

Alan L. Lockwood:
The Current Incarnation
of Character

Alan L. Lockwood is Professor and former Chair of the Department of Curriculum and Instruction at the University of Wisconsin–Madison. His special areas of interest are secondary social studies and values education. Best known for his careful critiques of values education curriculum, his examination of the Values Clarification approach to values education showed how ethical relativism and violations of privacy rights can be embodied unintentionally in treatments of values in curriculum. He is the co-author (with David Harris) of Reasoning with Democratic Values: Ethical Problems in United States History, *a critically acclaimed curriculum for secondary school students which incorporates the study of values in the context of United States history. A member of the National Council for the Social Studies' Task Force on Character Education, Lockwood's recent writings have examined assumptions and issues related to the current character education movement.*

Unlike many people interested and engaged in issues related to the teaching of ethics, values, and character, Alan L. Lockwood assumes a deliberately critical stance when evaluating the efforts of the current character education movement. Interested in discovering if his definition of character education differs from that of its current proponents, I asked: How do you define character education? How does it differ from terms that have been used in the past to describe educative efforts related to the teaching of values, such as moral education or values education? Why does the public only hear of character education currently, rather than moral or values education?

"It is helpful to think of all those terms as forms of what can be called intentional values education," Lockwood began. "That is an umbrella term that covers any curriculum that is designed to address directly value questions—as opposed to the idea of the hidden curriculum, which suggests that people and institutions unintentionally send value messages. Or, if you are a conspiratorial type," he added dryly, "you might believe that schools are intentionally designed to create a sub-citizenry.

"Under that broad umbrella of values education, one can identify Values Clarification, moral education, and character education."

Although definitions, Lockwood warns, can be slippery, he thinks of character education—in what he terms "its current incarnation"—as distinguished from moral education and Values Clarification by its emphasis on changing the behavior of young people. "Current proponents of character education are trying to change what they perceive as an epidemic of negative, anti-social behavior of young people," he said.

"The moral education approach, at least in its early affiliation with Lawrence Kohlberg and his group, was seen as tangentially related to behavior, but primarily focused on getting young people to employ high levels of ethical reasoning and to use defensible moral principles when making judgments that affect the rights and well-being of other people—as opposed to selfish, antisocial reasoning.

"On the other hand, Values Clarification is quite different. It is most commonly understood—to use an old phrase—as helping young people 'get in touch with their feelings' about a wide range of value-laden issues. Again, Values Clarification was not disinterested in behavior but was tangentially related to it. Its primary goal was to create a better understanding for youth of what they believed was right and wrong for them."

Why is the current, popular term—a term brandished by everyone from William Bennett to university professors—the term universally used? "Everybody has to have a label to identify with," Lockwood responded. "The current dominance of that term is a consequence of the primary leaders, people who have chosen to label their advocacy work as character education."

Character Education's Previous Incarnation

He points out that a similar—and ill-fated—character education movement flourished briefly in the 1920s. "That movement," he explained, "was motivated in many ways by the same social conditions that motivate the current movement—a perception of social disorder and anti-social behavior among young people, along with the withering away of what might be considered a traditional moral compass in society. In the 1920s, the family, the church, and even respect for governmental dictates in the form of laws were perceived as no longer providing the social cement that allows civil decency to prevail. Of course, the leaders of the current movement have the same general fear."

What brought the character education movement of the 1920s to a close? I inquired.

"My theory," Lockwood replied, "is that the early character education movement promised more than it could deliver. It hoped for substantial effects on young people that it did not—and could not—produce. The watershed for the movement, in my judgment, was the publication of what was for that time a highly sophisticated and extensive set of research and evaluation projects conducted by Hugh Hartshorne and Mark May, which were published in the late 1920s. Hartshorne and May were strong advocates of character education and also had a firm religious motivation that inspired their promotion and endorsement of efforts to change the behavior of kids."

He continued, "Their quite sophisticated research on the effects of character education showed no effect on behavior. In particular, they looked at behaviors related to altruism and honesty and could not find—hard as they tried—increases in honest and altruistic behavior in young people who had gone through some form of character education."

As a result, Hartshorne and May concluded that the behaviors they were seeking were largely situational, Lockwood added. "They were unable to identify character traits or personality traits. They discovered that the world can't be divided into people who have good character and others who have bad character.

"Instead, they found that moral behavior seemed unconnected to any stable personality trait and clearly unconnected to any educational experiences the kids had or didn't have," he continued. "In other words, in some circumstances some people would cheat; in other circumstances, the same people would not cheat. To the chagrin of the leaders of the character education movement—and to their credit—they acknowledged that the efforts to change character didn't appear to have any real effect on the kinds of behaviors they were hoping to influence."

Was the way character education was approached in practice in the 1920s similar to the way in which it is approached currently?, I asked.

"I suspect so," Lockwood said judiciously. "It is problematic, because when people talk about character education, it is not clear to what they are referring. It is clear that they are referring to an effort that schools and other organizations are making, but that effort is not tangible and clearly defined, such as new math. It is easy to find out what people talked about in new math a couple of decades ago. Character education is much more diffuse. It was then, and it is now. Because character education efforts differ by school, it is difficult to know what actual practices are being used."

The underlying motivation behind the character education movement of the 1920s and the current movement is remarkably similar, he points out, as are many of the broad assumptions of character educators. "Primarily, the character education movement of the twenties—like the current movement— was distinguished by the belief that one can transform the character-related behavior of young people through education," he noted. "Character educators, then and now, believe that the behavior of young people can be shaped to be more socially acceptable."

The Evidence: Is Character Education Effective?

It would appear there is ample evidence that society is eroding, I said. Isn't that why character educators push for a program of character education in schools, believing substantive, value-related interventions need to be undertaken by social institutions to reverse the negative direction of society?

In his reply, Lockwood points to lists that frequently are produced by character educators to buttress their belief that schools are obliged to provide character education, and that such educative efforts will succeed in changing youth behavior. "Character educators such as Ed Wynne and Tom Lickona commonly refer to youth disorders, such as rates of teen pregnancy, drug use, violence, homicide, and suicide. In fact, William Bennett has produced what he calls 'The Index of Leading Cultural Indicators'—a deliberate effort to parallel the 'Index of Economic Indicators,'" he said.

While these indicators exist, Lockwood remains dubious that character education provides the solution that will either stem the anti-social tide or reverse it into a more positive direction. "Character education is the ten percent solution," he stated flatly.

What can character educators realistically hope to accomplish, especially when they confront the lack of evidence that character education directly changes youth behavior?, I asked.

"Less than they think they can," Lockwood said immediately. "In their most rosy moments, character educators believe that if schools really work at it, they can overcome many of these manifestations of trouble among young people.

"That is naive," he added. "Anti-social behavior is not simply a consequence of an individual's moral failings. To the extent that character educators perceive all anti-social behavior as primarily a consequence of the failure of individuals to be good people, they make a major mistake. They ignore the profound effects of poverty, economic deprivation, and familial disorder that affect the behavior of young people. They certainly know these factors exist. Unless they are taken seriously, the expectations of character educators are doomed to modest success at best. One thing they can develop is a moral vocabulary in young people, a way of describing situations that goes beyond whatever is expeditious."

He added, "Establishing a moral vocabulary is no small achievement, however."

Setting Character-Related Goals

Why have you emphasized an approach to value-laden issues in terms of moral reasoning in your own work—and yet see yourself as an observer, rather than a proponent, of the current character education movement?, I asked.

"What I and other curriculum developers influenced by Kohlberg have done is certainly not antithetical to character education," Lockwood said carefully, "but it sets a much more limited goal for schools. Our goal is to promote thoughtful consideration of moral decisions that people confront, both in the public or personal domain, although we focus more on the public domain. There is reason to believe that systematic opportunities for young people to debate openly ethical issues increases both their understanding of the moral context in which decisions are made, and, to some extent, the sophistication with which they make their moral decisions."

He added, "We don't claim any immediate clear effect on behavior, nor does responsible research in the area. Works summarized by James Rest show a modest association between the moral thinking of individuals and the behaviors in which they engage, but there is no simple direct relationship between moral thought or the values that people espouse and the actual behavior in which they engage at a specific time.

"Actually," he noted, "this kind of work lies in the critical thinking tradition. This tradition seeks to enhance people's ability to think clearly and in complicated ways. The fact that it focuses on ethical dilemmas and that it is derived in part from research on moral development makes it seem like it belongs in the character education domain, but its goals are much more modest."

Modest, attainable goals are clearly important to Lockwood, who returns to his concern with the causal relationship that character educators draw between character education efforts and youth behavior. "Character educators, unfortunately, are often guilty of allowing that simplistic equation to be at the heart of their psychology of moral behavior. At worst, character educators appear to say: Good values equal good behavior. Bad values equal bad behavior. In order to change bad behavior to good behavior, you need to change the values of the individuals. That is an equation with a lot of common-sense appeal to the general public, but it has absolutely no psychological validity."

How, I asked, should public school staff deal with the religious overlay inherent in the current character education movement?

"You don't have to have religion to have good character," Lockwood said with some force. "Some individuals in the character education movement do have strong religious motivations. Certainly they believe that people should have the right to express religious opinions in schools. There is nothing unconstitutional about that. I don't know of any character educator who publicly would advocate that schools represent a particular religious orientation.

"But I want to emphasize," he continued, "that one can have good character, one can behave decently and honorably in one's life without a particular spiritual, religious affiliation. Some character educators may disagree with me on that."

Many teachers appear to be reluctant to engage in any teaching that has to do with values, or issues related to values. Why is this the case?, I asked. How might it be overcome?

"We should distinguish between teachers who work with little kids and teachers who work with older kids," he pointed out. "Most elementary teachers, particularly in the early grades, believe that part of their job is to help little kids get along with one another and not fight on the playgrounds, not to throw food at each other during lunch time, to be reasonably orderly in the classroom, and so on. It is not difficult to persuade elementary teachers that part of their responsibility as teachers is to get little kids to behave well."

This belief completely breaks down at the high school level, however. "The reasons are fairly obvious," Lockwood said. "One is that high school teaching lies in the particular academic discipline. Teachers are hired by public schools and licensed by the state to be experts in their content area. Therefore, the definition of a good teacher at the high school or secondary level changes to mean someone who makes that content interesting and exciting to kids while communicating the learning objectives of their discipline effectively to young people."

Teacher training and licensure requirements do not include specific coursework or practica on transmitting moral values—and therefore provide no stimulus for teacher education programs to focus on character education. Instead, typical programs emphasize the accumulation of credits in the content area, such as social studies, English, or math. "An examination of transcripts at the preservice level will reveal that there is no list of courses in moral philosophy or how-to's on shaping and affecting young people's behavior," Lockwood pointed out.

Other significant barriers to instruction related to values at the high school level include high school teachers' perceptions of their role. "Few would see it as directly trying to change the behavior of young people," he added.

One distinct difference between elementary and high schools that affects programs related to character education is what he terms the "batch processing" of high schools in which teachers see large numbers of different students every day versus spending the entire day with the same group of children. "Elementary teachers have a greater opportunity structurally," Lockwood said, "to deal with little kids and see that their behavior is controlled—or at least modified."

The fear of political controversy also steers high school teachers away from value-laden issues, he emphasized. "It is very difficult to work with values issues, for all these reasons, at the high school level. Most of the examples of character education that are found in literature and are reported at conventions are done at the elementary school level. The most famous current program, the Child Development Project in California, was initiated at the elementary level, although recently it has expanded its efforts to the middle level."

Lockwood sees an irony in this discrepancy. "Earlier, we talked about various indices and descriptions of social disorder among young people. Most of those behaviors are reported among youth who are fourteen years old and older. Occasionally there will be a story about a third grader who has done something outrageous. Yet character education focuses almost exclusively on little kids. Now, why is that? One could theorize that we need to start with the little kids, but why is so little done with teenagers?"

What does current research suggest about the effectiveness of character education efforts?. I asked. Is the evidence the same as the Hartshorne and May studies of the 1920s, which discovered what the researchers did not want to find: the absence of a link between character education efforts and desired youth behavior?

Lockwood begins his answer by re-emphasizing that character education can mean almost anything, according to how one defines it. "Therefore, I would prefer that the question be formulated as: 'Is there any evidence that schooling intentionally designed to affect kids' behavior actually has any effect?'

"The Child Development Project has been identified persistently as having a positive effect on kids' behavior. If one wants to call that project character education, that's fine, but actually examining the project shows a mix of role-playing exercises, ethical discussions, and a wide variety of curricular innovation. It is difficult to separate out exactly what is character content. While there is some promise at the elementary school level that systematic hard work on value-related behavior can have an effect, whether it will be a long-term effect is up in the air."

Goals and expectations in the values arena should be restrained rather than overly ambitious, he believes. "We should not have unrealistic expectations," he said. "Behavior is complex. It is not totally determined by what people in education do or don't do, or what values they espouse. It is influenced by the social conditions in which people live. It is unrealistic to assume that children are totally malleable and will be affected only by the experiences they have in school. Character educators do acknowledge this, because they advocate extensive family and community involvement.

"It's just silly to think that schools can somehow have this profound impact on kids' behavior," he added. "The evidence is all to the contrary. If schools were such a potent influence on what kids think and do, we wouldn't have half the problems that we have. For instance, schools teach literacy and believe in it, but we still have a very high illiteracy rate."

What would it require for character education efforts to be effective?, I asked. "I don't claim to have a good answer to that," he responded. "At minimum, we need to know much more about what young people think and what influences their moral behavior before we invest great energies into programs which miss the mark.

"For example, in a survey sponsored by the Girl Scouts of America—a survey of beliefs and moral values of America—they asked kids what they rated as social problems," he continued. "The problems reported from a representative sample—not just from the Girl Scouts—were not problems such as violence or drug use. Instead, they worried about getting good grades, preparing themselves adequately for the future, and coping with the pressure on them to do well in sports and get along with their peers.

"They also asked the kids to whom they would turn for advice if they had a moral problem and teachers were at the bottom of the list."

Mulling over his words, he added: "To put it metaphorically, when kids don't respect what teachers have to say about matters of morals or morality, how effective can teachers be if they adopt that responsibility? My guess," he noted somewhat darkly, "is that the average fourteen-year-old is more influenced by his or her peer group than by five teachers talking all day long."

He concluded on a note of inquiry: "What are the implications of the possibility that young people do not see teachers as great sources of moral wisdom? Are character educators urging teachers to be preachers to a congregation that doesn't recognize the clergy?"

B. Bradford Brown:
Who Adolescents Really Are

B. Bradford Brown is a Professor in the Department of Educational Psychology and research scientist at the Wisconsin Center for Education Research at the University of Wisconsin–Madison. He has written numerous articles for scholarly books and journals on coping with stress in adulthood and on peer relations in adolescence. He is especially well known for his work on teenage peer groups and peer pressure and their influence on school achievement patterns. From 1986 to 1990, Brown was a Principal Investigator at the U.S. Department of Education's National Center on Effective Secondary Schools at the University of Wisconsin–Madison. In addition to providing inservices to schools and parent groups, he has served on the Science Policy Working Group of the Carnegie Council on Adolescent Development, participated in the Wingspread Conference on Adolescents and School Reform, and been a featured speaker at the U.S. Department of Education's Conference on Student Motivation.

The picture that the American public draws from media portraits of adolescents is grim: reckless youth bent on pleasure, recreational drugs, and sex, addicted to computer games, devoid of morals. What is the truth about American adolescents today?, I asked Brown. In what ways do they differ from American adolescents of twenty years ago?

"One major difference is exposure," Brown began. "Adolescents today are exposed to a much broader array of experiences prior to achieving adulthood than was typical for teenagers even twenty years ago. A higher proportion of teenagers are products of nontraditional household situations for at least part of their childhood or adolescence. A higher proportion are involved in serious risk-taking behavior as well as more nominal sorts of activities. Some sexual activity is more extensive than it was thirty years ago, perhaps not twenty years ago. Drug use is a little more common or at least accepted within teenage culture than it was twenty years ago."

But the biggest difference is the dramatic expansion of diversity within the student population. "A greater proportion of adolescents are in environments with a broader diversity of peers than was normal twenty or thirty years ago. This diversity is a function of school desegregation as well as demographic changes towards ethnic diversity within our society."

He noted that it is important to realize that researchers' understanding of adolescents has changed also over the past twenty years. "It is difficult to separate our understanding of adolescents and the actual change in adolescents," he pointed out, "because as our society has become more diverse, researchers have become sensitive to the diversity. That has worked into our studies of teenagers, in part because there is more diversity within society, but also because we've become more sensitized to the diversity."

One of the biggest changes in adolescents in the last twenty-five years, he reports, is a difference in the way they view their personal futures and the world around them. Where youth of twenty-five years ago were optimistic that they could make an impact on their times, today's adolescents are considerably more cautious and modest in their aspirations.

Brown said, "At the beginning of the 1970s, adolescents believed they could change the world and believed they had the resources as well as the time to do so. Today, teenagers are much more wary. They are not certain their marriages are going to last, not certain their careers will last. Twenty years ago, teenagers believed that they would not only change their own personal lives but the lives of the country as well."

Even ten years ago, adolescents were somewhat ambitious about their own careers and about the opportunities available to them, he says. "Now, adolescents are driven more into themselves and show their ambition in their values and interests, in what they can make personally of their lives. They are more pessimistic about their capacity to make any impact on society, more pessimistic about the direction in which it is heading, and more pessimistic about their capability to grab the brass ring early in their careers."

What accounts for this pessimism, these diminished expectations?, I asked. What influences on adolescents tilt them in this direction?

"There are two main forces," Brown replied, "economic and technologic. The economy is very different from the economy that carried from the late sixties into the early seventies. At that time, the economy still was expanding. It appeared that there were tremendous opportunities for individuals at all ages, particularly for individuals at the start of their careers."

The social movements of the 1960s and 1970s also shaped youth's belief in the future, he emphasized. "The women's movement, the equal rights movement, the civil rights movement—all appeared to reshape the nature of our society and the relationships among different groups. It was also a time of curriculum experimentation in the schools.

"Over the course of time, those social movements sputtered and faltered. So did the economy, to the point where prospects for the future were grim.

We have learned in recent years that one generation cannot have the dramatic impact that it expected to have. We can learn lessons from the baby boom generation, which started with a dream that turned into a different kind of vision."

The fact that baby boomers ended up trimming their ambitions is a lesson that was absorbed by youth who currently are coming of age, he remarked. "Adolescents tend to believe that perhaps it is not realistic or rational to dream idealistic dreams. This is not to say that teenagers today are not idealistic, but I think they are less idealistic than any other teenagers in recent history."

The impact of technology has had a stunning effect on adolescents, who are confronted with a dizzying area of cable channels, interactive computer activities, computer games, and rock videos. "We can easily tune in to thirty or forty channels at a time as opposed to three or four at a time," Brown pointed out. "Adolescents can sample a wider array of the media; they can chat with people around the world on interactive computers, not knowing who they are in any great detail."

How does their sense of diminished expectations affect adolescents' attitudes toward school?, I asked. Is there an appreciable difference between current youth and youth of twenty years ago?

At a superficial level, Brown sees little change. "Twenty years ago, kids would say that school was boring. Today they say that school is boring. So, on the surface, there are not tremendous differences.

"However, below that statement that 'school is boring,' there is a message. Twenty years ago, adolescents seemed to believe that high school was something that they had to endure before they could get on with their lives. There was a sense of a certain anxiety that they were ready to move on with their lives, but they would get what they needed later on. Today, the pessimism comes out in the belief that school will not prepare kids for the future, that they are entering adulthood with that big strike against them."

Again, Brown sees this in economic terms. "As the economy tightens," he added, "adolescence is extended."

The Influence of Peer Group Affiliations

In what ways do peer groups affect how well adolescents achieve in school? Do peer groups significantly influence adolescents' attitudes toward life and school?, I inquired.

"There are dramatic differences among members of one peer group as opposed to another," Brown reflected. "These differences include their school orientation and, to a certain extent, their orientation toward their future and school performance as well. In some schools, the difference between the 'brain' crowd and the 'druggy' crowd is as great as two full points on a four-point GPA scale.

"Whether this is a function of peer influences is another issue. Our perception as researchers is that students arrive at high school from middle school already equipped with an ability level, an interest level, and a set of academic orientations. They already apply themselves to schoolwork at differing levels and have varying senses of the meaning of school in one's greater life plan. Those components, among others, are factors that establish one's image or reputation among peers. Crowd affiliation or crowd assignments are made from that image and reputation that an adolescent has among his peers."

This is not an unconscious process, Brown emphasized. "Kids realize that they have certain interests and abilities, and they realize they seem to qualify more for one group than for another. They are just like adults. We gravitate toward individuals who share our own attitudes, orientations, and opinions—and then are nurtured and reinforced by the norms, values, and expectations of that particular group.

"In adolescence there is a vicious circle," he continued. "Teenagers feel a need to fit in or belong or establish a reputation that associates them with a particular crowd. If that occurs and peers recognize their crowd affiliation or their reputation, they begin to treat them in accordance with that. If they naturally form friendships among people who are part of certain crowds as opposed to part of other crowds, those values and orientations get reinforced. What we find is that crowd affiliation is a naturally divisive force that takes small, sometimes subtle differences between groups and accentuates them."

The popular image of peer pressure as some powerful, inexorable force that teenagers cannot avoid—a fulcrum that pushes them into action—is simply not accurate, Brown contends. "This image of peer pressure is overblown," he said. "This is as true today as it was thirty or forty years ago. Today, there is a real reluctance to acknowledge that peer groups exist and that they do have effects on individuals, although not to the extent that has been portrayed in the popular media."

Why a reluctance to acknowledge the presence of peer groups?, I asked.

"As Americans, we believe we should all row our own boats," Brown answered. "If I am acknowledged as a jock or a druggy or a black, I'm falling into someone else's marching line—but that is what adolescence is all about. A second factor is that this generation has grown up with a powerful dose of school programs telling them the horrors of peer pressure and how they should never give in to it."

The campaign against peer pressure, Brown says, began in the mid-1970s with a concerted emphasis on individualism. "There were lots of strategies put forward for building personal self-confidence and self-esteem, along with decision-making strategies for the individual. The impact of these programs on individuals is that they resulted in adolescents' adopting negative attitudes about belonging to groups or crowds. In some communities more than in others, there is also increased sensitivity to divisions that are racial or ethnic.

"In other ways, the pendulum is swinging in the other direction. There are thoughts that maybe the whole notion of desegregating schools wasn't such a good idea. Perhaps the prices of busing are not worth the benefits it was supposed to produce. We start to drift back and forth, thinking in terms of neighborhood schools on the one hand versus an Afro-centric curriculum on the other. As schools become more culturally diverse, crowds tend to crystallize along ethnic lines as opposed to interests or abilities. That is uncomfortable and disquieting for many people, and I can understand teenagers' concern about it."

Teenagers and Race Relations

Do you see teenagers today as forging new race relations for themselves, or are they mimicking race relations that they see within the greater society?, I asked. What do the actions and attitudes of high school students tell us about the future of race relations?

"Today's adolescents won't lead us into a new age of racial relationships," Brown responded, "but it isn't because of teenagers themselves. Rather, they seem to reflect what is going on in their own families and communities rather than charting a course for themselves.

"Racism is very much alive," he continued. "Ethnic prejudices are still brewing, but they are subtle. They are not expressed openly and blatantly, and consequently they are not easily recognized or dealt with. We are venturing into an age where we recognize that ethnocentrism, racism, or ethnic-oriented prejudices cut both ways. One can see that among the individuals of ethnic minority groups as well as ethnic majority groups. There has been," he added, "an interesting change among adolescents in the past ten years."

Ten years ago, Brown emphasized, racial harmony was a goal that teenagers believed possible and desirable. "Today, you still hear some of that, but teenagers also acknowledge some concerns, frustrations, and resentments, particularly among the majority. They feel they have tried to achieve harmony and don't feel they have been accepted. There seems to be tension between the races in the schools, and no one feels he or she is to blame. Actually, teenagers are a little angry or disappointed or bitter about the status of race relations. As they begin to articulate their feelings, they also begin to realize that maybe they are not as prejudice-free as they originally presented themselves. If there is hope for the future, there is hope in that honesty—and the possibility of exchanges of honest opinion on racism."

A backlash has begun?, I asked.

"You see it among parents as well as adolescents," Brown responded. "And it's not a function of desegregation or busing because those efforts naturally were thwarted at the level of social interaction patterns. For example, at the same time that school systems were making concerted efforts to integrate the races, children and adolescents—particularly adolescents—found ways to fend those efforts off.

"In studies of human development, we see that as kids go through grade school and into high school, cross-race interaction diminishes. That occurred historically, even at a time when opportunities for cross-race interaction were theoretically abundant."

Something about adolescence works to separate the races, he added. "It is very subtle. If you walk into a high school, you still see lots of cross-race interaction. If you ask teenagers to list their friends, there are a fair number of kids who will include some individuals from different racial groups. That's not uncommon among adolescents.

"Yet, kids will say that when they march into middle school, everything changes. There is a pulling back, particularly among minority youth. It seems that peers send subtle messages that it is not right—not cool—to spend too much time with individuals from different ethnic groups."

What causes this behavior at the middle school age? I asked. Why middle school?

"Adolescence is a time when individuals need to come to grips with their sense of identity," Brown observed. "That has been one of the mainstays of our understanding of adolescence for the last twenty to thirty years. We used to think that coming to terms with one's identity was a generic process within any given culture, and that everyone went through it in pretty much the same way. We thought that identity was in part individual but also in part cultural. We saw our identity as being our own person but also an American, or a Cuban, or whatever I may be.

"Today, as we become more aware of the diversity within our particular culture, it begins to mean more. If it means more, it needs to be incorporated into that sense of self. For me to really and truly discover who I am as a person, I need to withdraw a little from cross-racial interaction patterns in order to explain what it means to be black or Native American or Cuban or whatever it may be. There are, of course, social consequences for that withdrawal."

What Brown terms "the subtheories" about identity formation appear to suggest that individuals will go through this stage of individuation as a normal part of growing up, and then move back to relationships with individuals from other racial groups—"in a different form," he added.

What about group affiliations such as gangs?, I asked. How does affiliation with a group change to membership in a gang?

"We have little understanding of how that process emerges," Brown said, "but my sense is that gang membership begins as a particular image or style, easily understood by adolescents who watch MTV at home. I can adopt that particular culture if I want to and become a gang 'wannabe.' The 'wannabe' is still a real outsider to the gang.

"There are screening processes for individuals who want to get into the gang on a deeper level. At that point, we need to look at gangs as businesses or corporations rather than some sort of adolescent-oriented group. The leadership positions in gangs are held by adults, not adolescents, and there is a huge profit motive that fuels them."

Gangs are corporations, literally, Brown emphasizes, with individuals filtering through the ranks and promoted to higher positions for superior accomplishments and contributions to the group. "As they move to higher positions, there are tremendous rewards. Sometimes there are tremendous risks as well. When individuals cross the bridge from being a 'wannabe' to full-fledged gang membership, some of the affiliation is psychological and some is a function of the community."

He notes that gangs are not completely anti-social, but also serve pro-social needs as well. "For example, they often sponsor young aspiring athletes with cash so that they can afford the latest in clothes and equipment for their athletic efforts. They are not terribly different from corporations, except that the gang's economic means are illegal."

Particular "types" of adolescents do gravitate to gangs, he clarified. "There are teenagers who are establishing a reputation as a punk or a headbanger, and those who embrace that image in a more extreme fashion, cutting off all relationships with people who do not fit that image. Relationships with parents, teachers, and other adults are put aside. Relationships with peers who are not punks or headbangers become more antagonistic.

"Who is engaging in this behavior?," he asked. "Usually it is a kid who has problems. His problems, however, are not the creation of his particular peer group but more likely relate to experiences of long standing in the family and in the school. To liberate that child from that environment is a real challenge because it is hard for adults to get close enough to do so, and to do so one has to address many issues."

Is gang membership anything that the school has the power to affect?, I asked.

"I'm hopeful," Brown commented, "that the school has a major role to play with gangs. Because gangs are so difficult to study, people have not studied them very carefully. Instead, they've plunged forward with gang prevention or violence prevention programs without really understanding the phenomena with which they are dealing.

"It is not uncommon for gang members at age 20 or age 25 to look back and say: 'That was a bad choice. I wish I had not done this. And you should not do this either.' The money that rolls in is great, but the personal insecurity is a high price to pay. Schools can latch onto those feelings if they can provide teenagers with some hope, some reason not to join gangs. In many communities, gangs are a real avenue toward some form of success."

Schools cannot work alone, he added. "It isn't possible for schools to do it all, and our society has expected schools to deliver on this problem. However, the hope that teenagers are looking for is contingent upon their prospects for a reasonable future at age 20 or 30 or 40, not at 12, 13, or 15. In other words, there is no reason for kids to buy into schools and school culture if they don't see a community that is going to support the efforts of kids. In the interim, schools can help by featuring some success stories. They also can help by meeting teenagers at their level of need rather than at the school's level of need. They can do a better job of understanding the nature of an adolescent's life, to try to fulfill some of teenagers' needs in their school—above and beyond academic lessons. Some schools do that effectively, and as a result, they don't realize they already have an effective gang prevention program."

Many educators have arrived at responses to youth behavior problems, I said, with the result that some believe in violence reduction programs, others in gang prevention programs, and others in broader programs such as concerted efforts focused on character education. What kind of response to anti-social youth behavior do you suggest on the part of schools?, I asked.

"We're too quick to pass judgment on the different approaches that schools and communities have taken to the array of problem behaviors among youth," Brown reflected. "Essentially, we decide that if there is not a certain percentage that indicates a success rate, then the program is a failure. That is based on a curious American notion that life is simple and that there is one single answer for any particular dilemma."

As a result, he believes, a whole variety of problem behaviors have been clustered together when they should be separated and targeted for intervention. "Human beings aren't put together that simply. As a result, programs don't work that simply. For a while, we thought that if we just nurtured self-esteem in early adolescence that kids would avoid peer pressure automatically, shy away from drug and alcohol abuse, and avoid violence and aggression toward each other.

"If self-esteem wasn't the answer, then preparing for jobs or planting the fear of the consequences of unprotected sex or drug use was the answer. If we really and truly are addressing a very diverse audience—not only diverse in terms of social and family backgrounds, but also in terms of developmental characteristics—we need to develop a whole variety of approaches to different problems. Instead, it's much more expedient for a school system to look at the array of violence prevention programs, pick one, train everyone to do it, and then have everyone work with it in the same way so that all students are exposed to the same program.

"The problem with that approach is that it doesn't recognize the inherent diversity of the American teenager. It ties into the stereotype that teenagers are all alike, instead of realizing that teenagers are even more diverse than are adults. Some will respond to one program that others think is silly."

A program with a 20 percent success rate may not sound effective, Brown pointed out, but is very effective for the teenagers that are part of the 20 percent. "Over time we would hope to find the appropriate audience for that program as a means of increasing the percentage of effectiveness. An alternative program, targeted to different kids, addresses the same issues in different ways. Of course, the difficulty is that this approach demands more resources."

How can schools afford to provide such a plethora of programmatic responses?, I asked.

"It has to be a community effort," Brown replied. "How do specialty stores exist in a mall? How can they afford to target such a small audience? They do so with low inventory and knowledge of their clientele. They keep on hand what will sell, what will get out the door. They use marketing strategies that hit hard on the people who are the most likely to respond.

"What that takes in resources is quite a lot. But we might think about how we address a diverse set of shoppers when we think about reaching diverse students in schools."

Parenting Practices and Academic Achievement

What parenting practices, I asked, appear to affect academic achievement in adolescence—both positively and negatively? Are there practices that have no effect at all?

"In recent years," Brown said, "the work on parenting practices has described basic differences in the orientation that adults take toward the task of parenting. The most common form of that is parenting styles. Researchers concentrate on two major dimensions: first, the degree to which parents place demands or expectations on their children; and second, the degree to which they maintain or foster warm and caring relationships with their kids as opposed to cold or distant relationships.

"If we think of these two as separate, independent aspects of what parents do, we can cross them and come up with four basic strategies. The research suggests that parents who place certain expectations on their kids and simultaneously maintain a warm and caring stance toward them—often called an authoritative parenting style—have kids who tend to do best in school."

But people are complicated, and it is impossible to impose a template upon parents that will produce uniform results. "No one strategy works consistently," he added. "That may be because there are certain environments where parents have an authoritative parenting style that aren't the most adaptive for the kids. For example, this particular parenting style doesn't seem very effective in our studies of school achievement among African-American or Asian-American youth. The best sense we can make of that is that in environments that are inner-city, parents cannot afford to be authoritative. They need to be authoritarian. That is, they need to be more iron-handed—not as warm and accepting—because the dangers in the environment are so strong. If they don't keep a close hand on their kids, they will escape. The other pull in these environments is that parents often sense they have lost control by the time of adolescence. They feel they have lost control to the streets or the gangs. At that point, whatever parents do isn't going to make much of a difference."

The reason why the authoritative parenting style may be less effective with Asian-American youth is different, he contends. "It appears that the environment around Asian-American high school students is so nurturing of academic achievement that even when parents are laid back the kids still tend to perform very well. It is not easy to prescribe a particular course of action. Parenting styles need to be placed within the larger context of influences in both the peer environment and the neighborhood environment particular to the kids."

But there is a general lesson, he believes, and it is that parents still have the power to make a strong impact on the academic and social lives of their children. This is a hopeful message, he emphasizes, and one from which parents can take heart.

Part II

Dealing with Difference:
Race, Culture, and Ability

Differences challenge assumptions.

—Anne Wilson Schaef, *Women's Reality*

Overview of Part II

As B. Bradford Brown observed in part I, one of the most profound changes in the contemporary student population from previous student populations is its diversity. Some educators are bewildered by the diversity they encounter: great ranges in income level, family backgrounds and ethos (including the definition of what actually constitutes a family), differences in parenting styles, racial polarities, widely varying levels of English-language acquisition, and varying levels of ability and achievement. Conversely, other educators appear to welcome this diversity as a provocation that spurs their best practice. Why? Is this a matter of individual temperament or can all educators learn to teach in a manner that is respectful and nurturant of individual differences, abilities, races, ethnicities, and levels of language achievement?

The educational leaders included in this section offer a variety of responses to the topic, "Dealing with Difference." First, I talk to Christine E. Sleeter, who takes a broad view of multicultural education, emphasizing that it should not be reduced to the programmatic level, but instead must be seen as an entire way of viewing the world and the people in it. Next, Gloria Ladson-Billings advances her theory of culturally relevant pedagogy, drawn from her research as a Spencer Foundation Post-Doctoral Fellow. Ladson-Billings argues for pedagogy that draws upon students' cultural experiences as the wellspring for authentic instruction that will not leave them conflicted about their racial or ethnic identities but simultaneously will prepare them for mainstream society. Lily Wong Fillmore discusses the particular role that language plays in any consideration of diversity, specifically addressing issues of pedagogy for students learning English as a second language, and more largely, dissects the ambivalence Americans have as a society about diversity and immigrants. Anne Fairbrother, an English and ESL teacher at North Salinas High School in Salinas, California, roots both the issues of ethnic/racial diversity and English language acquisition in examples drawn from her classroom teaching experience.

Next, I turn to conversations that focus on ability, talent, and "giftedness." Joseph S. Renzulli advocates an expanded definition of talent, one in which as many children as possible participate in enrichment programs distinct from the regular curriculum. He is followed by Mara Sapon-Shevin, who critiques existing gifted and talented programs for their inequity, insisting that education needs to change systemically to provide all children with the type of peda-gogy and curriculum offered in programs for those children identified as gifted and talented. Next, Howard Gardner discusses his theory of multiple intelli-gences and the reaction it has received in the educational community, advances some reasons for the widespread interest in the theory, and insists that education must be as personalized as possible to maximize each child's talents. Finally, Thomas R. Hoerr illustrates how Gardner's multiple intelligences theory has functioned as a framework for reform at the New City School in St. Louis, Missouri, and provides concrete examples that show how staff used the theory both to legitimize, enrich, and extend their practice.

Christine E. Sleeter:
Understanding and Embracing
Multicultural Education

Christine E. Sleeter is a professor and planning faculty member at California State University, Monterey Bay. Previously she was a Professor of Teacher Education at the University of Wisconsin–Parkside. She consults nationally on multicultural education and multicultural teacher education. Sleeter has received several awards for her work, including the National Association for Multicultural Education Research Award and the American Educational Research Association Committee on the Role and Status of Minorities in Education Distinguished Scholar Award. She has published numerous books and articles on multicultural education. Her most recent books include Keepers of the American Dream, Developing Multicultural Teacher Education Curricula *(with Joseph Larkin), and* Multicultural Education, Critical Pedagogy, and the Politics of Difference *(with Peter McLaren). In addition, she edits the series entitled "The Social Context of Education" for SUNY Press.*

When Christine Sleeter began teaching in the Seattle public schools in the early 1970s, her eyes were opened to the way most schools view multicultural education: a program that can be patched onto the regular curriculum. "The Seattle schools had undergone the desegregation process before I started teaching," she recalled, "and had programs in place to try to deal with some of the most overt manifestations of tensions between the kids."

She added, "Often white educators are concerned most about the tensions between the kids, whereas educators of color are more concerned with academic expectations."

At the time she began teaching, a group of Seattle educators received funds through the Ethnic Heritage Act for the purpose of developing curricula to help elementary school children relate to one another in the relatively recent desegregated context of the Seattle schools. "This was a very real problem," she noted, "and I don't think any of the people in that group conceptualized kids relating to each other as the whole of what needed to be done. They worked hard to develop materials that could be infused into the curriculum. But if you

53

were to pick up the materials they developed today and think that was the sum of multicultural education, you would be mistaken."

To Sleeter, in order to understand the wellspring of multicultural education and its goals, it is crucial that educators and the public recognize—and grapple with—the power of institutionalized oppression. Many well-intentioned multicultural educative efforts fall short of their goals, she maintains, because they do not deal directly with racism. "If you look at many curriculum materials developed by people who don't know anything in depth about racial oppression in the United States, then you will see that multicultural education too frequently becomes a cutesy program that is added on to what you are already doing in the classroom. The whole idea of the struggle against racial oppression from which multicultural education emerged then turns into a little program that is dropped into what you're already doing."

The Roots of Multicultural Education

Sleeter draws a fundamental distinction between multicultural education as an entity and misguided programmatic efforts to patch it onto the existing curriculum: First and foremost, multicultural education must not be reduced to a "program."

"When I think about multicultural education," she said, "I think about it in the context of the history from which it came. It emerged in the context of the civil rights movement, as people of color were striving to break down various barriers that were excluding them from full participation in American society."

The hope and optimism held by leaders of the civil rights movement fueled the belief that, as minority students entered previously segregated schools, obstacles would melt away, yielding new opportunities to achieve and succeed. Instead, other barriers to their full participation in public schooling emerged, Sleeter says, and are just as potent today as previously.

"Some of the barriers are still present," Sleeter noted, "and include such things as teachers holding low expectations of the ability of students of color to learn; curricula that focuses on white people and people of European descent; and systems of grouping and tracking, which place African-American kids, non-English-speaking kids or Latino kids into the lower tiers and institutionalize lower expectations in the process."

Multicultural education challenged these obstacles in a serious way, she contends, that was just as much political as educative. "When multicultural education is downsized into a program, it happens through a couple of different, but related, processes," she pointed out. "One is the capacity of a bureaucracy to be able to absorb changes without really changing, or changing minimally and keeping many other things as they were. Another process is through the teaching profession, which consists primarily of white, upwardly mobile working-class or middle-class people constructing education from a vantage point that fits their own worldview."

She believes that the coupling of these processes has resulted in the institutionalization of discrimination, inequality, and oppression in the ways in which teachers think about students of color.

Sleeter reports that she frequently sees this institutionalization of discrimination in the white student teachers with whom she works. "They cannot understand oppression beyond individual stereotyping and individual acts of discrimination. In fact, they have real difficulty with the whole idea of systemic oppression."

Another contributing factor to the trivialization of multicultural education, she reports, is the way that multicultural education is often reduced to its ethnic component, and that ethnic component is condensed further into food, music, dance, and literature. "White people think about their ethnic identity in terms of food, folk tales, and stories our grandmothers told us. Those things are indeed a part of ethnicity. But deeper ideas about what culture is, as well as other things that are really important to the struggles of people of color, aren't things we tune in on.

"A number of my students, when they think of multiculturalism, think of what ethnicity means to white people. White people generally don't see our everyday lives as cultural. We take for granted much of how we think and live as 'normal.' To identify what is cultural, we think in terms of Old World customs that have been passed down and tagged as such. I, for instance, love the ethnic festivals in Milwaukee during the summer. But those festivals are a concrete manifestation of the food, dances, and music of an ethnic group. If you don't study another group's history, you may never get beyond the food festivals, dance, and music approach to what multicultural education is."

The Goals for Multicultural Education

Given the varying interpretations and applications of multicultural education—and all the barriers it confronts—what should be its goals? I asked.

To Sleeter, these goals are intimately intertwined with the ideals of the founding fathers of the United States: democracy, justice, and equality. "I don't think these ideals are exclusive to European people," she adds. "Indian people were living those ideals already on the North American continent.

"But those ideals haven't been a part of how a good deal of business has been conducted in the United States. Until 1954, people of color were legally excluded in a whole variety of ways. This blatant exclusion flies in the face of the ideals upon which this country was founded. So does the genocide of Native people."

Multicultural education cannot be other than political, economic, social, and cultural, she maintains, since it attempts to redress the wrongs and inequities of society. "The goals of multicultural education include learning how to bring the realities of the political, economic, social, and cultural processes of this country in line with the goals that we espouse."

She added, "It is clear that this country will not sustain itself if it doesn't work very seriously on that."

The importance of high expectations for all students is the key underpinning for multicultural education—something much more difficult to attain than rhetoric would suggest. "We must teach low-income and minority kids as if they are capable of brilliance. This is fundamentally important to what multicultural education should be about. Although there are people who do this, and do it very well, often it doesn't happen at all."

She points out that too frequently educators regard racial, ethnic, and economic status as barriers not worth trying to overcome. "I recently met a principal of a predominantly African-American and Latino elementary school in Dallas. For a long time, her school was one of the lowest-achieving schools in Dallas. Many people jeered at them. The attitude was: 'These kids can't achieve because their parents are on welfare.' In a relatively short period of time, she was able to transform the school and the expectations of achievement. Now it is the top-achieving school in Dallas.

"Her basic message is: 'This isn't magic. This is hard work and it means that we expect a lot from the kids. We follow through with more hard work.'"

Differing Approaches to Multicultural Education

In broad strokes, Sleeter swiftly outlines different approaches to multicultural education, describing briefly their limitations and strengths.

"Clearly, kids who are not achieving very well need to achieve at high academic levels," she said. "Carl Grant and I call one approach teaching the exceptional and culturally different. It asks: How can we help kids to achieve? Teachers then work with strengths and cultural resources kids have, building learning on the bases kids—all kids—bring with them. Jaime Escalante would be a wonderful example of someone who uses this approach extremely well. He teaches kids calculus very successfully. But he doesn't teach them to critique the dominant ideology, which other approaches do.

"What is known as the single group studies approach occurs in the intellectual scholarship of university departments of ethnic studies, black studies, Indian studies, women's studies, and so forth. Rather than seeking to integrate knowledge about different groups, scholars have been retrieving information and reconceptualizing the disciplines from the vantage points of different oppressed groups. For instance, in women's studies, people theorize about what history would look like if it was centered around the study of women. They ask: What would count as the best literature written by women, and on what basis do we make that decision?"

While these studies are an attempt to reconceptualize curriculum around a single group, their power often is forfeited in schools. "What often gets lost in schools," Sleeter said, "is the part about drawing on the intellectual scholarship and intellectual leadership of ethnic studies or women's scholars. When teachers do single group studies, too often they end up relying upon their own assumptions about what they think is worth teaching—without backing up their assumptions with solid research."

In contrast, the multicultural approach, she says, looks at how a classroom and school can be built around a pluralistic model in terms of race, ethnicity, language, social class, gender, and disabilities. "Everything that goes on in the school is pluralistic," she continued. "The multicultural approach takes the best of the ideas from the other approaches, such as a strong emphasis on academic achievement. It takes the best of the ideas from the intellectual scholarship in the single group studies approach, and works to synthesize those into a coherent curriculum. The school in Dallas that I mentioned probably works with that approach."

The final approach, the social reconstruction approach, Sleeter describes as "a politicized version of the multicultural approach, in which people focus on analyzing structures of oppression. People who work from the multicultural approach tend to focus more on cultural aspects and people who work from the social reconstruction approach tend to politicize cultural aspects and focus on structures of oppression when they talk about what multicultural education means."

Can people who do not understand the nature of oppression work successfully with a truly multicultural approach to education?, I asked. Could their self-consciousness about teaching something in which they are not invested ultimately doom their efforts to failure?

"The schools don't exist in a vacuum," Sleeter responded. "All of us have grown up and lived in a racist society, a sexist society, a capitalist society. We bring our life experiences with us into the schoolroom. Teachers can teach academic content and skills more effectively without understanding oppression, if they believe in the kids. You don't have to rework your whole perspective on the world before you can become a better teacher. But at the same time, we can't just walk into the schools and think we will be able to teach in a multicultural way without expecting to do a lot of learning, some of which may be difficult and painful."

She believes that people should be willing to undergo the arduous struggle that results when grappling with issues pertaining to race and oppression. "This would be much better than trying to segment their lives into living in one way in their lives outside school, and then trying to be 'multicultural' when they get to school. If you try to do multicultural teaching without engaging with people of diverse backgrounds in your everyday life, you end up doing things in the classroom the kids don't buy into because they know that you don't believe in or really understand what you're teaching."

Perhaps the best place to begin with multicultural education is the most difficult: an honest self-scrutiny of values and attitudes about race, ethnicity, and culture.

Is it realistic to think that staff development, in its most frequent current incarnations, will either facilitate or encourage such relentless self-examination?, I inquired.

"Certainly there are many issues that relate to staff development and multicultural education," Sleeter said, "but there are also profound issues about who we hire to teach our children. I have seen schools hire, then try to inservice, an all-white staff in the belief that staff development will produce multicultural education, but that approach clearly does not work—especially when staff development means an occasional half-day inservice. You wouldn't teach someone who can't read how to read that way. Most people know that reading is complex and takes lots of time and work. So does developing a multicultural perspective."

She added, "There is also the issue of how much you can develop people who already are in the schools. I think we should put much more energy into recruiting a culturally diverse teaching force, which means doing some serious re-thinking of the whole certification process."

She reports concern about the people who enter teaching. "Who are we certifying to teach? What do they bring with them? What are their attitudes; what are their beliefs? How can we work with them to help them understand the nature of institutionalized oppression?"

But staff development aside, Sleeter puts a great deal of her energies into prospective teachers, because the future of multicultural education lies in their attitudes, beliefs, and practice. "In the preservice teacher education that I do, I work to get people to deal with what is inside themselves, and it is very difficult to do. But it is not impossible, and a strong teacher education program can make a positive impact. It isn't and never will be a substitute for a pluralistic teaching force, but it is important."

Teacher Education for Multicultural Education:
What is Needed?

What are the essential components needed in teacher education programs, I asked, so that multicultural education can succeed in schools?

"There are two critical components," Sleeter said. "One is getting prospective teachers out into different sociocultural communities for an extended period of time. The second is providing them some intellectual knowledge to help them interpret what they are experiencing and feeling." Isolated experiences, she adds, without guided discussion that seeks to explore their meaning and ground them in the proper context, can result in more stereotypes and increased prejudice. "I work to get my students into minority community centers because many students would never think of getting out into the communities. They need to learn that communication goes both ways. Instead, they may expect parents to come into the school and don't perceive a need for themselves to go into the communities.

"Many also are afraid of getting out into a place that isn't psychologically safe for them, so they avoid it. Also, forcing them out into an area where *they* are the minority is helpful. It gets them past their fear of doing that."

But their time in the community must be structured, she says. "One exercise I give prospective teachers is to observe the interpersonal communication styles that are used by a particular group. I have had students who have been in predominantly Hispanic settings and students in predominantly African-American settings who collect data on things such as: How do people use their hands? Language? What distance do they maintain from each other? When adults talk to kids, describe it.

"When they come back into class, I have them describe what they saw, compare the patterns they witnessed with patterns that white people use—usually something they've never thought about. Instead, they take for granted how people are supposed to interact with each other, how close they are supposed to stand to each other.

"Next, I have them talk about it in relation to shifting their behavior from one cultural context to another, which anyone can learn to do. All this is one way to help them see that when minority kids are in schools, taught by white teachers who have never been in the community or at best, have only driven through it, there is a gap between the cultural codes that children bring to school and the teacher's understanding of those codes. Teachers will often react very negatively to the behavior that they see children of color exhibit in the classroom, because they don't understand it in a cultural context. The result is a lot of kids are thrown out of class. That's how so many students of color end up in special education.

"Instead, if teachers or prospective teachers get out into the community and see where kids are coming from, they increasingly are able to see why they act the way they do. They can understand their behavior in a context in which that behavior makes sense. As a result, they are less likely to react negatively to the behavior."

She added, "I would rather see people genuinely struggle with the issues rather than segment their lives by living one way but trying to be 'multiculturally' acceptable. Otherwise, what you end up doing in the classroom is stuff that kids don't accept because they know you don't mean it. You're providing them with watered-down, superficial content while saying to yourself: 'This is multicultural enough.'"

White teachers can learn to identify with oppressed groups, she emphasizes. "They won't learn to identify with these groups by living in the suburbs and spending a little time with minority people like they are slumming for the weekend," she said, "but they can learn by truly getting to know people personally, spending quality time on someone else's 'turf.' While whites can never become black or Indian, they can learn to identify their own futures with oppressed groups instead of with the oppressors.

"This type of identification has interesting ramifications for what teachers do. For instance, with the passage of Proposition 187, if you really identify with immigrants whose services are cut off, you feel quite keenly that your own services have been cut off. And if you see it that way, you work to make sure no one is cut off."

Why Multicultural Education Falters: A Contextual Perspective

Sleeter concluded by pointing to a variety of economic and political factors that have made it difficult for multicultural education, in the true sense, to root itself in schools and flourish. "We see that people of color, until 1954, were legally excluded in a whole variety of ways. This legal exclusion flies in the face of the ideals upon which this country was founded."

In addition to the tardy legal recognition—and inclusion into American society—of people of color, the economic plight of the United States has worsened for all but the very wealthy.

"Economically, the disparities between the very richest to the very poorest have been growing, not closing. In the last several decades, wealth has been upwardly mobile, which means that the richest control a growing proportion of the wealth in this country. This runs contrary to the idea of equality.

"The goals of multicultural education are to learn how to bring the realities of the political, social, economic, and cultural processes of this country in synch with the goals that we espouse. This country simply will not sustain itself if it doesn't work seriously on doing just that.

"But the intervening factors are the anger of the middle class, which has felt the pinch of tax burdens shifted onto middle America, while corporate America has gotten out of the business of paying taxes to support a lot of public services," she emphasized. "As middle America has felt taxes going up and job opportunities eroding, they have become angry. Meanwhile, the upper class has used the media to steer the viewpoint of middle America to blame people of color, immigrants, and poor women as the cause of their problems—instead of looking upward to the elite to see what the elite has been doing.

"The upper class also has succeeded in cutting its own taxes and scape-goating immigrants, low-income women, and people of color—and many Americans have bought into their rationale. Multicultural education is a tool," she concluded, "that helps us look critically at all these factors."

Gloria Ladson-Billings: Culturally Relevant Teaching in Action

Gloria Ladson-Billings is an Associate Professor in the Department of Curriculum and Instruction at the University of Wisconsin–Madison. She is the author of numerous journal articles and book chapters on issues of multicultural education and culturally relevant pedagogy. Her book The Dreamkeepers *(Jossey-Bass, 1994) was the winner of two professional awards: the National Association for Multicultural Education Outstanding Research Award (1995) and the American Educational Research Association Division K Outstanding Research in Teacher Education Award (1995). Ladson-Billings is a former recipient of the Spencer Post-Doctoral Fellowship Award. Currently she is Co-director (with Mary Louise Gomez) of the University of Wisconsin–Madison's Teach for Diversity Program. She teaches courses in multicultural education, culturally relevant pedagogy, and social studies methods.*

The belief that instruction must change to boost the achievement of minority students in ways that respect their race, ethnicity, and culture is the foundation upon which the work of Gloria Ladson-Billings stands. In fact, her theory of "culturally relevant teaching" suffuses her research and her current work co-directing the Teach for Diversity Program at the University of Wisconsin–Madison, a theory derived from research she conducted as a fellow of the Spencer Foundation that resulted in her 1994 book, *The Dreamkeepers*.

Clearly, students of color are disproportionately represented among those who do not reach their potential level of achievement in school, due to a variety of factors including low teacher expectations, lack of teacher investment in their learning, and an attitude that some children will succeed and others will fail—a type of Darwinian belief to which many educators subscribe. As Ladson-Billings reflects back over her own educational experiences in public school as a person of color, she refuses to credit her own intellectual prowess as the primary reason she succeeded.

"I succeeded, in part, because I was the recipient of what I call sponsored mobility," she began. "The smartest person I ever met didn't make it. She wasn't sponsored because she wasn't very clean. My teachers saw in me someone who possibly could make it.

"My second-grade teacher never touched any of us. I remember it clearly because at the time it seemed so bizarre. She avoided any physical contact with us. Yet I was skipped a grade out of her class. Partly it was an issue of growing class size, because one thing they did with baby boomers was take the top students and move them ahead. There was another girl in my class whose hair was combed and whose clothes were clean—like mine were—and the teacher basically said: 'You two: Go ahead. You will make it.' The way we got to be top students was the perception that we came from families that were supportive, plus we were neat and clean, not because we were intellectual stars.

"Of all my teachers, it was my fifth-grade teacher who clearly believed we were all smart, that we all could learn. But in most of my classes, my teachers differentiated, and frequently on the basis on personal appearance."

Today, in her research, her writings, and her work co-directing the Teach for Diversity Program at the University of Wisconsin–Madison, Ladson-Billings is dedicated to developing what she calls "culturally relevant" teaching—pedagogical strategies she has discovered to be especially effective with African-American students.

Culturally Relevant Pedagogy

Should pedagogy focused on African-American children be different from what other children receive?, I asked her. Why? If so, to what extent are the successful practices she advocates different from practices that are successful with students of other ethnicities or races?

In her response, Ladson-Billings expressed her belief that it is only logical that what works with the most underserved population of students will work with other students.

"Frequently," Ladson-Billings said, "when I do presentations about culturally relevant pedagogy, people will say: 'That's just good teaching!' In fact, I have written an article entitled just that: 'That's just good teaching.'

"While I don't disagree that what is happening in culturally relevant classrooms would work really well for all children, I must emphasize that if we can improve instruction for the least well-served, then we have information that will help everybody."

Overcoming low expectations and the widespread conviction that some children will never succeed is at the core of Ladson-Billing's theory of culturally relevant teaching. She explained, "There has been such hopelessness and despair about teaching African-American children; so many people believe they cannot be taught. For that reason, people who learn about successful practices for African-American children—what I call culturally relevant teaching—have an opportunity to begin to reexamine their own teaching practices, realizing they can apply these practices to the children with whom they work."

Although each teacher that she studied as a Spencer post-doctoral fellow had a distinctively personal style and approach to teaching, some common themes emerged—sufficient to lift the notion of culturally relevant teaching above the level of individual temperament and personal characteristics. These themes, Ladson-Billings explains, developed into what she terms "the hallmarks" of culturally relevant teaching.

Above all, academic achievement is paramount in the culturally relevant classroom, she says, an emphasis that might surprise educators preoccupied with increasing self-esteem and personal self-worth in youth, especially those labeled at risk of educational underachievement or failure.

"If the kids don't learn something," Ladson-Billings stated, "it doesn't matter how good they feel in the classroom; it doesn't matter whether they have a wonderful, loving relationship with the teacher. The bottom line is that teachers have a responsibility to help kids achieve academically."

How precisely that might be accomplished is something she is careful to leave to the discretion of the individual teacher. "It does not mean, necessarily, that student test scores rise by a certain number of standard deviations," she accentuated. "It might mean that teachers can show they have documented a youngster's progress, that they show an example of an early attempt and a current effort. That is evidence of academic achievement just as much as showing on a standardized test that the student is capable of doing certain things.

"For all the teachers I studied," she said, "academic achievement was a clear priority."

The second criteria for culturally relevant teaching, she says, is "knottier, because it is a more complicated notion of cultural competence."

Achieving Cultural Competence

To Ladson-Billings, the idea of cultural competence is tied integrally to whether one understands the school experiences of African-American children and what happens to them in school settings. "In the Fordham and Ogbu work, we have seen the notion that the only way African-American children can be successful in school is to 'act white.' But teachers who teach in a culturally relevant way are able to pair academic achievement with the ability to maintain and support the kids' cultural competence."

For instance, rather than rebuke students for using African-American vernacular, students are allowed to use it in appropriate settings, such as informal conversation with their peers. At the same time, they are taught standard English.

"The kids in the classrooms I studied were so aware of the difference between African-American vernacular and standard English that when they were writing, they would ask: 'Is this supposed to be in standard form?'"

This awareness was the result of teachers' deliberate focus on the difference between casual forms of speech, such as talk between friends, and communicating with others who might not understand the vernacular form of communication. "Teachers would say: 'Your journal is a very personal document. If you want to write in it the way you talk, that is fine.'

"These teachers attempted to help them understand when informal forms of speech were appropriate and when they were not appropriate. Everybody also follows certain conventions when attempting to communicate to a broad audience."

One exercise she found particularly compelling in one classroom she observed was a letter-writing assignment to star athletes. "The teacher gave the kids examples of the ways in which they spoke—combinations of African-American language and youth culture—and then she gave them examples of the standard form. Her question was: Who will get the response if you write in each of these ways? The kids were savvy enough to realize that the star probably wasn't going to read his own mail; that he had a staff. They decided that if they used standard English, it had a higher likelihood of being passed on to the star by the person who screened the correspondence."

Accomplishing a Sociopolitical Consciousness

A third criteria that distinguishes culturally relevant teaching, and the teachers in Ladson-Billings' research, is developing in youth a sociopolitical consciousness. "That is, helping them realize that their education is not merely an individual achievement or attainment," she explained. "We have a responsibility to help others, both in the classroom and in the school—and more broadly, in the community."

The teachers that she studied skillfully juxtaposed issues their students faced in their communities with larger international issues. "During the time I was collecting data," Ladson-Billings remembered, "Nelson Mandela had been released and came to Oakland as part of his visit to the United States. A lot of the kids were going to see him at the Coliseum. One teacher worked with the kids to explain their reasons for wanting to see Mandela. She asked: 'What is the relationship between you and Nelson Mandela? Why are you going? Are you going just because he's black and you're black?' She worked to help them understand some parallels of political inequalities in South Africa and the United States."

In one classroom Ladson-Billings studied, children bemoaned the condition of their community, eager to abandon it as soon as possible. "The teacher used this as an opportunity to have them investigate the community, not in a stilted community study where people who worked in the community visited the classroom, but instead in an investigation of what the community used to be. The kids began to ask questions about why it became the community that it is today, and also asked: What can be done to restore it to its historic goodness?"

Ultimately, the class project became a land use proposal that the students presented at the city council. "This teacher," Ladson-Billings pointed out, "understood that this couldn't be just an exercise. Kids won't get engaged if they don't believe the work is real. If the work is done merely as an exercise, the work may be good, but it has no meaning.

"She felt compelled to get their proposal on the city council's agenda so the kids could be heard. They understood it wouldn't benefit them immediately, but they also understood that when you develop a sociopolitical consciousness, you are concerned about the community in the future, not just with yourself or the present."

Ladson-Billings contrasts this with a more common exercise, an exercise that points out how urban schools with significant minority populations differ from other schools. "In these exercises, the policeman or the friendly neighborhood grocer typically visits the class to talk about his work. When I was teaching, policeman came to my second grade class as part of a community helpers unit and all the kids started to scream. They screamed because all their interactions with them had been negative. The friendly neighborhood grocer? The kids knew that he was gouging their families."

From Expectations to Action

How does the belief that all children can learn translate into significant action? I asked. When the statement originally emerged from the work of Ron Edmonds, it had a certain power—especially in the wake of the Coleman Report—that since has diminished to a slogan.

"It has become very trite to say that all children can succeed," Ladson-Billings said, "but what I saw among these teachers was a sincere belief in the educability of the students. Unfortunately, my experience has been that some teachers believe that there are children who *cannot* be educated, that the best you can do as a teacher is keep them under control. These teachers may think: 'I can keep them under control and I can keep them from being kicked out, but they just can't handle the intellectual material.'

"Among the teachers I studied, I saw a way of talking about and referring to the children that was outstanding, particularly in relationship to other things I heard about kids in these kinds of schools. For example, never once was a child referred to as being from a single-parent household. Most of them were; in some ways it was normative. Why keep saying it? If you're in a setting where most children are from two-parent households, you don't keep saying, 'Most of my children are from two-parent households.' It sounds ridiculous."

Ladson-Billings probed the teachers about why they did not refer to the children in stereotypical, pejorative ways that alluded to their family life or socioeconomic backgrounds. "Their response was always: 'What does that have to do with teaching? Nothing!'"

Their perceptions of children, she emphasizes, "were as resourceful, intelligent, educable human beings." As an example, they did not want children to leave their classrooms and enter other programs such as special education, even when they clearly tested into them. "They would hide children from special education," Ladson-Billings reported with some amusement. "They would subvert special education. They felt obligated to the children that they had, since they had developed a relationship with them, and there was mutual trust between the teachers, children, and parents.

"They didn't see themselves as magical," she continued, "but they believed a child slated for special education could learn in their classrooms. They didn't know exactly what was going on in special education. They believed that they could create a community in that classroom in which people took responsibility for each other's learning. They sincerely felt that the other kids wouldn't let their peers fall behind, but would work with them."

Characteristics of "Culturally Relevant" Teachers

What was it about these teachers that compelled them to rise above stereotypes, low expectations, and hopelessness to become teachers who provided culturally relevant classroom experiences for children?, I asked. Were their attitudes innate or did they learn them at some point in their careers?

Interestingly, Ladson-Billings says she saw that each teacher in her study experienced a type of professional epiphany that changed her practice. "Each had a point of transformation," she said. "For Gertrude Winston, a woman who had taught for forty years, it was her experience in the Peace Corps. For twelve years, she taught in a rural, one-room school in Michigan. When the school consolidated, she joined the Peace Corps and went to West Africa. She had never been around black people in her life!" she exclaimed. "But she said the experience helped her understand how much she took for granted as a white woman. She made a vow she would not work in all-white settings again.

When she returned to the United States, she taught first in Watts and also in the Bay area.

"The world," she added, "opened up for her."

Another teacher approached her instruction with a quietly religious fervor that made her classroom a sanctuary for learning. "She was on the borderline of the First Amendment," Ladson-Billings remembered with amusement. "She began school every day by having the kids sing songs such as: 'Peace is flowing like a river.' She originally was a Catholic and changed religiously. This religious change made her rethink her work."

Yet another teacher, Margaret Rossi, began her career in education as a nun, teaching in exclusive Catholic schools. Ladson-Billings said, "She began to question the value of helping, and contradictions between the social justice principles of the Church and her role in helping elite students get into the best colleges."

Pragmatically, she questions the transformations. "What does this mean for novice teachers who are 22 or 23 years old? How much time does it take for them to reach the point where these teachers are? What do they have to experience in order for this to happen for them?"

The Role of Teacher Education Programs

What can teacher education programs with a careful focus on the tenets of culturally relevant teaching—such as the Teach for Diversity Program at the University of Wisconsin–Madison—do to prepare teachers?

"Our focus has been to help prospective teachers make visible their own culture," she observed. "We haven't focused on categorizing students in terms of learning style and silly cultural do's and don'ts. Instead, we look at a culture that is the dominant culture because we've normalized it to the point that it is invisible.

"Probably, that is the primary struggle we have as they begin in the program, getting them to understand that what they do is culturally mediated, culturally defined. They don't do something because it is right; they do it because their culture dictates it. In some ways, we have witnessed some epiphanies for students."

One such epiphany she reports followed an assignment to bring in something to the class that students believed was an accurate representation of their culture or their sense of cultural identity. "The students obviously thought carefully about this," she said. "They didn't bring in hot dogs, baseballs, apple pie, and Chevrolets. One of the young men chose to bring in a Stanley thermos, explaining that the whole reason he had one was that his dad had one his entire life.

"We talked about that in the group. You know, middle-class men don't carry thermoses. The ones they have are plastic, because they use them for tailgating. They don't carry them to work because somebody at work makes their coffee. This student said that the thermos really symbolized his background in the working class. It is not at all unusual to submerge and try to hide a working-class identity because it is not the norm of the dominant culture."

"Culturally Relevant" vs. "Assimilationist" Teachers

Ladson-Billings emphasizes differences between what she terms "assimilationist" teachers and culturally relevant teachers. I asked: What are the primary differences and how do they reveal themselves in subtle ways?

"I think of these differences as a continuum," she replied, "that teachers are not all way or all another way. I don't see assimilationist teachers as 'bad' people. However, they have a particular view of society and their role in it that undergirds their approach to teaching. They believe some people will be highly successful, others will be in the middle, and some people have to fail. Basically, they believe in a type of bell curve. They believe in competition; they believe in winners and losers. Above all, they believe in the primacy of the individual over the group."

Culturally relevant teachers try to balance individual and group concerns, whereas assimilationist teachers see their role as placing kids into the slots they are supposed to fill in society, Ladson-Billings pointed out. "Assimilationist teachers think society works the way it is supposed to work. They believe there is only so much you can do with certain kids. They have a belief in the system that says society is fine the way it is.

"In contrast, culturally relevant teachers are upset with the way society functions. They believe society has the potential to be better. Assimilationist teachers and potential teachers believe that even if you want to change it, how could it be different? Somebody has to be on the bottom."

Whereas an assimilationist teacher might discourage a student from aspiring to be a doctor, a culturally relevant teacher would ask students who express such an ambition why they think they would want to be doctors.

However, she reports that some teachers in her study were concerned about the devaluation of work they saw among her students. "Kids would say that their older brothers and sisters weren't willing to work at McDonald's—as if for a teenager that's a bad job. Rather than bringing doctors and lawyers to their classrooms, they brought in custodians, secretaries, and kids' parents as people who do productive work for the society."

Assimilationist teachers might not want to bring in doctors and lawyers for career day, she says, but for a different reason: they would think it unrealistic, far beyond what their students could hope to achieve. "The typical career day," she pointed out, "brings in these hotshot people who are so far out of the kids' realm that it is as if people from Mars are visiting the class. Another message it sends is that you have to leave the community to do this kind of work.

"Culturally relevant teachers," she continued, "prefer that the kids understand the value of work—of everyone's work—and what society could be like if we really valued the work that everybody does. This is the reason that one teacher always uses the custodian in her room as the first example of work done in the immediate outside world. She has two or three of the kids work with him for several days. They have to come in at 6 in the morning to do so.

"They come back and say, 'This is hard work!' They also are impressed that custodians make quite a bit of money. They are surprised because previously they had devalued their work. She also notices a different attitude toward the custodian after this experience. The ones who worked with him are constantly telling the others: 'Pick that up!'"

The professions are not neglected, she says. "These teachers don't say, 'This is your only possibility.' But the kids' first experiences of work revolve around the work that is going on in their community. There is a dentist who has made it a real mission to stay in the community. He spends a lot of time in the schools helping kids understand what it takes to become a dentist—and the kids know him because he is their dentist, one of the few in that community. Rather than bringing in a Nobel laureate and saying, 'You too can be this,' you help kids understand the value of work, you help them understand the various jobs and careers that are out there, not just in the elite sector."

The ability to work with student-produced material and draw upon the resources offered by their communities shines through culturally relevant teaching, Ladson-Billings maintains. "I really appreciated the way in which these teachers used the children's parents and communities as resources. One teacher, Ms. Winston, had an artist-in-residence program in which one of the artists was a parent who made wonderful sweet potato pie. Ms. Winston structured the residency so that the mother worked with five or six of the kids for two days.

"The first day, they made crusts and refrigerated them; the next day they made the filling. Ms. Winston surrounded the experience with literature, math, and other elements. One result above and beyond what the kids learned was that they looked at that mother in a very different way.

"She brought in another parent who was a carpenter, scrounging plywood and nails so that the kids could have the experience of building things themselves under expert guidance."

To Ladson-Billings, what culturally relevant teachers provide is epitomized by these examples of ways in which the children's outside communities are drawn upon as resources, parents and community members are respected and consulted as experts, and academic achievement is held paramount—

woven skillfully through the fabric of students' cultural background. "You don't come to school just to get skills," she concluded. "For so many kids, providing them the opportunity to talk with adults in low-pressure situations in which they're not evaluated yields the understanding that the people you live with do have knowledge and skills."

Lily Wong Fillmore:
Our Common Culture,
Our Ambivalence

Lily Wong Fillmore is an internationally recognized linguist, who is a Professor in the Graduate School of Education (Language and Literacy) at the University of California–Berkeley. Wong Fillmore has worked on issues related to the education of language minority children since the mid-1950s, when she was a volunteer teacher of Mexican migrant children in California farm-labor camps. Over the past twenty years, she has conducted six large-scale research projects examining the linguistic and academic adjustment of Latino and Asian background children in public school classrooms. Her research has focused on identification of the cognitive and social processes by which young children acquire a second language, the sources of individual and group variation on language development, and the influence of culture, social settings, and instructional practices on second language learning. She has conducted observations of parent and child interactions in Asian, Latino, American Indian, and Inuit homes. Wong Fillmore's own primary language is a dialect of Cantonese; she learned English at age eight, when the Mexican and Dustbowl migrant children she went to school with in Watsonville, California convinced her, as she says, that it would be "socially useful to do so." Thanks to these childhood influences, she has acquired a lifelong interest in language socialization.

Acquiring a second language in the United States is loaded with psychic baggage related to the symbolic meaning of being an English speaker. Issues such as the cost of losing the first language, not learning the second language well, and the impact of second-language acquisition on families who are left without a way to communicate with their children are seldom considered by educators eager to see children assimilate into American culture.

Lily Wong Fillmore is keenly, almost painfully aware of all of these issues. She first addresses the psychological and cultural meaning attached to speaking a second language in the United States. "The problem in the United States is that we have elevated English to the status of an ideology," she emphasized. "It doesn't matter any more what the language really accomplishes; what it stands for is what generally counts. There is a belief that if people speak another language, they are somehow disloyal to the symbolic meaning of English."

As an example, she points to a recent congressional study of all government documents, requested by advocates of English as the official governmental language. The study examined government documents to see how many were written in languages other than English. "With over 400,000 titles checked," Wong Fillmore said, "the General Accounting Office identified only 265 foreign language documents released by the Government Printing Office and a Congress departmental agency over five years."

She added, "What are these people worried about? Are these documents in other languages somehow diminishing the quality of American life? Are they causing the society to break down? What are people afraid of? What leads them to call for these kinds of examinations?"

A glance at any urban daily newspaper provides ample illustration why it is difficult for people to learn a second language and retain their first language and culture in the United States, she notes. "Imagine what it is like to be a person who does not speak English well," she said, "and you will have some sense of the experiences that immigrants have in this society. It doesn't take them very long to conclude that if they don't learn English, they will be separated from everyone else."

The fact that this extreme view—speak English or be an outcast from American society—dominates most people's thinking is illogical, she argues.

"Why should a language separate people?," Wong Fillmore asked. "We are impatient, terribly impatient with people while they're in the language-learning process. We suspect very strongly that they're not going to learn English. These days, we don't even give them two, three, or four years to do so— whereas we used to give people a generation to make that big adjustment. Currently, we expect people to make the adjustment within a year or two of immigration to this society. This may suggest that the problem is not language but rather is the presence of newcomers among us."

Recollection of our collective and individual pasts would help all Americans, especially educators, in all their dealings with people learning English. "We forget," she added, "that most of us are only a couple of generations away—at most—from the kind of status English-language learners have in our society. I puzzle over this question constantly, over the paradox."

Obviously, the better a person is able to speak English in our society, the easier their communication with others and navigation in the second culture, she says. But the price of second language acquisition, particularly as English is taught to increasingly younger children, can be considerable. "People who learn English sometimes come to identify completely with their adopted culture or society," she pointed out, "and in doing that, they come to deny their own native culture or identity."

How can second language instruction help children retain their primary language and culture while learning the new language?, I asked. How can educators help prevent causing a psychic wound as the native language and culture are lost or denied?

"It has everything to do with how people view the relative importance of the native versus the second language," Wong Fillmore replied. "The issue is not just the language learners themselves but rather the social context, the relationships that the language learners have with people in their environment.

"It is assumed that when students do not learn English it must be because they refuse to give up their native language or because the schools are emphasizing their native language over English. Actually, in many cases, people who don't learn the language well have already given up their native language and are not getting any kind of native language support at school."

Surprisingly, a great deal of the pressure to abandon the native language can come from home, she emphasized. "Parents are pressured not to speak to their children in the native language because of the belief that this will hold the children back from learning English well. Truly effective English-language instruction at school would support the learning of English in such a way that it would take some of that pressure off parents."

Wong Fillmore reports that one of her biggest concerns surrounding the entire issue of second language acquisition is the need to remove pressure from both parents and children. "The consequences go far beyond language learning. Children's self-esteem and the identity of their families are affected, as are their relationships with family members. In many families the kids start using more and more English in the home until it begins to affect communication with parents, and although the parents continue to use the native language with the kids, the kids respond only with English—a language that the parents really don't understand. This effectively shuts down communication between parents and children."

As communication between parents and children becomes strained and eventually collapses, the result is alienation. "This process usually takes place over a period of approximately four years. Yet another type of breakdown happens when the parents follow the advice of teachers to abandon the use of the native language at home with their children. This breakdown is very abrupt and difficult for everyone. I might add that the breakdown of communication is difficult in both cases, and totally unnecessary."

An unanticipated result of either type of communication breakdown occurs, ironically, in school as children's achievement plummets. "The children really suffer in school. When the parents can't communicate easily with the children, they can't teach them much of what they should be teaching at home.

While I won't venture a percentage of what should be learned at home versus at school, and while a breakdown in communication doesn't mean that nothing is learned at home, what is learned is simply not as complete."

Effective Second Language Instruction

What ensures that second language learning will work?, I asked. What mix of ingredients needs to be present so that children can advance?

"Schools need to recognize that no one learns a language just by being in classrooms where it is used," Wong Fillmore observed. "How a language is learned is not just up to the learner, and the failure to learn the language well cannot be made the sole responsibility or shortcoming of the language learner. In many situations there aren't enough native speakers of the language in the classroom to support language learning, so much of the responsibility for providing access to and support of learning the language depends on what the teacher does instructionally. It depends on what kinds of materials she uses, the kind of emphasis given to the language itself, the amount of feedback she provides the language learner, and the amount of practice the learners are given. It depends upon whether the language is used in situations that are meaningful and supportive of language learning.

"Educators," she continued, "have to recognize that many of the theories espoused by some language specialists suggest that the teacher doesn't have to do anything special to teach the language: they just have to use the language 'meaningfully.' These so-called theories are completely counterproductive, and cause the kind of poor language learning outcomes that we see. Educators need to recognize also that the kinds of grouping practices that are often used in schools may work against language learning. The practice, for example, of putting all the language learners into a class that is segregated from other kids who speak English works against language learning or they are grouped by language proficiency—thus isolating the language learners from native speakers of English. Children are too frequently placed into social settings that are not conducive to language learning.

"If schools insist on these practices," she continued, "educators need to know that a very, very heavy responsibility for instruction is going to fall on the teacher to provide all of the help and support that the language learner needs. They also need to know what while it's difficult, the level of instruction in curricular content does not need to be lowered for the sake of the language learner."

How might schools assist children in maintaining their original cultural identity, I asked, given the tremendous press for assimilation they experience typically in school and in their communities?

"Programs where teachers emphasize the importance of the cultures of the students can help," she replied, "and bilingual programs help, but the most helpful programs are those that place great emphasis on the culture of the home and celebrate it in the right sorts of ways, not just by paying attention to the music and food and visible aspects of the culture. Instead, the best programs pay attention to the type of relationships between children and teachers as well as children, teachers, and parents. They also show high levels of respect for the home culture in their relationships with children."

The most effective settings are schools that simultaneously respect children's native languages, acknowledge and celebrate their culture of origin, and also push students to acquire the English proficiency and the kind of education that they need to deal with life in American society, Wong Fillmore suggests. "A school can do a lot to help. It can also do a lot of harm, in making children feel that their home cultures don't stand for anything—or stand in the way of their progress."

So bilingual programs are not necessarily enlightened in the ways in which they deal with acquisition of the second language?, I inquired.

"They are as enlightened as the people who run them," Wong Fillmore responded. "Just calling a program bilingual doesn't make it a true bilingual program. In fact, in many bilingual programs, people don't really believe in the use of children's home languages in school or have an assimilationist view and see their efforts as a temporary exercise that will help students become mainstream. Transitional programs vary widely in quality.

"The worst," she added firmly, "are the programs that push children into all-English programs as soon as possible and emphasize Americanization and assimilation rather than help kids acquire English and everything else that goes with it, in addition to respecting their home languages and cultures."

Effective language instruction depends on the social setting, Wong Fillmore emphasizes, because without the proper social setting there is little or no interaction between the language learner and native language speakers—interaction that is essential if the language learner is to succeed. "There must be enough people who know the language well enough to support language learners in that environment," she said. "The social setting also must be structured in a way that allows the learners and the native speakers to interact. The third aspect is the type of relationship that speakers of the target language have with the language learners. Social divisions between the two deeply affect language learning."

Each element is important, she emphasizes, and must be carefully considered and manipulated. "If there are many more language learners in the setting than there are speakers of English, interaction is more likely occurring between people who don't know the language very well. If that happens, the learner doesn't receive much help in learning the language. The learners are mostly learning English from others who are themselves learners, and therefore imperfect speakers of English. But if the social setting is structured so that the influence of the people who speak the language well is maximized—the teacher, for example—then it is much more conducive to successful language learning."

Our Common Culture, Our Ambivalence

Returning to her puzzlement over the ambivalent feelings Americans have about diversity, Wong Fillmore points first to the accomplishments of American society. "We have incredible competence, talents, and resources because we are an immigrant society," she said. "We are diverse; we come from different backgrounds and societies where different sorts of talents and abilities are valued and therefore developed. We bring all of it to this society as immigrants.

"Yet as Americans we are afraid of immigrants and diversity. We are afraid of the elements of diversity within the society. If we look, for example, at the discrimination against Irish immigrants at the turn of the century, we see that many groups experienced hostility and prejudice initially. Having experienced discrimination personally does not mean we will try not to discriminate against others. Once people make the adjustment, become American, become a part of the society so that others no longer identify them as a foreigner, it's their turn to discriminate against the next group of immigrants.

" You're all American now," she added ironically.

"This is especially possible for whites," she continued. "Once people begin to fit into the society, they disappear. The so-called melting pot metaphor works for them because after a time, they are no longer distinguishable from other Americans or from the view we have of Americans, what they ought to look like. But the residual hurt remains.

"Not infrequently, people take on the views of their oppressors. We identity this more with immigrants of European extraction because they look more American, although many former Asian immigrants and Latin American immigrants become equally intolerant of newcomers."

She points to the vote in California on Proposition 187, which excluded alien immigrants from entering the state, as an example of closing the door after ourselves once we have reached our destination. "Over 60 percent voted against Proposition 187, voted to deny services to immigrants who are here without documentation—yet so many of us started that way. Many of us came to the United States without 'papers.'

"A lot of Latino people in California who voted for Proposition 187 only came here a generation ago, but now they're all American. I'm not saying that we don't need a good, clear immigration policy or that we can handle all people coming into the country who would like to be here. We can't accommodate that many people. We do need an immigration policy that makes sense and that we can enforce.

"But at the same time, we're talking about the denial of services to those who are here already, and in many cases, denial of services to children."

Achieving a Common Culture

Given all these factors, will it ever be possible to achieve a common culture that isn't an assimilationist melting pot where the original language and culture are shed?, I asked.

"We already have a common culture," Wong Fillmore responded firmly. "We succeed in spite of ourselves. Many, many of us have contributed to our common culture, although there is this crazy idea that nothing that the immigrants have brought to it is worthwhile. We do believe that what immigrants bring with them should be put aside as irrelevant once they become American.

"But, in fact, the American common culture consists of what you and I, in addition to everyone else in this society, natives or immigrants, have contributed to it. Look at the art, the music, the literature; look at our beliefs. One way or another, we have contributed to the common culture. It isn't just the British culture or European culture; it isn't that well-defined. Multiple influences are certainly present in our society, but we don't acknowledge the contributions of very many groups.

"Our society has been graced by the various people who have joined us, and as long as we push for the inclusion of the contributions of still others, the idea of a common culture is a good one. As long as the forces that are trying to drag the society back to the 1940s and 1950s are kept at bay, many of these positive changes will remain and continue to develop. To have all these contributions as part of our heritage is important, and the common culture does, in some interesting ways, include all of that."

Anne Fairbrother:
A Voyage of Discovery

Anne Fairbrother, a native of England, holds a B.A. in Sociology from the University of Hull in England and a graduate certificate of education from the University of California at Santa Cruz. Dedicated to multicultural teaching, she studies languages—including Spanish—on a continuous basis and has pioneered the teaching of Chicano and Native American literature at North Salinas High School, Salinas, California, where she has been an English teacher since 1989. An eclectic personality with a wide range of interests, in previous careers she managed a restaurant and also was a psychiatric social worker.

At North Salinas High School in Salinas, California, the student population is markedly diverse: approximately 40 percent Latino, 40 percent Anglo, 7 percent African-American, 9 percent Filipino, 1 percent Native American, and the remainder Pacific Islanders. Both the Latino and Filipino populations are growing rapidly with the influx of immigrants into the community, which means that students arrive at North Salinas varying widely in language proficiency.

Anne Fairbrother, classically schooled in the "Great Books," embraces multiculturalism with an open heart, striving to incorporate literature into her English classes in a manner that will speak to—and for—her students. Her current courseload also presents a range of achievement levels: 11th-grade college preparatory English classes and ESL. In the next semester of the current academic year, she will teach general 10th-grade English and ESL.

I questioned her first about the meaning and attitudes that currently surround the words "multicultural" and "multiculturalism." Do you find, I asked, that these words have lost meaning? Do your fellow teachers truly understand what it means to teach in a multicultural way?

Fairbrother reflected for a moment and then said: "I really like the word multicultural, because it is a very powerful word."

But hasn't it become, I asked her, a synonym in some quarters for "minority" students or students of color?

"Yes, but what it means to me," she replied eagerly, "is an alternative to a Eurocentric curriculum. When we talk about something being multicultural, we definitely are bringing in minority voices—the Anglo voice is just one of those voices. I can see that people might not like the word 'multicultural' because it is threatening; it does mean that the minority voice gets some kind of hearing or attention.

"However, 'multicultural' shouldn't mean solely students of color because after all, my European-American students are much less aware of their heritage than my students from Mexico, my Native American, or my Filipino students. When I have my European-American students do the type of research where they interview a relative about where they came from, they often say: 'I'm American!' I tell them: 'You came from *somewhere*, unless you're a Native American—and quite recently, too.' Their backgrounds clearly are a whole area of knowledge that's lost, which is sad."

In addition to being lost, is it denied?, I asked.

"Exactly," she agreed. "We talked about that, my students and I, about how assimilation works. At some point, the knowledge of their heritage was not passed on, which equals a form of denial."

Teaching in a Multicultural Way

What does it mean to you, I asked her, to teach in a truly multicultural way? Have you always taught in this way? What permeated your thinking and educational philosophy to make you aware of multicultural issues and how might they be applied to education?

Fairbrother replied, "They say that you teach the way you were taught. During my student teaching, I was very passionate about teaching, and my model was what I had received, very much the tradition of British literature. When I finished my teaching program—many years after coming to the United States—what I took away with me was the belief that the curriculum should be relevant to students' lives and should build upon what they already know."

When she discovered that many of her students at North Salinas High School were Latino, her first question to her colleagues was: "Where is the Latino literature?"

The thinking that prompted her question, she reports, was somewhat naive: she assumed that her colleagues would point her to specific works of literature with which they were already familiar, works they had taught successfully that they could share with a novice teacher. "Instead, colleagues said they would love to teach some Latino literature but they didn't know any."

Fairbrother swung into action. "I thought that was crazy," she said candidly. "I started researching it myself, finding materials. We now have five works that are supplemental works in our curriculum, and other works that are being piloted. This attention to this literature didn't come about just through me," she noted, "although I helped make it happen, and I feel good about that. Other people were ready for it to happen, but the books weren't there and people didn't have time to look for them. To me, it was so obvious that we needed them."

Once she began to find books, she reports, she shared them with colleagues, with the result that they began to search out books as well. "As time went on, I found more materials to use and also started reading Filipino literature. For the last three or four years, I have been studying Native American literature, taking classes in it. You need to know a lot," she emphasized, "before you teach a short story."

One reason Fairbrother enjoys teaching multicultural literature is that it reflects the United States. "I tell my students to look around them. 'This is America,' I tell them. 'It is a diverse country by definition. Look at each other in the classroom and you can see the diversity.' Obviously I want the literature that they read to reflect that America. I want them," she said strongly, "to get a true sense of America through the literature in all its diversity and all its variety.

"That is the first thing that it means to teach multicultural literature. We will read the core works, but they will be balanced by other works. Through doing this, they lose the sense that the predominantly Anglo works written by male authors are the most important, even though they are the works that most students get in their classrooms. Those core works will dominate until we actually change the core works, which is the next step. We do need to make the core curriculum in literature more diverse."

To buttress her point, Fairbrother lists the core works taught in English classes at North Salinas High School, adding her own comments: "*Romeo and Juliet*—white male author, *To Kill a Mockingbird*—written by a white woman, *Black Boy*—black male author, *Huckleberry Finn*—white male author, *Of Mice and Men*—white male author, *Raisin in the Sun*—black female author, *Cry the Beloved County*—white male author although it was written about Africa, *MacBeth*—white male author, *Lord of the Flies*—white male author, and *The Crucible*—white male author."

The canon, broadened only in the past few years by Fairbrother and others, now includes Native American writers, Chicano writers, and Puerto Rican writers. "Of course," she shrugged, "there are still some teachers whose curriculum is all white males; they haven't chosen to work with any of the supplemental texts—which is why we need to change the core works."

A district attempt to widen the core curriculum had somewhat odd results, she says. "We decided to change to one book per grade level on which the entire district agreed. For instance, every ninth grader in the district would read one book agreed upon by everyone. The second core work would be selected at each school, and then the rest of the books would be whatever the teacher chose. The belief was that this would allow some autonomy.

"What did we get? In our desire to be diverse in our core works for the district, we ended up with: *To Kill a Mockingbird* for 9th grade, *Black Boy* for 10th grade, *Raisin in the Sun* for 11th grade, and *Cry the Beloved County* for 12th grade. They are all African-American experiences, which is probably not the most appropriate choice for our population."

How do students react to books that are not part of the familiar Western canon?, I asked. Do you see any discernible reaction or significantly more interest in what they are reading?

"The only reaction I see in students," Fairbrother said with care, "is that because most of them don't read much, they don't think in terms of criteria for judging a book other than whether they like it or it's boring."

They are more straightforward about their preferences?, I suggested.

"It's either that the book is boring, which is usually a snap judgment, or their writing responses will show that they liked it. In their responses, they will relate what they have read to their families and to their own experiences."

What about students assigned Latino-centered literature, for example, who are white?, I asked.

Fairbrother reports that she was surprised by the layers of complexity of the responses she noticed pertaining to racism once she began to teach diverse literature. "I was not prepared for some of the white response," she admitted. "I'm white, but I have white students who had very odd reactions to it."

Impatience and a sense of waiting to "get to the real stuff" were common, she says. "When we looked into a lot of African-American or Native American experiences through the literature that they were reading, it triggered classic white guilt. Many students became hostile to varying degrees.

"There were also Anglo students," she continued, "who were quite delighted to explore the diversity. I know this, because I had them write responses to the literature. In that way, I knew how they felt about it. We also had discussions and group work. But it is in their writings to me that I get their real feelings. Some of them really appreciated it and liked the fact that the world is opening up to them, that they are learning more about different cultures in literature and that they understand different experiences."

In an attempt to increase the comfort level of white students, Fairbrother mentions some of the choices she felt were open to her. "When we read about Native American experiences in which whites treated them badly, of course I could have pointed out that just as there were whites who engaged in bad behavior, there were always white people who were on the side of justice. But I didn't feel comfortable doing that."

Instead, she had an insight while showing a fifteen-minute portion of a film developed for PBS, *The 500 Nations*. "I showed a section on the California

Indians, how the Spanish came and enslaved them. Then the Mexicans came, and then the Anglos came. It was factual, but very moving."

She arranged the class in groups in which they elected to be placed; their task was to view the experience depicted in the film from multiple perspectives. "If they were California Indians, how would they respond to what they saw? If they were African-Americans, how would they respond about the material they saw on slavery? Or if they were Mexican-Americans? Anglo-Americans? They had to imagine a whole range of responses, which they wrote down. The assignment was to tell me more than one response to each if possible."

A effort to encourage empathy?

"Exactly!," Fairbrother said. "I asked which of the responses would be the most sensitive or constructive way to respond. I tried," she added, "to get them to look at what their higher self, their better self would think of as a good, healthy response. I got a range of answers."

Going through their written responses at home, she created a continuum which she wrote on the board the following day. "The continuum ranged from responses that were totally uncaring, statements such as: 'That was the way it was,' or 'We had it worse,' to an understanding that moved from feelings of sadness to responsibility to moving on and learning through empathy. There was a whole range of possible responses, and we talked about them to show that every level of response was valid for people from different cultures and experiences.

"I supported them on the continuum in a way that allowed them not to be judged negatively for their responses, but also allowed them to move on and learn."

This approach diffused any latent tension that lingered over racial and ethnic issues, she maintains. "It did accomplish that," Fairbrother reflected. "It validated *any* response, and since it was all their work, it wasn't coming from me although I was there to talk about it. It was all theirs.

"This cut any hostility," she said. "I haven't felt a problem with it since. It diffused the defensiveness because in the context of the continuum I could say the things I wanted to about the responses that showed guilt and why not to feel guilt."

She says that she herself was helped through feelings of guilt about the experiences of oppressed people by an African-American man at a conference she once attended. "I asked for help: 'What do you say to students when they start to hear about the terrible things that whites did to African-Americans—and they're white? He said: 'Just tell them that the Underground Railroad could not have happened if there hadn't been white people helping with it.'"

What could have escalated into increased acrimony between racial and ethnic groups—rather than increased harmony—was thus averted. In an earlier incident, Fairbrother was brought up short by student reactions to what she considered a benign assignment. "I must admit," Fairbrother contemplated, "when I first moved into high gear in terms of the diversity in my literature and my curriculum, I was not prepared for the reactions. I thought everything was fine until I gave them an assignment to write a poem about themselves, their identities, and who they were.

"All sorts of white racist material came out," she remembered. "It was ugly. I talked to the young men who did it, but it was almost too late by that time. That is why I knew there had to be a way to diffuse the hostility and include everyone."

Inclusion is the message she wants to emphasize. "We are all part of diversity," she says in a matter-of-fact tone.

Multicultural Beliefs

What fuels your own beliefs about teaching in a multicultural way?, I asked her. What is the origin of your belief that literature should reflect the population that learns it?

In her reply, Fairbrother points first to her own love of literature and then to her conviction that it is crucial that one recognize, know, and accept one's cultural heritage. "I was grounded in British literature, since I went to English grammar schools," she emphasized. "Because I love to read, I started reading French, Russian, and modern American writers. When I discovered Chicano literature, that opened so many doors for me; I knew at that time I would develop a curriculum around it. The same is true for Native American literature.

"You learn so much about people and history through literature," she added. "I always remember when I first read Jane Austin, I loved reading her books because how else could I know what it was like to live in the last century? You learn a whole world: the way people eat, how they talked to each other, what they did to pass time, where they went for walks, what kind of clothes they wore. Literature brings the world to life for me, which is partly why I love it.

"I want students to have that experience, especially in their own cultures. Otherwise they may go through school without ever reading a book in which they find themselves. In the sense of my heritage, I know who I am, I know what it is to be English. I know my history, my literature."

When she began to teach in the United States, Fairbrother says she was shocked to discover that Chicano students, for example, did not know who they were. "They knew to some degree through their family and community, but in school, it was taken from them. I thought: This is wrong. They should know who they are; they should be allowed to make that same voyage of discovery. That is why I became involved in the community, in the history, and took additional classes.

"Even without any desire to look for multiculturalism," she added, "Chicano and Native American literature are vibrant and exciting. The main reason I teach it is because it is good literature. It reflects America. Because I'm not American, I don't have any vested interest in it, any part of it. That helps me, because I can stand back and see a diverse America, appreciate its diversity, and not have panic attacks when I see white superiority being eroded."

Many Mexican-American students do not know what it means to be Mexican, she emphasizes. "They don't understand that to be Mexican means you are both Spanish and Indian. For the most part, they have never seen the power and importance of their Indian heritage, which is the result of 300 years of colonization with the Indian as inferior and internalizing that sense of inferiority. Suddenly, they are faced with reading Aztec poetry in school and learning a bit about how great the Aztec Empire was. They gain a sense that Mexican-Americans are not really immigrants. This was Mexico and before that, Indian. This is their land. Literature nurtures a real sense of identity."

Along with literature, Fairbrother teaches history. "Gaining a sense, for instance, of the great civilization of the Aztecs is a wonderful thing for all students to know, not just my Chicano students. Other students also learn that suddenly there is something about being Mexican that is not the debased stereotype that they often see all around them."

Barriers to Multicultural Teaching

What, I asked, do you see as the chief barriers and obstacles to teaching in a multicultural way? Teachers themselves construct the biggest hurdle to multiculturalism throughout the curriculum, Fairbrother maintains. "There are a number of teachers in my district who are going ahead, making changes, trying out this literature, and pushing for it. But there are still teachers who close their doors and teach 99 percent white male–written material because it is the most easily available. They have been teaching this for twenty years, and are not comfortable teaching other things."

There is also an element of fear, she maintains. "If you are not familiar with a story, it becomes much more difficult. If you don't speak Spanish, and there is Spanish in the story, you may not want to risk it. I tell teachers to ask their students to help them with the Spanish. They may have students who previously have been quiet in class who may be happy to read the part that is in Spanish."

But that can symbolize an abdication of control. "If you find out that you can use your students as a resource," she said, "it becomes easier to understand the cultural context and references in the literature. This empowers students. The ones who otherwise wouldn't read normally are happy to have the chance to read some words in Spanish. They get to be the authority."

Some of this uneasiness, she believes, can be overcome if teachers succeed in connecting with each other. "One would hope that in time when they hear about a book that students like they will try it, and if they experience success, continue with this approach. Teachers are mostly white, and if they have been teaching for more than ten years, their training was Eurocentric."

Yet the time demanded by this active approach to seeking out new literature and learning everything that surrounds it is considerable, she acknowledges. "I couldn't do it if I had a family," she said frankly. "I love reading; I love exploring, but I can devote my time to it. Teachers with small children always have a conflict, which I understand."

Students with long-held attitudes about race and ethnicity can inhibit multiculturalism, she believes, as can families with provincial mindsets about racial relations. "One girl in my class said: 'Why do we have to read about Mexicans? There are enough of them around here.' I try to respond to this in a reasonable way. But I had a parent accuse me of teaching too much 'Mexican stuff,' which of course was an emotional response; an irrational, emotional response."

Yet she is heartened that these voices may be stilled over time. "They don't have the influence that they used to have because our school board is a mix of whites and Latinos, and our superintendent is Chicano. They are much more open to what some of us are doing, and they don't have any problem with diversity in the curriculum."

Some high school students themselves flaunt a type of arrogance around racial and ethnic issues that unnerves her. "Some students suddenly feel that they are being forced to do things that they're not used to doing and that they don't want to do. Unlike Latino students, they don't disappear when they don't find themselves in the curriculum. Instead, they become vocal or show their hostility because this isn't the way it is supposed to be."

This is but one reason that the process of transforming the curriculum in a multicultural direction, she believes, must be ongoing, never static, constantly striving for everyone's voices to be heard and recognized. "When we say 'multicultural,' we don't mean only minority voices and let's forget about whites. Instead, we embrace everybody."

Does she see, I asked her, a new type of racial relations evolving among students or are they mimicking race relations—destructive as they may be—that they see in the larger society?

"Students do have friends across the races," she said slowly, " but I wonder how deep it goes. Often students will speak in platitudes about how we're all people and there is no difference between us, but that sentiment doesn't necessarily go very deep. This country has a lot of racism," she added. "Part of the problem is its roots, its beginnings, which started with genocide, the subjugation of part of Mexico, and slavery. That is a difficult foundation to overcome. It is a troubling sort of scar tissue.

"Quite honestly, I don't know if this country can resolve it. Our students are caught up in it. They know it exists. They hear everybody always talking about race. But there is a mixture of idealism in students in the sense that they want to see everybody as the same and they have friends across the races to support that experience.

"On the other hand," she continued cautiously, almost feeling her way, "when it comes down to it, there is also a lot of skepticism. Latino and black students relate more readily to discussions of racism or prejudice or discrimination. I have told students in my classes that none of us can really know how another feels or experiences something, and I have had white male students immediately respond with: 'We know about reverse discrimination. "They" are taking our jobs away.' They make every kind of stereotypical comment about what they perceive other races or ethnicities to be doing.

"After one of these episodes, on his way out of the room, one of my Chicano students looked at me and shook his head. When black and Chicano students hear that rhetoric, they know that the negative can come out and prevail. On the other hand, in one of my classes I had a young black man who is very articulate and well-liked by students. When we dealt with issues like this, he would set the tone. Somehow, that changed the tone of the room because he made his comments, students accepted it from him, and there was an openness about exploring the ideas.

"In my other class, I didn't think there was a problem. It just took one trigger and there it was, out in the open. I think that is how racism is. It is very subtle most of the time but it doesn't take much to bring it out in the open and for people to polarize around their positions. Young people today have learned these polarized positions from our society. There is the hope that they may learn new things that can break down the ignorance."

Still, she ponders the future. "Malcolm X said that those in power won't give it up easily. I see a backlash now that I didn't see twenty-five years ago. The times then were more hopeful, more idealistic. Even though young people may not have scrutinized their own prejudices, they are inundated with a vocabulary about racism and discrimination—and they are already bored when you begin to talk about it."

Joseph S. Renzulli:
Providing Enrichment
for All Students

Joseph S. Renzulli directs the federally funded National Research Center on the Gifted and Talented at the University of Connecticut, where he is a Professor of Educational Psychology. Renzulli is well-known within the gifted and talented education community for a variety of research and development activities dealing with identification systems, program development models, a curriculum development model, and a model for evaluating programs for the gifted and talented. A consultant to numerous school districts and agencies, he served as a staff member on the White House Task Force on the Education of the Gifted. Renzulli began his work as a classroom teacher of gifted and talented students, and through his research and program development activities, maintains close contact with teachers and students involved in special programs for the gifted and talented.

According to Joseph Renzulli, the main educative purpose of schools should be to develop talent in as many children as possible—and if schools fail to provide a continuum of talent-development services to challenge all academic levels, interests, and abilities of students, he believes they fail miserably in their educative efforts.

Why, I asked him, should schools emphasize talent development, versus academic achievement, citizenship, the development of values, or any myriad of other worthy goals? "By treating schools as places for talent development," Renzulli replied, "we move the individuality and uniqueness of each young person to the fore. Critics of this programming would decry this; they would believe we concentrate only on a few students, neglecting the rest."

Clearly, Renzulli does not agree with these critics. When talent development for all students is the foremost objective of educators, he says, educative emphasis is placed on fostering students' individual strengths, instead of leaving them to flounder in what he perceives as a dark well of remediation. "This is not to say we should not deal with their deficiencies," he added, "but school has become a deficiency-oriented place for many kids, especially for minority children and children of the poor.

"What we do in schools," he continued, "is find out what kids can't do, won't do, don't like to do, and then we spend the rest of the year beating them over the head with it." Listening to Renzulli, who is a whole-hearted advocate of a schoolwide enrichment approach (for which he has developed a three-part model to guide educators), I realized that he views the experience of "regular" school as unpleasant, almost Dickensian: The school too often becomes a factory where mindless, disagreeable tasks are conducted in a numbing environment. In the factory, there is a distinct danger that students at all ability levels will not achieve their potential; society will suffer as a result.

Who is Gifted? Who is Talented?

Whether "giftedness" or "talent" should be developed in special programs is a notion that troubles many critics of special programming—because of its history of exclusivity, the frequent practice of pull-out programs that separate children from one another, and the emphasis on early and vigorous identification of gifted students mostly through strict IQ-score cut-offs.

The words "gifted" and "talented" themselves are used imprecisely, I said to Renzulli; what do they mean to him?

In his reply, Renzulli was careful—scrupulously so—to avoid using the words as labels that separate children and place them into a superior group. "I use the words synonomously," he explained, "but as adjectives, not as states of being. That is, we talk about the *development* of talent, or the *development* of gifted behaviors." He added, "Since many people do believe there is some sort of golden chromosome that makes them a 'gifted' person, I avoid using the words 'gifted' and talented' as nouns."

In spite of his disdain for standardized achievement tests as measures of what students can do and what they are good at doing—along with traditional, hard-nosed IQ test scores that qualify students for admission into talented and gifted programs—Renzulli remains a pragmatist where such measures are concerned. "We will never get by without standardized tests," he acknowledged, "but why must we base so much of our decision-making on them?"

Instead, he encourages a broad continuum of services for all students so that students with differing skill levels, varying interests, and diverse learning styles can find challenges above and beyond what he terms "the regular curriculum." In fact, he sees the talent development approach as the path to systemic school reform—an approach that works with schooling in its present, imperfect form but also augments the weaknesses of the regular curriculum.

Renzulli defines the regular curriculum as "anything and everything that is a part of the predetermined goals, schedules, learning outcomes, and delivery systems of the school"—whether those are traditional, innovative, or somewhere in the change process. The regular curriculum, he believes, is determined by what he calls "authoritative forces"—such as textbook adoption committees, policymakers, school boards, and state regulators—all of whom decide on fixed outcomes for student learning.

"The current emphasis on defining curriculum in terms of outcomes is a favorable development," he said, "but it could end up another ill-fated regression to a minimum competency, basic skills approach to learning. Instead, it is essential that the regular curriculum include procedures to challenge all children through adjusting levels of required learning, increasing the in-depth learning experiences in which students can participate, and introducing different types of enrichment into regular curricular activities."

The Politics of Gifted Education

Clearly, Renzulli is attuned almost exquisitely to the political volatility of the entire educative movement for gifted and talented children. While he provides a clear rationale for his broad-based approach to talent development, he simultaneously points out political realities that he perceives as constraints on well-intentioned efforts to infuse the curriculum with enrichment experiences based on student interests. "The equity issue, the anti-grouping issue, and the lack of representation of ethnic and minority groups in gifted programs have caused a tremendous outcry against many of the very favorable practices that initially found acceptance in special programs," he said.

While he concedes that parents of gifted and talented students are vocal advocates, and at times, skilled lobbyists for special programs, he pointed out that currently they are an unpopular minority in a social and political climate that favors heterogeneous grouping and the abolishment of all special programs.

"It is very difficult for a numerical minority to overturn the current trend, especially with regard to the grouping issue," he noted. "If opponents of grouping and gifted programs would examine the concept of a *continuum* of services, realizing that within that concept their kids would get as good or better treatment than they have always gotten, they would buy into it."

The power held by foes of gifted programming is substantial, and extends to states taking positions against ability grouping followed by elimination of state funding for districts that do not abolish grouping. "This includes *all* grouping," Renzulli added, "even reading groups. The grouping issue has gone beyond political correctness."

Since Renzulli believes that every child should be provided with "enrichment experiences" based on the child's interests, I asked his position on ability grouping. Is it justified? Advisable? Unwarranted?

"There must be some grouping," he replied, "but that doesn't mean necessarily ability grouping. There is interest grouping, common task grouping, working-on-a-project grouping. These types of grouping are just as valuable as other, more common types of grouping, such as putting kids together because they have high achievement in a particular area."

Grouping students by skill level, he maintained consistently throughout our conversation, is not the same as ability grouping, but will result in similar arrangements. "The majority opinion is that grouping is detrimental to the achievement of many kids," he observed.

Yet he believes it is impractical to conceive of education without some grouping arrangements, mostly so that students are not trapped in a group once the material has been mastered and they are ready to move on.

Leaving Compensatory Education Behind

The specter of an unchallenging curriculum is part of what Renzulli sees as a major weakness of U.S. public education: working from a deficit model that emphasizes remediation, rather than building on areas of strength. In fact, he insists that the compensatory education model is the main reason schools do not accomplish their desired ends.

"The compensatory education model in this country has failed," he said tartly. "Basically, it tells kids: 'You're not doing well, so I'm going to give you practice and drill in your deficiencies, and that will help you improve.' That seems logical. It's the medical model, the diagnosis of what is wrong followed by the prescription that will fix things."

An enrichment approach, Renzulli argues, is considerably better for all student populations. It has clear benefits, he believes, because it ensures that all students will be represented in an equitable fashion, and it also challenges students at differing achievement and aptitude levels. "If we want more underrepresented groups represented in so-called gifted and talented programs," he pointed out, "first we need to find out how we can improve their basic learning program so that it is different from what we've tried in the past—which hasn't worked."

Statistics that point to improved student achievement, especially among minority and low-income children, he said, frequently are manipulated to placate a critical and increasingly hostile public. "When we see reports that show how the scores of African-American students rose, we don't see how many more have dropped out. The reports don't tell us how many students are classified as learning disabled and therefore aren't taking the achievement tests at all."

Will a systemic approach to talent development help this sorry situation? I asked. It offers hope, Renzulli said in reply, because it is accessible to all students when conducted properly, and it is not dependent on students first achieving adequately in the basic skill areas—the educational equivalent of not being allowed to eat dessert until one's spinach is consumed.

A Ticket To Take the Test

In his own research and fieldwork, Renzulli uses his Schoolwide Enrichment Model (SEM), a triadic model that focuses on a wide range of enrichment activities infused into the curriculum for all students, at all ability levels, with widely varying interests. These activities are frequently, but not always, conducted in groups. Students have the option to work semi-independently, independently, or in changing combinations. Authenticity is imperative for the model to succeed—or for any program offering a range of enrichment experiences to work, he insists.

To Renzulli, authenticity means that students' interests and learning styles are considered carefully when determining or creating groups for students, rather than their aptitudes alone. In addition, his emphasis on inclusion for all children, including low-income students and students of color, directly addresses arguments advanced by critics of gifted and talented programming. Such critics maintain that gifted programming skims off the top students (usually white and middle-class), provides better services for them because of their "need," and serves up a mediocre or substandard education to the rest of the school's or district's students.

Authenticity also means that the program called "the gifted program" is a genuine program, not a program in name only, Renzulli says. "I've never seen an outstanding or a good gifted program in an otherwise poor or underachieving school or school district," he said, almost parenthetically. "These programs do not exist at their very best in other than schools that have very good services and lots of enrichment opportunities across the board.

"Sometimes if you have a good program in a school or district that has low teacher involvement or morale, the staff in the school or district will manage to ensure that the gifted program fails," he said, "because the rest of the district or school will pale in the shadow of it. If anything too good goes on, that means that other things that are not good become accentuated in the eyes of the public. But the program must be good; it cannot exist in name only."

Renzulli's model views groups of students as "multiple talent pools"—open to anyone who is interested in the topic of the group, whether it focuses on archaeology, photography, or music. Although the model argues for inclusivity, he is not timid about speaking up for the educative rights of those with a profile of consistently high academic achievement. "In any school, with almost any population, about 15 to 20 percent will perform at the 85th percentile and above.

"Those youngsters have mastered a fair amount of the content of a subject. In other words, if I went to any school—affluent or poor—and found the top fifteen percent, using the norms of that school only, what I would know is that in relationship to their peers, they are at the very top end of the continuum. Of course, using this identification, we only refer to standard, traditional, academic talent."

That type of achievement, Renzulli believes, means that those students do not need the length of time mandated for all students in the regular curriculum, if the regular curriculum is not adjusted for their achievement level. "Obviously, these students are candidates for curriculum compacting, for curricular modification, and for various kinds of enrichment experiences."

A question he likes to pose is: "What are the implications for knowing more than 85 percent of your peers?" According to his model and his beliefs, those implications are clear: For students at the 85th percentile or higher, a good deal of the curriculum has already been mastered or is not challenging enough, which makes school a place of tedium, where they wait for their peers to catch up before they can move ahead.

I asked: What about those students who do not score at the 85th percentile and higher? Are they automatically filtered out of special experiences, condemned to what the "regular" curriculum offers? "Not at all," Renzulli responded. "When a talent pool is selected, it needs to include kids recommended by criteria other than tests."

Criteria might include a strong bent for story-writing, or an interest in science—whatever abilities or interests are noticed by teachers and parents. "These abilities need to be just as important as a test score," Renzulli emphasized, "because if we do not include teacher observations, we do not leave the door open for the marvelous insights teachers have that no test will ever measure."

I asked: How do you feel about criticisms of gifted and talented programs that point out their exclusive qualities along with the lack of or under-representation of minority and poor children? "Those criticisms are true," he replied. "In my work, I place less emphasis on tests than do more conservatively-oriented gifted educators. In most states, admission to gifted programs has been based on the top two to five percent, and almost exclusively related to test scores. In states that claimed they used multiple criteria, they gathered teacher ratings, parents ratings, self ratings, peer ratings, and samples of work, but none of these got a child into the gifted program. It only got them a ticket to take the test."

As giftedness or gifted behaviors are defined more broadly, do they lose specificity, and thus force, I asked Renzulli? "As the definition—or concept—

of giftedness has been shifted toward the *development* of giftedness, we do all we can to develop a talent, such as the development of violin talent in a young person.

"Obviously some kids will go farther than others," he said. "All of the egalitarians in the world can argue that we can take any child and make him into a Heifetz, but that's not true."

Although Renzulli realizes that some children will go much farther than others in an area of interest or even in an area of clear ability, his main argument is that such differences in skills or abilities do not justify focusing only on those children and neglecting all the others. "We should sidestep the selection issue," he said flatly. "We need to get past the stage of not helping a child with his or her talent unless there is something on paper that says that child is a 'certified' gifted child. Once we remove that albatross from our necks, we can give lots of kids opportunities to experience new and different things in addition to the regular curriculum."

He points to talent clusters such as a group of children listening to a guest storyteller. "Many kids might enjoy it, but two in particular demonstrate a talent for storytelling. Does that make them gifted or nongifted?," he asked rhetorically. "I don't know and I don't care. I do know that if I have the resources, I should develop their talent if I want to be responsive to talent development as a goal of the school."

Rather than focusing on identification of children for talent clusters, Renzulli prefers to identify what topics and programs need to be offered. "There's a big difference," he said. "This is not a sneaky way of saying, 'You're gifted and you're not.' It's all about differentiation of the curriculum and about identifying the service, not the kid."

Underachieving, Undermotivated, Underdeveloped

To what extent, I asked, will an enrichment approach succeed with unmotivated kids or with students who are accustomed to failure? What evidence suggests this will be more successful than other approaches, particularly with underachieving kids? When he answered, Renzulli indicated some research he conducted with colleagues at the National Center on Research for the Gifted and Talented, in which they studied a group of students who were very bright but maintained a profile of underachievement.

The sources of their underachievement, he said, were threefold: "Personal, school-related without disability, and school-related with disability—that is, they were mildly learning-disabled. We saw two things occurring when these students were able to use a highly concentrated enrichment approach where they picked the subject, the topic, and worked on it in a style comfortable to them.

"First, they really got into what they were doing and did not show many of the signs of underachievement. However, in many cases it took them longer to engage in the experiences than it would another student. There were more false starts. Many didn't know how to focus a problem and work on it, and that's a skill we tried to develop.

"Second, we saw some carry-over into their regular school program. Some began doing better, but of course it may have been due to other reasons. We were unable to tell how much of the resources and encouragement that we provided them in the experimental treatment were directly related to a spill-over into their regular classrooms. Their work in the enrichment situations was far more than we expected—in some cases, exemplary."

Enrichment in Action

Renzulli differentiates in his model between three levels of enrichment, with the first tier designated as an awareness/exposure level. As an example of an activity he deems "Type One," a local crime photographer might come to school to tell students what he does at a crime scene. "The purpose of a Type One activity," Renzulli explained, "is to stimulate interest that might lead to further involvement."

The second part of the model modifies the regular curriculum so that students are challenged, so that what Renzulli calls their "in-depth learning experiences" are increased, and so that various kinds of enrichment are introduced into the curriculum. He looks to teachers to modify the curriculum in suitable ways, including eliminating repetitious material from textbooks, planning increased depth in the treatment of content, and employing a process he calls "curriculum compacting," or "organized common sense."

In curriculum compacting, the curriculum is modified to eliminate repetition of previously mastered material through defining the goals of an instructional unit, deciding which students can move through material more rapidly than their peers, and perhaps most importantly, providing activities to replace material already mastered (Renzulli 1994, 10). A key feature of curriculum compacting is its emphasis on student freedom to make decisions about the topics and methods that will be used to pursue studies during time gained as a result of the compacting process.

The third component of the model is enrichment learning and teaching, which draws upon a philosophy of the "whole child" with unique capabilities and interests, the belief that learning should be enjoyable and that more is accomplished when learning occurs within the context of a real-world problem. The ultimate goal of learning within an enrichment context, Renzulli believes, is to replace dependent, passive learning with independence and engaged learning.

Readily admitting that these aspects of his model could become "a glittering list of generalities," nonetheless Renzulli points to the success of field efforts and field tests conducted in schools with widely varying student populations.

Cooperativeness vs. Exploitation

Although it may be an unpopular political stance, Renzulli does not join in the current enthusiasm for learning cooperatively in teacher-chosen heterogeneous groups. "We must differentiate," he emphasizes, "between the honorable concept of cooperativeness and the institutionalization of it known as cooperative learning."

Cooperativeness is part of the American ideal, he says, that should be taught to youngsters. "We live in a very interdependent society," he pointed out. "But, if a group of kids works on an exercise together, the group will progress like the convoys of old, at the rate of the slowest-learning child of the group."

He continues, "Obviously, you're going to hold back a lot of kids. Those who can master the material in five minutes should not have to spend an hour or two on the material." This scenario violates fundamental principles of equity, he says.

Another drawback of cooperative learning, Renzulli believes, is that students should be able to teach and work with others if they would like to—not assigned and forced into groups. "I worked with one group in an enrichment cluster that was called 'The Female Mathematicians' Support Group,' and their members volunteered to help other young girls in mathematics. Contrast that with someone saying, 'Susie, you're smart in math so you must help other kids.'

"That is unpaid indentured servitude," he says bluntly.

On the other hand, if students are given opportunities to make choices about their learning and those with whom they are going to work, Renzulli believes cooperativeness becomes "much more authentic. Whereas critics of grouping believe that a good heterogeneous group can take care of everybody, our research clearly shows that it cannot."

The problems that plague schools currently, Renzulli adds, such as increasingly large numbers of low-achieving students, teenage pregnancy, drugs, and poverty, throw educators into a crisis mode in which he believes it is easy to react almost reflexively, without careful consideration of possible consequences. "Critics of gifted education are brandishing these savage inequalities in support of their views," he noted, "while the conservatives in the field are arguing that this is precisely why we need a better education for kids identified as gifted, because they are the ones who will solve society's problems. I take the middle ground, because looking at schools in an historical context, we see that fifty years ago there was a class called math and it was taught with a textbook.

"Fifty years from now, there will be a class called math, and it will be taught with a textbook," he continued. "It may be called 'Mathematical Induction,' and it may not be third period; it may not last 42 minutes. It may be offered fifth period and last 50 minutes. But it will be there. Schools in our society structurally stay the same."

"What I'm trying to do," he concluded, " is get a teacher to look at a student and know how to challenge that student, to bring that student up to his or her capacity. If that happens, we will all benefit."

Mara Sapon-Shevin:
What's Good for the Gifted
Is Good for All

Mara Sapon-Shevin is Professor of Education in the Division for Teaching and Learning at Syracuse University. The author of Playing Favorites: Gifted Education and the Disruption of Community, *she is a widely published scholar and a board member of the International Association for the Study of Cooperation in Education. Her work centers on creating fully inclusive schools, cooperative learning, and anti-racist curricula.*

There is a profound and disquieting silence that surrounds the issue of special programming, particularly gifted and talented education, Mara Sapon-Shevin believes, and it is a silence that must be dispelled.

"Talking about gifted education," she said to me, "is a taboo. Certainly it is taboo to talk about it in terms of questions of equity, meritocracy, work, value, or educational philosophy—the questions I want to raise.

"Instead, most people want to talk about how to develop a good gifted program, not whether you should develop a gifted program. They want to discuss how you get your group into the gifted program. They don't want to talk about what happens if you don't get into the program. Talking about the underlying reasons for gifted education makes some people very uncomfortable because they have to answer questions such as: 'Do you think it's right that this child is getting this education? Is it really all right that this other child is getting something very different?'"

I asked: Do you find that people have ready arguments in defense of gifted education? If one asks if gifted education is equitable, do parents of children identified as gifted have a ready response?

Sapon-Shevin said, "They can justify it largely in terms of the inadequacy of the regular education. They can say, 'My child is in fourth grade and he reads at twelfth-grade level. In fourth grade, they're doing worksheets and dittos. He's bored, he's not learning, he's not challenged.'"

Because this type of fourth-grade classroom does not meet the child's needs, she added, removing the child from such a stultifying environment seems logical. As a result, parents talk about schooling in ways that suggest they have given up on the kind of schooling that all children should receive and on the possibilities of changing the typical classroom.

"They say things like: In an ideal world, that would be nice," she said. "Then they add: 'But that's not the world we have now.' Pulling a kid out of a miserable situation becomes justifiable as a good educational practice instead of realizing that it is a stop-gap measure, fending off disaster."

If I have a child in third grade, I asked her, who has been labeled as gifted, the child is getting something special at school, and I am nervous about the equity aspects of it but am reasonably content because she is happy and doing well, what is the answer? Doesn't it seem that any real change would take so long to implement that my child would not benefit?

"Right," she agreed. "I don't want to blame parents, except that if all the parents got together and put their intelligence, resources, and expertise to work, they might be in a position to look at the whole system. But the way it is now, it is such an individualistic solution. People don't see how embedded the problem is.

"If a parent's fourth grader is bored and not challenged sufficiently, the parent's probable scope on it is: 'Fourth grade wasn't good for my child.' It might be more useful to pursue an analysis that begins, 'That's not a good fourth grade. My child was unhappy, and there are other kids who weren't happy either and aren't having their needs met. I wonder how fourth grade could be organized differently.'

"Schools don't encourage parents to look systemically," she said with vigor. "When the wheel squeaks, we tend to find a solution for that wheel. We *may* need to disassemble the whole car!"

Making changes systemically takes time and massive commitment. "We do a lot of patching," she added. "Schools don't work for some kids, so we pull them out and put them in resource rooms. Others are pulled out into a gifted program. We don't look at the whole structure."

Where Can Change Start?

Where would parents begin to exert pressure, I asked, if they were unhappy with their child's school experience? "First, meeting with administrators and school boards, and looking at alternative models," Sapon-Shevin replied. "There would have to be some districtwide commitment so enough pressure could be placed on the district so that they would look at the entire system."

When beginning any change effort, she emphasized, it is crucial to question everything. As an example, she relates an anecdote: Recently she was asked by a school district to be an expert witness in a law suit brought against it by a parent whose child was identified as "gifted," and who believed the child should spend 100 percent of his time in gifted programs. The district wanted support for its position, which was that heterogeneous grouping was appropriate for the child. Sapon-Shevin shared her belief that it would be important to look at the whole school and ask if heterogeneous grouping, in fact, was meeting the child's needs.

"I would never say automatically: 'What you're doing is fine.' she said. "Instead, I would ask: 'Are you really doing the best practice out of all the things you could be doing to meet this child's education needs?'"

But philosophically, she is aligned with heterogeneous grouping, and is opposed to tracking and ability grouping. "Do I think that the child's education needs can be met within a shared regular classroom? Yes, I do," she said. "Is it done very often? No. So part of my argument is that we must keep holding out the vision of creating different kinds of classrooms. We need to discard whatever gets in the way of the vision. That's part of the problem with gifted classes: They divert us from seeing that vision, or from even needing to see that vision."

Sapon-Shevin has written about the "educational assumptions" that underlie gifted and talented programming. I asked her to summarize them.

"Basically," she said, "these are assumptions that justify the need or even the inevitability of segregated programming. One assumption is: You can't change the regular classroom. If you're going to do things for a group of children, you're going to have to do it outside of the site."

Another powerful assumption is that gifted children need something different, "qualitatively different," she added, from what other children receive. "There is the belief that this cannot be provided within the regular classroom. In fact, there are gifted educators who say, 'If these things are done in the regular classroom, they still can't meet the needs of gifted children.'

"In other words, there is a belief that there is a population that is so different that there are no broad-based changes that one could make that would do the job. By definition, if it's a good 'regular' classroom, it can't be 'right' for this child. It is a very narrow conception of what a regular classroom is."

One especially pervasive belief held by many advocates of special programming for gifted children is that in a regular classroom, all children do exactly the same work at the same pace. "It's hard to conceptualize that there might be a regular classroom where children are reading different books or working at different levels or using different modalities," she noted.

What about the justice assumption, I asked, that gifted children suffer when special programming is denied to them?

"Oh, yes," she replied. "People argue that we wouldn't deny special education to a child that needs it, so how can we deny gifted education to a child that needs that? The problem with this argument is that it assumes that *special* programming is inevitably delivered as *segregated* programming. Special education is changing radically—looking at how to meet students' individual educational needs within a shared context. Saying that we should attend to children's unique needs doesn't necessarily tell us *where* or *how* to do that."

But all children are not born with the same intelligence or talents, I said. What about those children with clear, pronounced talents and abilities that the regular classroom—for whatever reasons—does not and perhaps cannot accommodate?

"I would never argue that all kids are the same," she responded, "but kids differ in how fast they learn, what they learn well, and what attracts them. So it's not a question of making everybody the same. Instead, the question becomes: How can we develop the school system so that it looks at the full range of students' abilities and talents, and really works to develop them?

"My daughter, for instance, is an incredible writer. She needs and deserves a lot of support for her writing, but that is not to say that she is the only child who should get support for her writing. And she also doesn't need a generic 'gifted program' even if it's wonderful."

She points to different conceptions of talent, such as Suzuki's belief that most children can learn to play the violin. "His whole approach is based on giving those skills to as many children as possible. Does that mean they will all be equally fabulous violinists? No, but lots of kids can learn to play the violin."

Sapon-Shevin is obviously familiar with most arguments and rationales for gifted education, but they do not give her pause. 'We have no clue what will catch a child's attention or interest. In Syracuse, they just put on *Midsummer Night's Dream*, which was a production of very high quality. Which students did some schools elect to send? The gifted English students."

This doesn't make sense for several reasons, she maintains. "The kids in gifted English are often those whose parents have money and season tickets to the theater. Many of those students would have been able to go anyway."

But children not in a gifted class are those who might benefit most from seeing a professional production of a Shakespeare play, she said. "How better to capture the interest of a child who has never read Shakespeare?," she asked. "What a great way to get nonreaders interested in literature and theater!"

How does her position on gifted education vary from liberal gifted educators who believe in enrichment experiences for all children?, I asked. "Enrichment programs for all make the most sense to me, especially when there are multiple entry points. But often they still think in terms of levels, and believe that only some kids can do certain things," she responded. "There are two issues that have to be examined. Most of our gifted programs are for kids who excel in verbal skills as well as score high on tests like the Stanford-Binet.

"But if we look at Gardner's work on multiple intelligences, the new learning on the kinds of intelligences, we see that there are very few schools that do a good job of nurturing more than one or two of those kinds of intelligences. We also have to work on developing programs in lots of different areas so that different kinds of gifts and intelligences can be developed."

What kind of training does a teacher need to be able to deal with different talents and learning styles in one class, and then go beyond merely coping to truly succeeding in nurturing those differences?, I asked.

"One, the teacher must be a learner, someone who doesn't believe in a transmission philosophy of teaching. Two, the teacher needs to be willing to acknowledge that there is more than one teacher in the classroom. Children can serve as teachers, and there are considerable community resources. We need to get away from the belief that the teacher is exclusively in charge of the thirty kids in the class."

Willing to relinquish control?, I asked.

"Yes," Sapon-Shevin replied. "The teacher has to be willing to take risks, to be comfortable with change—not to be a control freak. Those are 'givens.' Teachers also need skills in organizing curriculum that is multilevel. They need skills directed toward developing integrated curricula, and multilevel, multimodality teaching. They must get away from the notion that there is one body of information that has to be transmitted and that every child learns the same thing in the same way."

She points to a teacher she worked with who looked at her peers who were ordering textbooks within the parameters of the budget given them, and asked: "Why would I want thirty copies of the same book in my class?"

"Just think about that statement," Sapon-Shevin said. "Why would I? I can take that money and get six different texts, historical novels, computer programs, whatever. Where is it written that every student has to have the same textbook in front of them? Why do all students have to learn the same ten facts about the Civil War? Why not look in ten different books and see what they say about the Civil War and whether it is the same?"

I commented that the first set of things Sapon-Shevin discussed seemed related to individual temperament, and the second part related directly to skills. How will teachers get the skills they need?, I asked. How can the system help them? What needs to change in the system to ensure that adequate support is present for teachers?

In her response, she pointed to the need for collaboration above all else. "Teachers need to actually work with other teachers, to have time to meet, think, plan, and talk to one another. When they have the time, I have found teachers to be tremendously creative and innovative. I don't believe they need an outside expert."

She added, "I really believe that none of us is as smart as all of us. Teachers also need encouragement for following kids' leads and developing curriculum. They don't need administrators who demand lesson plans in advance or who evaluate everything by standardized test scores."

Finally, societal regard for teachers needs to be elevated, she said. "We need to treat teachers as professionals who can make good, thoughtful, intelligent, and ethical decisions about what children need because they are close to students. Those are structural factors, and they all require support. When I see teachers doing innovative things, usually the school supports and encourages them."

Innovative Practices, Innovative Teachers

Are the innovative practices Sapon-Shevin sees mostly occurring at the elementary level?, I asked. "It's definitely easier in elementary schools," she said, "but I just finished working with a middle school and exciting things occurred when they were able to talk to each other. Clearly, the quality of their teaching changed."

Does Sapon-Shevin see enough individuals with the temperamental characteristics of risk-taking, flexibility, and willingness to share authority entering teaching as a career? "No," she said bluntly.

Is there a mismatch between teaching the way it is currently and the people who have those characteristics?, I asked. "Probably," she said, "so one of the questions would be: 'How do we attract the kind of people with these characteristics to teaching?' And once we have students in preservice teacher education programs, how do we teach them to be flexible, creative, and collaborative?"

To Sapon-Shevin, one of the most compelling arguments in favor of parents rallying together to change the structure of schools is the changing face of American society. "If we are to have a real democracy," she said, "we need all kids to do well in school. It is very short-sighted to think that we only need to care about our own children.

"As we increasingly become a country of 'haves and have nots,' we see people sticking each other up on the streets to steal each other's coats. What are we going to become? A nation of people with security systems? Will we have to spend the money we make at our jobs to protect us from the people who are poor, who don't have an education? It's the equivalent of sawing off the branch you're sitting on."

I asked Sapon-Shevin how she would work with teachers who are frustrated by students who have been mainstreamed into their classes; teachers who feel frustrated by the amount of time they perceive the students need and by their own lack of preparation to meet their needs.

"They need the same things all teachers need," she said. "They need support, time to share, and resources. They also need people to honor their questions and help them find answers. The number one question in this country for teachers working on inclusion is: 'What do you need?' And the answer is: 'Planning time.'

"They need to know kids won't be dropped on their doorstep, that the people who drop them off won't be running like hell to get away from the situation. If I'm working on a unit on dinosaurs and I have one kid who doesn't read, I need to know someone will be there to say: 'How about trying this?' or 'I know we have some dinosaur activities that she can do on the computer.' Someone who can provide that type of support can keep teaching from being isolating, being in a room alone with thirty kids."

A culture within the school that makes it permissable for teachers to ask for help is crucial, she emphasized. "In a lot of schools when the teacher asks for help, it's seen as a flaw, which is very different from the school in which it is accepted that all teachers need help and support."

Although collaboration may be the ideal, it can present its own set of difficulties, she acknowledged. "It's like having someone else in my kitchen," she said. "You have your way to do dishes and I have my way. We have to figure out how to share this kitchen, which means communication, negotiation, and problem solving. We know that collaboratively taught classrooms are often the most wonderful, because there's another set of eyes, of ears, another brain. I'm not good at everything; you may be good at the things I'm not. How can we work together?"

The Effects of Gifted Education

What happens to the children who are not selected for inclusion in gifted programs?, I asked Sapon-Shevin. Are there observable effects?

"There are effects at different levels," she said. "At the educational level it's pretty clear that certain types of opportunities and experiences are provided for some kids and not for other kids. Not going to see *Midsummer Night's Dream* is just one example. You don't do 'gifted curriculum' with nongifted children, so we start discriminating based not on any real knowledge of a child but because of a label. Therefore, certain kids just don't have certain kinds of experiences, experiences that could be exciting and educational."

The inequities of special programming for the gifted are illustrated amply for Sapon-Shevin by an anecdote. "A woman went to visit an elementary school classroom. In one corner, there was a table around which four kids were using metric measurement to assemble a gingerbread house. The other table had twenty-five children doing worksheets.

"What are the feelings that kids have about that?," she asked. "And what does the teacher tell them? 'You can't do that because you're not smart enough?' The difficulty people have explaining this is one of the signs that something is not right."

I asked what effects she thinks gifted education has on teachers. "One of the effects it has on the teachers of 'regular kids' is that it keeps them from doing those kinds of activities because they become activities for the gifted kids only," she noted. "Other teachers say they're glad there is special programming because some of the kids can have their needs met, needs they weren't meeting before. In other words, 'I wasn't getting enough support, so thank goodness someone else is doing it so I don't have to worry about the kids.'"

Gifted education is a painful way to teach children who counts in the world, Sapon-Shevin maintains. "There is a tremendous amount of hurt that is embedded in the gifted program, in who goes and who doesn't go. If we think the kids don't know and don't talk about it, we're deluding ourselves."

Is programming for children identified as gifted secure, I asked, or will the pressure brought by its critics prevail?

"I have a two-part answer," she said. "I'm concerned that people will use anti-tracking or anti-gifted education arguments to deny resources to the school. Instead of reallocating monies spent on special programs or grouping, they will cut that amount completely. This is very different from asking how the money can be spent differently.

"At the other end of the spectrum, some schools have used the rhetoric of inclusion to drop special education programs and have literally dumped kids back into regular classrooms with no resources, no support, and no training for teachers."

"Inclusion," Sapon-Shevin said with emphasis, "is simply not the same thing as dumping. I'm not advocating that we put all students in 'regular' classrooms with no attention to the quality of that classroom. I'm asking that we look at curriculum, pedagogy, teacher development, and the school community so that *all* children have their needs met well—*including* differentiated instruction and curricula—within a shared, community context."

Howard Gardner:
Educating for Understanding

Howard Gardner is best known in educational circles for his alternative concept of intelligence that negates intelligence as singular and easily quantified with standard psychometric instruments. He is Professor of Education and Adjunct Professor of Psychology at Harvard University, Adjunct Professor of Neurology at the Boston University School of Medicine, and Co-director of Harvard Project Zero. The recipient of many honors, including a MacArthur Prize Fellowship, he is the author of fourteen books and several hundred articles. Recently, he and colleagues at Project Zero have been working on the design of performance-based assessments, education for understanding, and the use of multiple intelligences to achieve more personalized curriculum, instruction, and assessment. He has joined also with Theodore R. Sizer and James Comer in Project ATLAS, an initiative funded by the New American Schools Development Corporation. Members of the consortium, which also includes the Education Development Center, form Project ATLAS (Authentic Teaching, Learning, and Assessment for all Students), and have worked in 800 different schools with students of all ages and economic strata.

When *Frames of Mind* was published in 1983, the attention of the education reform community was seized with a novel and powerful notion: Gardner's conception of intelligence as multidimensional, with jagged profiles of different intelligences existing in everyone. Gardner provided hard data to support his theory, including test results of stroke victims and others who sustained brain injuries that impaired some, but not all, abilities. Cautioning that the number of intelligences is arguable, he identified seven intelligences—musical, spatial, bodily/kinesthetic, artistic, linguistic, mathematic, and interpersonal/intrapersonal—but insisted that his main point was to debunk long-held notions that intelligence is a single, unitary entity as specified by Spearman with his "g."

Although Gardner has expressed some surprise at the intensity of educators' reactions to his theory of multiple intelligences (MI)—especially in light of the fact that *Frames of Mind* was written primarily for an audience of psychologists—he seems comfortable, even pleased, with the reaction MI has sustained among educators. In the years since the publication of *Frames of Mind*, national seminars have been held on MI theory, entire schools have drawn up their educational programs based on their interpretations of the theory, and Gardner has entered into a partnership (Project ATLAS) with James Comer, Theodore Sizer, and the Education Development Center, actively aimed at reforming education around the fundamental concepts of multiple intelligences and personalization of curriculum and instruction.

In a previous interview with me, Gardner explained how he accounts for educators' eagerness to embrace MI theory. At that time (Lockwood, 1993), he spoke of the theory as "a provocation" which has galvanized many educators around the notion that a single conception of intelligence is neither accurate nor equitable—and, in fact, may hamper significantly educators' work to educate the "whole child." Its popularity in educational circles, he said, speaks to MI's "Rorschach-like" qualities: Educators and reformers appear to use the theory almost as an in-school test upon which they can project their own ideas about education—some of which may vary widely.

For example, some interpret MI theory as an endorsement to develop a child's areas of strength, rather than focusing on his or her weaker areas with remediation. Others disagree, believing that all intelligences should be as equally developed as possible, and warn against premature tracking of children into areas in which they show clear ability.

Rather than posing a concern to Gardner, he sees this lack of consensus among the educational community about MI's application as one of the theory's strengths, along with the fact that the theory remains a theory—it does not prescribe solutions to schools. Also, in order to personalize education so that what he calls "education for understanding" is achieved, educators have to reach the realization that they must provide a differentiated curriculum and divergent teaching strategies. Above all, he is convinced that with the right constellation of leaders and differentiated roles for school staff, a multiple-intelligences approach to learning can make a difference.

Hence, the uniformity of instruction customarily provided by schools is deplorable; personalization and individualization of curriculum, coupled with performance-fair assessments, are necessary for schools to transform themselves into places where each child's true potential can be realized.

Personalizing Education

In the years that have followed the publication of *Frames of Mind*, Gardner has made himself accessible to educators who have expressed an interest in MI theory, either because it offered them an opportunity to expand their educational repertoire, or because to some degree it verified their intuitive beliefs and validated their existing practice.

He believes the key to an improved education for all children lies in individually centered schooling, rather than mass schooling in which a uniform curriculum is offered to all students and children either fit into it and succeed, or never mesh with its aims and goals, and fail. What specific actions, I asked him, should school administrators, teachers, and parents take to aid a move toward individually centered schooling?

After a thoughtful pause, Gardner changed my question. "I tend not to put it that way," he said. "I ask: Are schools happy with what is going on? If they are, then they should not move toward individually centered schooling."

But often, I countered, the answer is: "No, we're not happy."

"Right," he agreed. "Then the question becomes: What is it that makes you unhappy? What would you like to do better? We hear time and again from teachers that there are many kids they do not reach. We also hear it from parents, who say their kids are bored and not engaged in learning. When you hear such statements, multiple intelligences, personalization of learning and individualization become an answer to the question.

"But," he emphasized, "I am very wary when someone comes into a school district or school and says: 'You need X, Y, or Z.' It is up to the school or the school district to say what it means, to articulate the options. I always ask educators: Before you embrace a position, whether it is multiple intelligences or Sizer's work or cooperative learning, what will you get out of it?"

Gardner sees a prescriptive, "canned" approach to education's woes as simplistic. Instead, he believes that school staff need to enter the sometimes painful work of learning to articulate and envision what they want, and then plot their strategy so that they can attain their goals. This may sound easy, but often schools want change, see the need for individualizatiion, but balk when confronted with the need to relinquish coverage.

The pervasive emphasis on content coverage, especially at the secondary level, is pernicious. In fact, Gardner sees it as one of the biggest philosophical and practical problems plaguing schools. "Many, if not most, would rather have coverage and sacrifice understanding, which seems one of the most foolish conclusions one could reach," he said.

"When you use multiple intelligences as your frame of reference when working with children, you give up the notion that you can rank kids first to last—which is an appealing concept, of course, if it is your child that is ranked first."

Critics of special programming for children identified as gifted or talented, who are committed to an egalitarian ideal, may discover that their egalitarianism works against the best education for all children, he maintains. "If you hold an ideal that you should treat every kid exactly the same, you will not get the best education for each," he said. "Even in societies that have that commitment, it is not happening.

"What MI says is that one size does not fit all," he added. "We need to learn as much as we can about the minds, personalities, and styles of all kids in school."

To what extent, I asked, does MI theory appeal to educators because it affirms what they are already doing? To what degree does it prompt new practice? "Everyone likes to be validated for what they do," he responded. "When I say that kids are different, they learn in different ways and have different strengths, everyone nods. It's common sense.

"It would be worrisome only if people think they are doing something very different because they have embraced MI and yet, if you look at their track record, it's not different at all. There are some people," he said dryly, "who confuse good intentions with the achievement of something new or different.

"Nevertheless, everybody who takes multiple intelligences seriously is likely to see eventually that they can do a lot more than they are doing. I also doubt that many teachers really serve all of the intelligences. I doubt that many teachers look as carefully as they could at all their students, really trying to personalize education as much as possible.

"Even if what teachers are doing is quite consistent with MI theory, MI shouldn't just be an endorser: It should be a prodder. Any new idea or any idea that presents itself as new is initially going to be applied in a superficial way. That's human nature. MI theory is both common sense and radical, depending on how seriously you look at it."

It is clear that Gardner is not pushing one more "model" onto schools, and, in fact, shows a researcher's caution when speaking of implementation in schools. Longitudinal studies are required to see how well implementation efforts stand up, he pointed out.

"That is the real test, to see if, five years down the road, the idea has long been forgotten," he said, "or if it is being implemented in the same sort of wooden way it was five years earlier. In that case, nothing has been gained. Or, has working with the ideas of multiple intelligences gotten people to deepen their thinking, to try out new things, to adopt those which work and reject those that didn't? I believe it really can transform their practice."

Multiple Intelligences: Implications for Teachers

What staff development or continued education do teachers need in order to transform their classrooms into places where each child's intelligences are nurtured, especially at the secondary level?, I asked him.

"The most helpful thing for teachers," Gardner replied, "is to see where this is done. All of us benefit from an existence proof. If we see a place working with kids somewhat like ours, we see they are human rather than superhuman. And yet, in these places, we can see that individual differences are taken much more seriously; the reports reflect that, and the curriculum reflects that."

Without a structure that allows or encourages teachers to collaborate within an environment of experimentation and risk-taking, little will ensue, Gardner added. "Teachers need a structure within which they can talk and try things out and critique each other. Most things don't work the first time they are tried out. If you think that an attempt followed by failure is a kiss of death, then you're not going to try things out."

Large national or regional conferences on MI theory have served a networking role, he said, bringing hundreds or thousands of people together who are interested in the theory. "A main benefit is that people are able to share experiences. In that kind of grass roots movement lies the best chance for jump-starting a more individualized approach to education.

"In Project ATLAS, which is just in its early stages, we are very committed to this personalization, getting to know kids better and getting kids to feel they are known better," he noted. "If the ATLAS approach works and catches on, then there will be many places we can look at to see a good demonstration of individual differences being taken seriously. In some places, we see these demonstrations already."

How, I asked, can educators ensure that they are developing all the intelligences present in each child? "I don't see education's primary goal as developing all seven intelligences in every child. That would be wooden and pointless," Gardner retorted. "Most people want productive citizens who use their minds well, who can make a decent living, and who serve the community. Because people are different, they will do this in different ways. The job in schools is to make sure that kids find stuff that they're good at, can connect to, that has some kind of social value—both in the sense that they could make a living at it and in the sense that it is not criminal. Consideration of more than the conventional view of intelligence, attention to the cultivation and deployment of the intelligences most appropriate for each child, is more likely to bring about this desirable state of affairs."

Gardner worries most about youth who never find something in which to be interested. "They don't get a kick out of anything," he observed. "The problem in America is not that kids don't have all seven intelligences. So many kids are bored. Yes, they should be exposed to lots of stuff, and we should make the decisions for them when they are young. But when my son, who is nine, wants to try new things, I have to say to him: 'You already have a lot of activities. Do you really want to take on something new?' He's old enough that he understands that he must make choices.'"

What about youngsters who are shuttled around on an exhausting round of music lessons, acrobatics, soccer games, dance lessons, and the like?, I asked. "They are still better off," Gardner said gently. "The ones who aren't interested in anything are the ones headed for gangs."

Programs for Gifted and Talented

I asked Gardner: Where do you stand on the question of special programming for students identified as gifted or talented? Do you believe it should be abolished? "Most programs that call themselves gifted programs," he replied, "are really programs for the scholastically gifted. The intent behind these programs is to find kids who are good in school and give them some enrichment to push them ahead more rapidly. Of course, there is a long tradition behind this programming with pros and cons to it.

"It's just silly to pretend," he continued, "that kids who can do work more challenging than what they're given should stay where they are. I also believe, however, that it is a mistake to cordon off kids who happen to be good scholastically from other kids. There are many positive benefits for kids with varying abilities when they are together for at least part of the day. There are many activities where a scholastically precocious child can learn from someone who sees things differently."

If special programming for students identified as gifted is a district or schoolwide commitment, Gardner has some caveats about its implementation. "If such programming were in place in my school district," he said, "I would want some attention paid to kids who are gifted in the arts or in leadership or in athletics, as well as attention paid to kids who are scholastically gifted. Obviously, I do not assume that the kid who is gifted in one area is going to be gifted in another area."

Even scholastic giftedness, he said, consists of putting many things together to reach a coherent whole. "The notion of scholastic giftedness deserves to be disaggregated. A person might merit enrichment in the language area, but not in math or science or vice versa."

But the typical way of placing those children identified as gifted into special programs alarms Gardner. "If you have a 131 IQ, you get all the marbles," he said. "If you have a 129 IQ, you don't. Almost no place looks at what comprises the score."

I asked: Do you think special programs persist because what is usually offered in schools is so stultifying? "Yes," he said. "If you have a child who is reading much further on his own and doing science much further on his own, the parents have a right to be frustrated. While I'm not opposed to special programs per se, there are probably 100 programs to which I am not opposed.

We cannot fund all 100, so communities have to decide where they will put their extra resources. It is not a foregone conclusion that those resources should go to the gifted program, but I certainly would not eliminate it as an option."

Diversity and MI Theory

Given the increasing diversity of student populations nationwide, I asked: To what extent does MI theory—which focuses on diversity of intelligences— respond to the diversity of race, ethnicity, and culture?

"There are claims the population is more diverse now," Gardner replied. "Diversity is clearly with us, but it is actually fairly difficult to determine whether we have substantially more diversity now or whether the diversity is more noticeable and more attention is paid to it. In the last analysis, the basic idea of multiple intelligences boils down to the fact that kids are different from one another; they have different kinds of minds.

"In uniform schools, where they resolutely ignore those differences, they treat everyone the same, believing that it is fair to do so. And it *is* fair—if everyone is just a smarter or less smart version of the same kind of mind. You could say it is arguably fair in that case. But if, in fact, we aren't all cut out of the same cookie cutter, but have very different kinds of minds, then perhaps schools should do something else.

"I hope that people happen to have the kind of mind that school serves, and if we have 100 different kinds of schools, they will serve 100 different kinds of minds. In fact, we would have to look at a particular kind of school to see which minds are being well-served and which minds might be served much better.

"MI theory says: Forget about one size fits all. Learn as much as you can about the minds and the personalities and the styles of kids and schools. If you want to help a child develop as much as possible—and I haven't heard any- body oppose that goal—you can begin to think about curricula, pedagogy, and assessment in terms of the individual."

Assessment needs to be personalized as well, Gardner maintains. "Stu- dents don't have to show what they have learned all in the same way," he said. "Again, MI theory encourages one to pluralize the forms of assessment and evaluation. If you believe in just one kind of intelligence, what would follow from that? Would it mean you would have to treat everyone the same? What would be gained and what would be lost in doing that? Once you have recog- nized different kinds of intelligence, you are selectively driven to try to per- sonalize education as much as possible."

I asked Gardner: Do you refuse to accept the notion that schools cannot move to individually centered schooling, given their current structure? "Clearly, you can't personalize as much if you're teaching classes of 30 kids and you're in a high school with a total student load of 120 to 150," he said. "Nonetheless, that doesn't mean that if you have a bad ratio, you have to give up. You have to do what you can.

"One way is to outsmart the system. If you can't get to know the kid well, you could set up a classroom where at least other people could get to know kids well. You could do this by using aides in the classroom, or cooperative learning, or through using exhibitions with some kids and letting others see how their class-mates are doing them and joining in critiques of the work that has been exhibited.

"There are many options available to you once you buy into the notion that you *should* know kids well," he added. "Also, once the school system buys into individualization, it realizes that kids can help in the process. The student can tell you: 'This is the sort of thing I learned well, and this is the kind of thing that is difficult for me.' A passive child can break out of that by realizing that it's a part of the game to try to make use of all the knowledge you have about yourself."

Depoliticizing Education

I asked Gardner if the current conservative political climate—or the con-servatives who make their voices heard at the district level—will have a mea-surable impact on how MI theory is absorbed into schooling. In his reply, Gardner suggested that education be depoliticized; in so doing, he said, the public might discover its common ground.

"Many things that I say are not particularly left or right," he observed. "If you pay attention to individuals and help them learn, is that left or right? If you want kids to be able to understand and be able to perform what they understand, is that conservative or liberal?

"A lot of the political characterization of schools is a pseudo-activity," he enlarged. "It doesn't look very deeply at what a particular approach is trying to achieve. Even with something like national standards, most advocates have taken a middle-of-the-road position. They believe we ought to have national standards to see how our kids are doing, but the ultra-conservatives and the lib-erals have rejected them. Only those in the middle still like the concept."

Why do many cling to the concept that school can be a uniform place for all children and, without differentiation, meet all their needs?, I asked. "Basi-cally, until recently it wasn't important to educate people in this country," Gardner reflected. "People were prepared to be farmers or to work in factories, and an education didn't matter too much for either occupation. The educa-tional system's goal, as I put it humorously, was to pick out who would be the best law professor. A good law professor is someone who is very scholas-tic. If you show me a law professor, I'll show you someone who did very well in school and scored well on the standardized tests.

"But we no longer can afford to have a society where 80 percent drop out of sight, and the law professors get it all. We were able to get away with it because the stakes weren't very high. In Europe, which is a heavily tracked system, assessments are made before adolescence as to who will continue and in what way. In Europe, you know something if you have a secondary education. But in America, in college all too often you're ready for remedial work. But we can't compare secondary education in Europe with America because they have very different standards."

Multiple Intelligences at the Secondary Level

I asked Gardner: How can MI theory be implemented best in secondary schools, given the pressures visited upon them and their usually rigid structure? He immediately acknowledged the complexity of the secondary school, saying, "It is probably a mistake to lead with MI in high schools. It would divide people unnecessarily. If I were interested in the MI view in high school, I would begin by talking about kids who aren't served well in the present system, and how anything worth teaching can be presented in a number of different ways."

Gardner added, "I firmly believe both of those statements are true. If one can get consensus around that, namely, that kids aren't being well-served and that material worth teaching could be taught many different ways, then we could introduce the MI way of thinking. But the things that are rather attractive to a second grade teacher or even a middle school teacher, are the types of things that disciplinarians and high school teachers get very nervous about. They say, 'What's going to happen to me? What's going to happen to my subject?'"

Despite their fears, teachers at the secondary level can be powerful change agents, Gardner believes. "Many are keen observers of the high school, and they recognize that many kids aren't well-served. If they are good teachers and know their subject matter, they are aware that the subject matter can be presented in various ways and that people can show their understanding in various ways. Unfortunately, some believe there is only one way to teach geometry or geography, and there is only one way to show what has been learned. Those people will never be sold on MI."

Making Education Reform Succeed

In *Multiple Intelligences: The Theory in Practice*, his 1993 reader aimed at a diverse audience, Gardner wrote that for education reform to succeed, five main prongs needed to be integrated actively. He pointed to assessment, curriculum, teacher education, professional development, and community participation. I asked how he envisioned that this integration would occur.

"Not without leadership," he said, "and leaders could be important people in the community: teachers, administrators, and parents. They have to take this as a goal and they can't shove it down people's throats. They would have to provide a story, which means a vision that other people want to buy into. They also have to provide an embodiment for the story and their own behavior.

"In other words," he continued, "if you are a leader, you can't call for the school to respect learning if you don't respect learning yourself, if you are not a learner. Excellent leadership is required more and more, and it is in short supply. But any place which has moved in this direction hasn't seen it happen without brave, supportive leadership."

If schools want to move toward personalized learning, the way Gardner believes they should, leadership is especially crucial, he maintains. "We would make a grave error if we underestimated the importance of leadership," he said, "whether it's a Deborah Meier, a Ted Sizer, or a James Comer. These people are leaders, and even though they are genuine democrats, they would always admit that nothing happens without very powerful, dedicated, hard-working leadership."

Effective leaders must drive change, but not force-feed school staff, Gardner said. "If schools are going to move in an individually centered direction, somebody has to help them get the conversation going so that people can articulate what they are unhappy about in their schools, whether they are unhappy, how they would like to change."

Gardner concluded, "In the long run, we wish for that type of infrastructure, because when the charismatics die or get exhausted, nothing is left. There is little staying power. But if people grow and become opinion makers and leaders in their communities, they are no longer one-issue people; they're there for whatever the issue is."

Thomas R. Hoerr:
One School's Application of
Multiple Intelligences Theory

Thomas R. Hoerr directs the New City School, an independent elementary school of 360 students, ages 3–12, located in St. Louis, Missouri, where he has been instrumental in leading the school's implementation of Howard Gardner's multiple intelligences theory. He also has been a principal and teacher in public schools, and holds a Ph.D. in Educational Planning and Policy Development from Washington University. The creator and Director of Washington University's Non-Profit Management Program, which prepares managers of non-profit organizations for their leadership roles, he continues to provide instruction in the program. Hoerr is a frequent presenter at national educational organizations and has written several articles on the application of multiple intelligences theory in school settings.

For Thomas Hoerr, encountering Howard Gardner's multiple intelligences theory (MI) while on a sabbatical from his duties at the New City School, was both a personal and professional epiphany. Here, he thought as he finished reading *Frames of Mind*, are ideas that are consonant with what I have believed for a long time about children's capacities to learn. His only frustration, he reports, was the lack of people with whom to discuss Gardner's ideas. Returning from his leave, he invited staff at the New City School to meet and discuss the book.

"I knew it was important for the entire faculty to be as excited as possible about the theory in order for us to apply it," Hoerr remembered. "As we proceeded through our discussions, teachers took on the responsibility of teaching other teachers."

The faculty kept three informal lists before them as they worked. Hoerr describes them as: "This Is What We're Already Doing"; "These Are Things We Could Do Pretty Easily"; and "These Are Things We Could Do If We Had Money."

"These lists," he recalled, "reminded us both how easy it is to have some quick successes, and also that we were already working—almost intuitively—from a multiple intelligences approach."

The original one-third of the faculty who were keenly interested in MI theory were outnumbered by two-thirds who were what Hoerr terms "unfamiliar" with the ideas. "At every faculty meeting we would give an update of what the committee was learning, so that everybody in the school felt some level of knowledge. When the Association for Supervision and Curriculum Development (ASCD) held an MI conference at the Key School in Indianapolis, we decided as a committee to send eight people to it. We further decided that four of them would come from the committee; we would take two cars and have two people from the committee in each car. We were that deliberate about continuing to widen the circle and pull more people into it."

The following year, formal implementation of MI theory began with abundant time committed to teacher inservice. To Hoerr, one reason it was relatively easy to gain faculty support for the theory was the fact that New City's curriculum had never been locked into a rigid use of textbooks. "Our feeling is that our curriculum should not be determined by a publisher in Palo Alto or Albany or San Antonio; it should be determined by people in our school."

Why MI?

MI suits the purposes and philosophy of New City perfectly, Hoerr maintains, because it does not prescribe or recommend particular steps for implementation. Rather, it is a collection of ideas, almost a philosophical template that individual schools can use with their own overlay placed upon it. "We use MI as a tool," he said, "in three major respects, dealing with our three constituents: our kids, their parents, and our faculty. The more we have worked with MI, the more it has helped us focus on strengths and what kids can do rather than working from the traditional deficit model where you find out what kids can't do and have them do it until they are better at it."

But Hoerr is quick to qualify New City's approach to MI. "This doesn't mean we are stepping back from a commitment to reading, writing, and computation," he said. "If you cannot do those well, you have a disadvantage, just as if you cannot do well on standardized tests you have a problem. With MI, kids have found more ways to succeed."

One of those ways, he believes, is through a heightened self-concept. "If there were an instrument that accurately measured self-concept and we had administered it five years ago as well as currently, there is not a doubt in my mind that we have improved in making kids feel good about themselves."

As with any reform, parents are an integral part, and New City's staff has focused heavily on parent educative efforts in order to convince them of the importance of the MI approach. "Parents become more comfortable with the school when they truly understand what is going on and are willing to buy into it. Understanding the school's mission also helps them look at their kids differently;

they see their strengths in the same way we see their child's strengths."

Finally, MI has provided the philosophical foundation for teacher collegiality. "MI has given us a common language," Hoerr noted. "It has given us a common vision and shown us areas in which we need to work together."

In fact, an unexpected development since MI theory was introduced into the school is teacher commitment to collegiality.

"We believe very strongly in Barth's notion of collegiality, that teachers first must be learners, that they must be students themselves if students are to learn and grow. As one example, each teacher has been given $250 to use for staff development in any way that he or she chooses. This is above and beyond what we have allocated in the budget," he said. "The idea is that since you are the teacher, you tell us what you want to do."

Options might include waiting four years until $1,000 has been accumulated and the teacher embarks on a trip to Europe to study the Mediterranean. "We like the fact that this money is above and beyond our regular staff development money, but we also are telling teachers that we trust their judgment.

"Of course, the problem we are experiencing are the people who want to use the money to buy books for their students. My response is: Hold on, put yourself first. Where do *you* need to grow?"

Because schools tend to be hierarchical organizations, Hoerr believes they often attract staff with a certain temperament that has to be nudged to take risks. "The people who are attracted to the profession are those who work well in organizations. The real accomplishment won't come out of the way the money is spent, but out of the thought process that takes place before the decision is made, when teachers talk with their teammates and ask: 'How are you going to spend your money? Where are you going to go? What books have you read? Can I borrow yours?' All those questions advance teachers toward becoming reflective practitioners rather than people who go to a workshop because the boss said it would be good for me."

Educating for Understanding

I asked Hoerr for his interpretation of Gardner's term, "educating for understanding." What does this term mean to you? I inquired. How does New City's faculty interpret "educating for understanding," and how do they work with students to ensure it occurs?

Hoerr reports that he and his staff refer to Gardner's term as "genuine understanding," and it is an issue with which the staff continues to struggle. "We began working on the concept about two years ago," he said, "asking what is genuine understanding? Can it be demonstrated? Does genuine understanding involve synthesis and a certain amount of skills? We discussed this quite a lot, and ended up defining genuine understanding as the use of skills or knowledge in new or novel situations."

As the staff proceeded to grapple with the concept, individuals tried different approaches to see how genuine understanding, or educating for understanding, might be assessed. For example, a first-grade teacher worked with her team partner to see if the notion of genuine understanding could be used to assess what their students learned about plants. "At the first-grade level, for example," Hoerr said, "our feeling originally was that the kids learn such limited information about plants that it is hard to demonstrate genuine understanding. They know that plants need sunlight, they need water, they grow toward the sun, they breathe oxygen, but these are isolated facts. But once the teachers began to work around the concept of genuine understanding, they found ways for kids to put facts together.

"The teachers were able to go beyond that to show kids how they could use genuine understanding to demonstrate what they knew about plants."

The result, Hoerr said, was a student-created plant museum. The process of building the museum was broken into several discrete chunks: a teacher-led student discussion about the purpose and contents of museums; the development of a checklist of things students liked in museums; and trips to different types of museums with student reports to the rest of the class on what they saw. The museum visits were not pell-mell field trips, but instead were carefully organized to ensure students would apply what they learned in the museum setting.

"The kids took clipboards and rated what they saw in terms of how easy it was to understand," Hoerr said. "When they returned, they had a list of criteria for what they wanted in their museum. They then talked about what they knew about plants and created displays of the things they had learned. That is where MI came in; some kids actually potted plants, others worked with graphics for the exhibition and so forth. For three days at the end of the year, we have had a first-grade plant museum with games, exhibits, and a gift shop."

Key to the success the children experienced when demonstrating their genuine understanding of plants, Hoerr believes, was a staff consensus that the easiest area for children to show their understanding lay in social situations such as planning and working together on a project. Hoerr himself waxes passionate over the need for development in what Gardner terms the interpersonal/intrapersonal intelligence—what in other quarters has been termed "works and plays well with others."

Getting Along with Others

"If you have strong intrapersonal intelligence, you know what your strengths and weaknesses are, you can make the accommodations necessary to enable you to do what you want to do," Hoerr emphasized. "Because we believe that so fervently about our kids, we also strive to do it in our work with each other."

Students at New City are urged from an early age to learn to accommodate one another. "In our first grade, we have what we call the Red Chairs," Hoerr reported. "Kids know that when they are not getting along with somebody we guide them to the Red Chairs to talk about it. We think we have helped kids have a genuine understanding of how to resolve conflicts, because we see them in situations we would never have anticipated, moving to the Red Chairs to talk."

With the exception of one little girl who enjoyed the Red Chairs so much that, as Hoerr says, "She overused them," the technique has been remarkably successful and, in fact, has generated teacher reflection about staff differences.

"People need to feel comfortable about making mistakes," Hoerr noted. "If you haven't made a mistake lately, that says to me that you haven't stretched yourself, you're not willing to try new things. Of course, it is one thing to say that and another to put it into practice."

How, I asked, does he offer critical feedback to a teacher with a "perfect lesson"?

"I come in with a laptop computer," he said, "and type my notes. An hour later, the teacher gets a copy of my notes. Three-fourths of my comments will reflect what I saw and one-fourth will ask questions such as: What if? Why did you? Why didn't you? In my session with the teacher, I will acknowledge the quality of the lesson, but I will also ask what would have happened if he or she had tried new things. I do it in a way that says what the teacher did was wonderful, but let's talk about how that teacher can stretch herself. I may say that the next time I come to observe I would like you to try something that you're not sure will work. If it does work, that is wonderful, and if it doesn't, it is okay too, because we are both going to learn from it."

Measuring Genuine Understanding

Another piece of genuine understanding revolves around the school's progress reports, which are being redesigned around multiple intelligences— and again, highlight the intrapersonal and interpersonal intelligence.

"The first page of our progress report focuses exclusively on personal intelligences because we believe that is the most important part of a child's progress," Hoerr said. "These are the skills such as gets along with peers, works well with others. But since we have such a strong commitment to diversity, we ended up adding an item that says: Can appreciate the perspectives of others, particularly those of other races and cultures.

"We thought it developmentally appropriate," he continued, "because it is different for a kindergartner and for a sixth grader. Also, if we can get our kids to do it, we have succeeded. We are currently in the process of reconfiguring the rest of the progress report around the intelligences. Next we will develop rubrics for linguistics and mathematics, and finally we will do the most difficult part, creating rubrics for assessing genuine understanding."

Clearly, Hoerr is intrigued by the task. "In my mind," he said, "there is a question about whether one can really develop a rubric that is specific to genuine understanding if by definition genuine understanding is a unique and novel situation. One way I like to look at it is to explore the question that asks: How different would this country be today if instead of being settled at Plymouth Rock it had been settled at Sacramento?

"This question can be answered at every level of development because it is open-ended. Or we might ask: What if instead of the Magna Carta we had the writings of Confucius? How would that have affected the Declaration of Independence and the Constitution? Questions such as these require kids to come up with novel solutions to demonstrate their understanding. On the other hand, how do you design a rubric that captures that? We don't know that answer but as we work on it, we are a faculty that is moving forward, working as a collaborative, collectively trying to find answers."

Gifted and Talented Programming

I questioned Hoerr about his attitude toward special programming for gifted and talented students. Given the present structure of public schools, does he think the programming is necessary because they otherwise will not be able to meet the needs of all students, especially the most intellectually able?

"When you have a gifted program," he replied, "by definition you have a nongifted program. That bothers me. I would much rather say that every kid has a gift; let's find out what those gifts are and develop all the gifts.

"Can you individualize for every kid? No, you can't. Does that mean you pick some kids and individualize for them and not for others? No, I don't think you do. Instead, we ought to be saying that every kid has a profile, every kid has some gifts. Our job as educators is to find those gifts and nurture them."

But fiscal and political reality often collides with good intentions and goals, I pointed out. Hoerr agreed, saying: "In this culture, the reality is that some intelligences are valued more than others if we look at who makes money. Our gifted programs replicate those intelligences. Success in life and success in school are not the same thing, and many educators think they are."

So he believes in a totally inclusive classroom?, I asked. "Every teacher is a gifted teacher," he answered, "and every teacher is a teacher of the gifted.

Many would scoff at this. That is because they are in situations where kids have been taught for years that they are *not* gifted, whether it is what is said to them or how they are treated.

"If we look at most high schools, we see offerings that reflect all the intelligences: athletics, choir, shop, a myriad of choices. Theoretically, all of these intelligences can bloom and be nurtured, but the reality is that by the time many kids reach high school the damage has been done. For instance, I might believe that I'm a good athlete but someone else is really smart. We ignore leadership skills and teach compliance. Then we wonder why kids won't play a leadership role. If every teacher said: I am a teacher of the gifted, we would be much better off."

One gets the sense that if Hoerr had not found the ideas of Gardner's MI theory, something else would have provided the reform framework he wanted. Is this so? I asked him. "Probably," he said, "but I can't imagine what it would have been."

I then asked him how he sees his role as the school's director. How do you see yourself as a leader?, I inquired. What sorts of things do you feel you have to do to encourage the collaborative culture within which the ideas you believe in will flourish?

"People ask me what my job is," Hoerr said in response. "My most important role is helping my faculty grow and develop. If I do that, everything else falls into place. If anything, I see myself as a developer of people. Because I run a private school I also see myself as a developer of my board. The function of everybody with whom I come into contact is going to grow. That doesn't mean I am super-skilled at helping people grow, but it means that in today's world we all must move forward. In that way, I am a catalyst."

Part III

"You Can't Lead Where You Won't Go":
Professionalism, Unions, and Leadership

You can't lead where you won't go; you can't follow where
you won't lead.

— Roland S. Barth

Overview of Part III

The context in which teaching and school administration occurs is highly political. Almost everyone—from national blue-ribbon commissions to parents—claims expertise on how schools should function, what should be their goals, what content teachers should teach and in what way, how school administrators should lead, and whether teacher unions are a positive or a negative force. A common theme that runs through this rhetoric is that of "professionalism" and "professionalization." Teachers are exhorted to be "professionals" or long for the improved working conditions, higher pay, and above all, the societal status afforded physicians and lawyers. Teacher organizations, such as the American Federation of Teachers, demand professional status for teaching, arguing in part that if society held teachers in higher regard, significant school improvement would occur.

I begin this part with the views of Roland S. Barth, who dissects the meaning of "professionalism," and then describes the heartless school culture that resists teachers' and principals' efforts to be professional. As he details the many types of dysfunctional relationships common in schools due to their structure and culture, he progresses to a scenario through which real school change can happen. Kathleen Densmore then takes up the discussion, arguing against the professionalization of teaching on a democratic basis. As part of her intricate argument, she maintains that teachers should not be elevated to the societal status of professionals because this would separate them further from the people that they serve. Wayne J. Urban provides an historical context for teaching as an occupation that never succeeded in elevating itself to professional status, and explains the role teacher unions played. Although unions, he points out, did not contribute to the professionalization of teaching, they should not be blamed: they had another agenda. Kent D. Peterson turns his attention to the role of the professional leader in the contemporary school, delineating the challenges leaders face, and urging a combined role upon school leaders: visionary and manager. I conclude the section with the views of Patricia K. Anderson, an urban school principal who has been active in school reform. She contemplates the meaning of professionalism, the push to professionalize teaching, and the effects of teacher unions upon school reform and improvement efforts.

Roland S. Barth:
Professionalism and
School Leaders

A veteran of both public schools and universities—and thus the two, often conflicting worlds of practice and research—Roland S. Barth has spent his career furthering the self-renewal of schools. He has done this in several capacities: as a teacher, a principal, a professor, and as founder and Director of the Principals' Center at Harvard University. Currently a consultant to numerous schools and districts throughout the United States and Canada, he is the author of numerous articles and books, including Improving Schools from Within *(1990),* Run School Run *(1980), and* Open Education *(1972).*

What is the role of "professional" teachers and principals in the large picture of school improvement? Does "professional" status for teaching translate into improved working conditions, higher pay, and improved social status? Or is "professionalism" a different, more elusive concept that has little to do with social status and working conditions? What difference, ultimately, will "professional" status make in the lives of teachers and students? When I posed these questions to Roland Barth, his reactions revealed how difficult it is to grasp the concept of teacher professionalism—and to reach consensus on its meaning.

Professionalism, he insists, has little or nothing to do with higher social status and public respect for the work of teachers. Admittedly, Barth's view runs counter to much of the current thinking about the professionalization of teaching, yet he makes a convincing argument that, when applied to teaching, professionalism translates into highly ephemeral and personal variables that link inextricably with personal responsibility, self-respect, and self-motivation. In some ways, his view is quasi-therapeutic, as he refuses to cast teachers and other school staff in the roles of hapless victims, instead stressing their individual ability and responsibility to effect change for the larger good.

"Whether you are a teacher or a snow-plow driver, you are paid from taxpayers' money, which contributes to the often demeaning place where teaching is held," Barth said. Yet he is emphatic that money is not what professionalism is about.

Instead, professionalism begins in the head and the heart. "Professionalism means," he enlarged, "that one has a clear conception, a clear set of values, a clear vision about one's beliefs. It also means that together we can create a community of learners within the school, an enterprise in which everyone—students, teachers, principals, parents—is engaged. Furthermore, all can recognize this as the most important enterprise in the schoolhouse. The mark of the professional is someone who takes responsibility for sustaining and making visible himself as a voracious learner."

Although "professionalism" has become almost a Rorschach upon which people project their individual and varying interpretations of the word, Barth told me he wants to make it clear that the philosophical underpinnings of professionalism—as applied to education—are the heart and soul of school improvement. "If you are an educator, you are engaged—or should be engaged—in a continuous search for the conditions under which people's learning curves go off the chart," he said. "That's what it means to be a parent, a professor, a teacher, or a principal. That's also what it means to be a professional."

A teacher can learn more about how to teach effectively, but the act of learning transcends the actual content, he said—placing the responsibility for one's own intellectual renewal squarely on the shoulders of teachers and principals. "You know, when you board an airplane, the flight attendant instructs the passengers how to proceed in the event of an oxygen failure: first place the oxygen mask on their own faces and then on the faces of small children traveling with them. This assumes a dead person cannot save anyone."

He added sardonically, "We who work in schools should take note of this fact. There are many corpses in schools," he continued, "faithfully, conscientiously, *desperately* trying to administer the oxygen of learning to kids while they themselves are anoxic."

Clearly Barth has grappled with the concept of professionalism in his career as a teacher, principal, professor, and founder/director of the Harvard University Principals' Center, one of the nation's first systematic educative efforts targeted exclusively to principals engaged in school reform. Many years of work in both public schools and the research university setting have left him with the belief that before one embarks upon a full-scale philosophical and practical consideration of the effects of professionalism in schools, first it is necessary to acknowledge the ambivalence both educators and the public hold about teaching and teachers as professionals, ambivalence that is profound in its effects upon schools.

This ambivalence, he suggests, can be seen in public policy that demands more technical training for teachers, more supervision, and closer adherence to increasingly prescriptive requirements from state departments of education and national commissions proposing "voluntary" standards. Yet the rhetoric of reports from national commissions urges "professional" status for teachers, more autonomy and freedom from supervision, and a voice in the decision-making process of schools.

To make the double bind complete, Barth points to the prevailing assumption that unless outside agencies, or "experts"—including state departments of education and education reform groups—intervene in the lives of schools, school people will continue to do exactly the same thing next September as they did last September. "A very chilling assumption," he said with care, " is that schools, and people who live under the roofs of schools, cannot get their own houses in order." To Barth, this assumption is the antithesis of professionalism, yet is commonly held by the general public, by the business and university communities, and by school staff as well.

A whole constellation of powerful sources beam out this single message, all bent on a single target: the public schools, he noted. "I hear it from the reform movement; from universities; from new legislation passed in the state capitals which now requires that your school improve by next June by mandating you have a mission statement, a vision, a strategic plan, a school improvement council, and annual audits. The world is giving schools, by and large, a vote of no confidence, no belief that they are able to improve themselves in ways that the times now demand."

But if school improvement were that simple, I asked, would there be any need for outside forces to concern themselves with the life of the school? In his reply, Barth first pointed to the vicissitudes of human nature and demonstrated his deep, even weary understanding of its operation in social organizations like schools. Teachers, like their students, he maintains, have been inculcated into a culture of passivity, a limbo-like place where they wait for direction before setting their course. He indicts passive teachers as "dependent variables," who have become accustomed to having things happen around and to them because they are demoralized, because it is safer, and because they do not know what exactly they are supposed to do in the face of escalating directives and exhortations—national, state, and local—governing the life of schools, and because they may not know what they really *want* to do.

"You cannot have a *profession* of dependent variables," he emphasized. "It's an oxymoron. It is much safer to ask: 'What am I supposed to do?' and then either do it or complain about it, or do it *and* complain about it. It is much more risky—and much more professional—to offer and act upon one's plan, one's vision, one's hope."

I asked Barth about the common first step of school improvement plans that suggest working from a collective, rather than an individual, vision to change the school. Isn't the process of developing a collective vision—although it holds the seeds of contention and interpersonal conflict—the most common starting point for school improvement? "It is difficult," he acknowledged, "but perhaps more important than developing a collective vision, at least initially, is unlocking and honoring people's individual *personal* visions."

If an administrator or school board articulates a collective vision and then imposes it upon staff, they then can decide whether or not "they want to play," he noted. "Frequently, school visions are homogenized bromides—window dressing—in which no teacher can find her own personal vision."

But the power of the individual vision means that school staff are invited to devise different solutions to problems—"those can be contentious," he admitted—"but if they have the encouragement to articulate individual visions, I have found there will be surprising congruence among their visions.

"Most of all, there is a wonderful energy and hopefulness that comes with the invitation to invent," he added. "This is what professionalism is all about."

Although Barth articulates a hopeful vision for school renewal, it is a vision suffused with pragmatism. Many forces collude to work against a spirit of professionalism, he said, including teachers themselves. "Too often teachers work against their own professionalism by behaving in unprofessional ways, by not aspiring and taking the risks to be professional, by not having a high enough self-concept, by not holding high expectations for their peers as well as themselves.

"Administrators work against teacher professionalism—and their own professionalism—by perpetuating a factory mentality where the administrators are the shop foremen, the plant managers, the bosses. They do the quality-control checks and the evaluations."

In all, adversarial relationships in schools stem from what he terms a "union-management mentality that is embedded in the culture, and frequently plays out with administrators pitted against teachers. It is very difficult to overcome."

Indeed, the way Barth speaks, many schools have not evolved very far beyond the schools of the nineteenth century, and the factory metaphor often promulgated by school administrators—and furthered by the complaisance of teachers—contributes to the already adversarial relationships found in schools. "These adversarial relationships make the whole concept of shared leadership so volatile," Barth noted, "because it means that the keys of the store have been given to the enemy. Many administrators perceive the enemy as parents, teachers, or even students. And indeed, many have become so."

Nonetheless, he points to examples of administrators who find the superordinate/subordinate relationship nothing less than demeaning for all. What distinguishes them from their peers? Are there basic temperamental distinctions that can be drawn? Barth believes the need for control is deadly, and identifies less preoccupation with control as a positive trait that informs the practice of true professionals in schools.

"If you're preoccupied with control," he explained, "you can't give anybody much of anything because you don't have enough of it yourself. But it you're more preoccupied with process or with creating a culture of engagement and an evolving organization, you release yourself from being in control and you begin to think of yourself as yeast, as having the ability to bring out the best in all the ingredients. Yeast is not in control."

Despite the embedded adversarial quality of relationships between teachers and administrators, Barth points out that the larger system is perhaps more at fault. He says that it is the larger system that demands and even fuels administrators to maintain tight, top-down control of their schools, under the press of increased state regulations that monitor teachers against highly specific outcomes. In many states, administrators become little more than middle managers, shuffling between the demands of the state and the disaffection of the teachers in their schools. "The good administrators," Barth added, "are the mavericks who do not play the game totally but who play enough of it to enable and then create and sustain their own culture."

Given the synergism of these negative forces, I asked Barth how teachers can be leaders in school climates that discourage and even fear shared leadership. In his reply, he paradoxically takes heart in the complexity of the problems facing schools, and the growing recognition that the problems educators face are too large to be solved by one person or lone committee. "A big part of professionalism is every teacher taking responsibilities for some schoolwide leadership, no matter how modest. These responsibilities could include designing a new fire drill system, developing a science curriculum, finding ways to involve parents more, or helping with new discipline procedures."

He added: "There is no shortage of opportunities for the professional teacher to show her professionalism through initiating and even demanding ways to demonstrate leadership."

Out of the tangle of human nature and outside mandates, he identified the question that to him is the most pressing: Under what conditions will it become likely that school people will become reform agents? "I do see schools where these conditions exist," he said, "and I do see self-renewal occurring." Self-renewal of educators and of their schools, Barth insists, lies at the heart of professional behavior.

Admittedly, the culture of schools is "cruel," Barth observed, "very cruel. It makes teachers competitors for scarce resources and recognition. If you get more money for your field trips, I don't get as much money for my science equipment. If I say nice things about you, parents are going to want their kids in your class and not mine. It places us in these roles as competitors for scarce resources and recognition—and I would say this is not professional."

In fact, the nature of the adult relationships found in a school are central to whether the school can improve, Barth believes. "These relationships can be very invigorating, or they can be corrosive as hell. In my journeys through schools, as a resident and as a tourist, I find adult relationships take three very different forms."

One he terms "parallel play"—independent relationships carried on side by side with no interaction. "Parallel play is a term from three-year-old pedagogy," he explained, "where one youngster sits in a sandbox with a bucket and a hoe and another one sits in the corner with a rake and a shovel. They will go for days and weeks without knowing someone else in is the sandbox, let alone will they exchange a bucket for a rake and build a sand castle together." The quality of their relationship is characterized by self-absorption and self-interest; it is oblivious to the interests or the welfare of anybody else.

Another, equally destructive adult relationship he sees in schools is interactive, but adversarial. "People interact, but they aggravate each other, serving contentiously on committees. Sometimes teachers tell parents: 'You don't want your kids in that class over there; all they do is fool around.' Or as one teacher said: 'We teachers have gathered our wagons in a circle and trained our guns on one another.'"

For this reason—overt hostility—parallel play is welcomed in many schools because no one relishes confrontation, which is too frequently accompanied by conflict and anger. Barth elaborated, "You hide in your corner of the sandbox as a way to escape interaction, that is to say, conflict."

A third type of adult relationship seen in schools is collegiality: the goal. "Sadly, I have seen it the least frequently," he mused. "One teacher might have a collegial relationship with one other teacher, but such one-on-one relationships are limited and do not characterize or pervade or permeate the whole staff."

In his comments about teacher collegiality, Barth pays tribute to the work of Judith Warren Little and her indicators of collegiality. "The best descriptions I have seen of collegial relationships come from her work. She talks about three or four qualities. One indicator of collegiality, she says, is teachers actively talking outside their classrooms about the work that they do inside their classrooms.

He recounted an experience. "One faculty room I went into had a sign on the door that said: 'No students allowed in the faculty room.' I thought that was a bit unfriendly, but I went in and asked a teacher about it. She said, 'That's the written rule in here,' and then added, 'The unwritten rule is no talking about teaching in the teachers' lounge.'

"Yes," Barth agreed, "teaching *is* intense, but not talking about it is unprofessional. Talking about teaching with our colleagues is a hallmark of professionalism.

"Another indicator of collegiality is to actively help others become better at what they want to become better at. It's one thing for me to talk about it; it's another for me to invite you into my room; it's another thing for me to take ownership for your success as a fellow teacher."

One reason teachers are reluctant to observe each other and talk about their work is the fear of negative evaluation. "Every educator—and I speak for myself—at some level knows we are living a fraud, a lie. You have these sets of marching orders and you are not even sure what you're supposed to be doing, what the state wants, what the school board wants, what the principal wants. What you know is that you're not doing it just the way *they* want, so to make yourself visible is to risk discovery that you are fraudulent, which is why teachers hide behind closed classroom doors and principals dread site visits from superintendents.

"Another reason to hide is the competitive culture. If you see my new ideas about grouping kids in math, then your math class is going to be better than mine. Of course, this is not professional. It is professional to make one's practice visible to others in hopes it will stimulate a good conversation, some reflection of the practice of one another, and maybe provide some help."

Difficult as it is to have such a generous spirit in a culture that may discourage it, because it makes everyone in the school a staff developer, it is possible. "Show me a school," Barth challenged, "where there are abundant personal visions and conceptions of a desired future for the school, where the grown-ups are first-class citizens of the community of learners, show me a school where everyone is a leader in some way, show me a school where the relationship among the adults is collegial, and I will show you a school that is not only capable of significant improvement from within, but I will show you a school that is already improving in dramatic ways from within, and will sustain that improvement. And I will show you a school full of professional educators."

How do teachers and administrators reach these positive conditions? Barth laughed. "First, you acknowledge that most of the world doesn't think teachers are very capable of very much. Second, you experience some moral outrage over that. Third, you say we can do quite a bit, if these conditions are in place. Those three steps alone sound a wake-up call."

Next comes the real work. "You announce what you value. You can announce it as a teacher in a classroom, as a school principal. You can say: 'I value us working as colleagues, not as competitors or adversaries. I care about sharing leadership.'"

Modeling is equally important. "If we want to build a community of learners," Barth observed, "somehow principals and teachers have to convey that they are not the wise, learned priesthood; rather, they are the head learners in their domain. In one school, the principal comes on the PA system just before dismissal every day and says, 'Boys and girls, I want to share with you what I learned in school today.'"

The importance of modeling cannot be underestimated, he insists. "If kids view the important people in their lives as all finished with learning, they want to be finished with it too. They want to be important people, after all. But if important people are actively, voraciously involved in learning, they will pick up on that."

Rewards are also crucial, and they do not need to be limited to financial incentives. Barth provides examples: Rewarding three teachers who want to work together by giving them a big space in the school or rewarding a teacher who presents a personal vision by recognizing it and publishing it in the newsletter. "Schools need to develop a bigger repertoire of rewards for desirable behavior. Right now, people who do desirable things don't get more out of it than people who do undesirable things. Sometimes people who do undesirable things are the ones who get the recognition and the attention.

"So you announce what you're about, you model it, and you reward it. You also must protect people who engage in those behaviors, because if they were so fluid and easy and self-evident, everybody would be behaving like colleagues. Somebody has to run interference, and at first protect people who are violating the taboos of the culture. After a while, more and more people can do so without protection.

"The teacher who stands up in a faculty meeting and tells the other teachers: 'I've got this great idea about grouping kids that I want to share with you,' will be shot down by all too many faculties. The others will say: 'Big deal. I've been doing that for twenty years. Who does she think she is? Why are we wasting time listening to her? Let's get moving so I can get my coat on and get out of here.'"

The school culture, in addition to being cruel, is "ruthless," Barth continued. "All of the four conditions I list for self-renewal and professionalism are taboo. Sharing a vision is a nondiscussible. It doesn't happen. Shared leadership is a taboo as well. If not everybody can be a leader, then those who are leaders are going to distinguish themselves from those who aren't—and they are going to pay for it. There are taboos also against behaving in collegial ways. If I come into your classroom, you're going to kill me, unless it's a recess. So we must protect the teachers who violate these taboos in order to change the culture of the school in these desired ways."

I asked Barth if all the conditions for self-renewal of a school and professionalism for staff should exist simultaneously in order to be effective. "It depends," he answered, "on who you are. If you are the superintendent, how do you proceed? If you are the principal, how do you proceed? If you are a classroom teacher, or the head of the PTA, how do you proceed? It really depends on from whence the energy for change and renewal is going to come."

Principals, he maintains, currently have the unrelenting scrutiny of the public fixed on them. "The central office is saying the school is the largest unit of change. Business people understand what a plant manager does, so they think they see the importance of the principal. Teachers, too, have a tendency to sit back, wait, and see what develops from the main office. So a finger—or several fingers—point to the principal.

"The good news is that we're acknowledging that the key to improving a school resides under the roof of the school, not under the state department of education, but the bad news is that teachers are further deprofessionalized by the current focus on the principal."

Barth recounted, with wry amusement, a conference of educators he attended where each principal wore a beacon-like button that announced his or her importance. "Principals make the difference!" shone off every principal's lapel. While not offended by the message, he suggests it is not sufficiently inclusive. "Some teachers who were there asked: 'What does this say to teachers?'

Changing one word in the message might be sufficient, he noted mildly. "I would like teachers to wear a button that says: 'Principals make *a* difference and teachers make *a* difference.' They make a difference not only in the eyes of the kids in their class, but through the development of a healthy culture in the school. That is the difference that teachers need to be invited to make, and need to want to make, because principals are not going to make the difference. The ones who do make the difference do so by engaging teachers in making the difference, and parents too."

He asked: "Aren't the qualities necessary for school improvement within and the qualities of a healthy teaching profession congruent? We shouldn't be surprised if they are parallel or preconditions for the other. After all, the concept of having a strong healthy teaching profession and terrible schools is as absurd as having a wonderful school staffed by nonprofessionals."

Self-renewal for staff and schools becomes one and the same as professionalism, he suggests. "As a principal, I have found that if I could help a group of teachers and a group of parents to agree on something we believed in and we moved forward with it, in what we considered to be the best interests of youngsters, very few people from outside are going to complain. It is a wonderful way of creating diplomatic immunity, immunity to all the little petty dictates of the system."

In the face of the obstacles of which he is almost painfully aware, Barth remains hopeful that schools can transform themselves into self-renewing communities in which the spirit of professionalism flourishes. "Tip O'Neill said all politics is local. I say that maybe all professionalism is local. I have seen highly professional teachers and principals thrive, even in the quagmire of nonprofessionalism."

He concluded thoughtfully, "The good news is: It is possible for professionals to exist and rise up through the murk, through the mud-flats of non-professionalism. Now the task is to extend professionalism so that it pervades all schools, transforming them into communities of learners—where all who are involved in the educational enterprise become, themselves, engaged in the process of learning."

Kathleen Densmore:
Democratize, Don't Professionalize

Kathleen Densmore is Assistant Professor of Education in the Division of Teacher Education at San Jose State University in San Jose, California, where she teaches courses in the sociology of education and educational foundations. She also works with beginning student teachers in public high schools in East Side San Jose. In the College of Humanities she teaches in and coordinates a community service program. In this program students combine scholarly reflection with volunteer work in local community centers, for example, homeless shelters, an immigration and refugee center, a center for the aging, and local schools. Densmore worked as a technical advisor in a pedagogical research institute at the National Autonomous University in Mangua from 1987 to 1988. She also has taught postgraduate courses in pedagogy at the Jose Varona Pedagogical Institute in Havana, Cuba. She has written on teacher professionalism, school-community relations, and literacy.

Kathleen Densmore has two keen and critical points to make about teacher professionalism and the professionalization of teaching: Teaching cannot and should not become a profession, she avows, for a whole panoply of reasons—reasons she believes have been overlooked by a large number of education reports and commissions.[1] "Historical evidence strongly suggests that teaching cannot become a profession," she said to me, "not in the sense that law and medicine became professions. Doctors and lawyers had to be very aggressive; they had to work together to be ruthless in separating themselves, the elite, from less elite occupational groups."

Physicians and lawyers engaged in fierce competition with other occupational groups in society to gain public consensus that they deserved the elite status that they sought—and ultimately gained, she pointed out. "But education reforms, most of which recommend professionalizing teaching, seem to suggest that if you, the teacher, just do good work, the public somehow will bestow this recognition upon you."

Densmore's opinion of that is clear: "It is foolish," she insisted. "There is plenty of sociological research on the professions of law and medicine to show

how they became professions.[2] It is questionable whether or not most teachers in our country want to engage in politically or socially aggressive competition with other major occupational groups."

She added: "I can't imagine most teachers taking on that kind of fight—because many enter teaching for reasons that are more altruistic or because of commitments and values that otherwise conflict with such ruthless occupational self-promotion."

Whether or not teaching can become a profession, the heart of her argument is that teaching *should not* become a profession. Although "professional" status carries with it the designer-label baggage of prestige and social status, it is exactly that baggage that she sees as problematic. If teaching is viewed as a profession—similar to law and medicine—teachers, Densmore states, will be elevated to a position above and apart from the people they serve, especially low-income parents and parents of color. Distances between teachers, parents, and community representatives—already large—will enlarge. The term "professional" actually may do more harm than good in the context of building bridges between teachers and parents, she persists. "We need instead to look for our commonalities, our common interests, and find ways to work together."

But to many, if not to most educators, not to aspire to professionalism is antithetical. What then, I asked, constitutes a profession, as opposed to an occupation? In response, she listed three broad characteristics: Autonomy, or the ability to make decisions based on individual discretion; university training versus on-the-job training; and prestige in the larger society.

"We do need," Densmore said, "the type of teachers referred to as professionals, teachers with technical expertise. We need skilled teachers. But education depends on some kind of participatory approach in which we discuss our purpose. What kind of students do we want to produce? What kind of growth do we want to see in our young people? How can we evaluate how well we have done?"

She sees dangers of elitism in the arguments of education reformers who urge professional status on teaching—the danger that professional status might be conferred only upon a few teachers, rather than the entire occupation. Further, she warns of reformers who believe professionalism for the few is more desirable than professionalism for all. Clearly, Densmore sees that as antidemocratic and divisive.

"Individuals who support the notion of professionalism for the few believe this approach has the potential to motivate the rest of the teaching profession," she explained. "For instance, if a teacher passes a national exam, she will be paid more, and will enjoy higher status than other teachers. Some believe that is a good idea because it will be an incentive for teachers either to take the national test or to do whatever they need to do to enter the ranks of fully professionalized teachers—few as they may be."

Advocates of professionalization believe they speak directly to demands for teacher accountability. "They believe that in this scenario good teachers will be recognized and rewarded; the cream can rise to the top," Densmore suggested. "While I share the sentiment that wants to see good teachers rewarded, I see several problems with promoting professionalism for the few."

In addition to only affecting a few teachers, professionalizing teaching could serve to deepen divisions between teachers because some will be rewarded with supervisory responsibilities that recognize their "professionalism"—as opposed to their fellow teachers who remain unrewarded, she noted.

I suggested to her that a key conundrum in the professionalism/professionalization struggle is the implication that perhaps the most powerful reward available for good teachers is a supervisory position—traditionally the destiny and sole reward for the most competent teachers, who then are removed from the classroom. Admittedly, this confirms that the rewards available for teachers in many school systems remain limited and traditional. Densmore responded, "This concept is very troubling, because looking solely at resources, it would mean that the school's money will be devoted to higher salaries for supervisors, which is questionable."

While it is understandable that reformers and the public are focusing on key questions that include how good teaching should be defined, how teachers should be evaluated, and how teachers will be held accountable for their practice, Densmore argues that professionalization as the answer to these tough questions presents more problems than it solves. For instance, the emphasis on teachers as the key variable can serve to scapegoat individuals who are relatively helpless in the face of larger, systemic problems. "Individual teachers have become the focal point of reform," she pointed out, "but if I named the top five problems in the educational system, I doubt that individual teacher competence would be number one or two."

Targeting teachers as the focal point for reform is constructed upon reasoning, she believes, that if the best and the brightest can be attracted into teaching, everything will change: in particular, achievement gaps between different groups of people, between white students and students of color, will be greatly lessened. "That reasoning is ill-conceived," she said. "The best teacher in the world can't turn around student achievement single-handedly. Yes, we need good teachers, and we need more rigorous teacher preparation. But teachers as individuals are scapegoats for all the failures of the educational system—failures beyond their power to address."

One of the most egregious educational problems facing the nation's educators, she believes, is the lack of progress in reducing achievement gaps between white students and students of color. "How does focusing on more rigorous tests to obtain certification address that problem?," she asked. "Instead, I would think that disparities in funding between wealthy districts and poor districts are certainly key. Of course, these are political and social issues. I work with one student teacher in a school where most kids are getting a free lunch and breakfast. They are not coming to school ready to learn. Again, the best teacher in the world can't overlook the consequences of poverty.

"In many cities across the country, even if students graduate from high school, they are facing high unemployment rates. It is very difficult for a teacher to say: 'You learn this because this is going to help you get a better-paying job.' We as teachers can't solve these problems but we can think about what we can do about them and who we can work with to mitigate the effects they have on achievement in a classroom."

Since much of the literature on teacher professionalism, she says, revolves around the notion of the teacher's technical expertise, the result may be that the important questions she outlines may be deserted by educators. "We do study technical material about teaching strategies and techniques," she remonstrated, "but I have never seen that knowledge as separate from the uses to which we put it, separate from social questions. What should we be teaching? How to teach is one question, but when one talks about *what* one teaches, one begins to talk about what should be taught. What do low-income students need to learn? What do African-Americans need to learn? What do women need to learn? What do *all* students need to learn to prepare them for the future?"

She summed up: "What do students need to learn to function effectively in a democratic society? Those are questions in which all people hold a stake."

Why, then, I asked her, is the allure of professionalization so powerful? How did the professionalization of teaching capture such a prominent position on the agendas of education reformers?

Answers to these related questions can be found, she replies, in a variety of synergistic reasons that make "professionalization" almost indisputable as the correct direction for teaching. "Teachers are under many pressures," she said with obvious empathy, "and under increased expectations. School districts and states are placing greater demands on teachers for accountability; usually these demands are translated into increased standardized curricula and more standardized testing of students."

Just because expectations for teachers have burgeoned in an increasingly technical direction does not mean that they are correct, she maintains, because they do not challenge teachers to design learning activities, create new curricula, or draw directly upon their skills and abilities in other ways. In fact, despite the increased specificity of external demands placed upon teachers, their working conditions remain poor—a source of continuing demoralization. "Teachers are frustrated with inadequate salaries, bureaucratic work conditions, and their overall low status in society," she declared. "It makes sense that a label that suggests that teachers are worthy of respect and higher status—including deserving of higher salaries—would be invoked by teachers toward that purpose."

She added: "Just thinking of yourself as a professional also makes you feel better."

The barrage of external and internal demands upon teachers—many of which conflict with each other—encourage many to seek some type of leverage so that they can experience an increased sense of efficacy in the classroom, she said. "A view of teaching as a profession and oneself as a professional can be used as a buffer between yourself and the external demands placed on you," she emphasized.

Teachers are not the only school staff affected by cries for increased and higher expectations. "Many school administrators," Densmore added, "are in a bind as well, because they are working with frustrated staff, and the existing institutional arrangements just do not work in many schools, in many districts. Principals have to deal with teachers who recognize that they cannot do the job the way it is being defined."

As a result, "professionalism" can become a motivating word used by administrators to exhort teachers to a new level of effort to meet the public demands for accountability—effort that does not result in improving the quality of instruction. "Administrators," she added, "really do not have the resources or the authority they need to change significantly working conditions that might enable teachers to do their jobs better."

One of Densmore's most particular points is that efforts to professionalize the teaching occupation are attempts to make teaching apolitical, somehow pure in a technical, scientific sense. "With that viewpoint, the way to improve teaching and learning is to take a very rational, scientific approach to it," she noted. If stakeholders in the educational process can view it in a "pure" way, the hope, of course, is that a scientific approach to teaching and learning will lift it above the heat of local conflicts, such as controversy surrounding school prayer and whose values should be taught.

"That is one part of the issue," she said, "and another part has to do with the relationship between teaching and the state." This is definitely not apolitical, and Densmore emphasizes the disparity between the state's role and the teacher's role in the local school. "The state is under pressure to save money, to be efficient, to demonstrate that schools are doing a good job."

At the nexus of the late 1990s with the twenty-first century, the state joins many education reformers in viewing teaching as a scientific enterprise, something, she said, that can be approached dispassionately, technically, rationally. "We refer to that approach as 'professional.' The relationship between the occupation of teaching and the state is squeezed by the state's need to demonstrate that it is doing a good job—and one way to demonstrate that is to prove the schools are doing a good job. This technical, rational, 'professional' approach helps define for teachers what it means to be a good teacher."

Densmore added, "Professionalism means different things to different people; the term is used in different ways by different groups." To the degree, I suggested, that it has lost meaning.

"Yes," she agreed. "Maybe at one point in history professionalization of an occupation served democratic aims, but it is doing the opposite now. It serves to exclude people from participating in educational decision-making. I see professionalism and professionalization as a symbol that has outlived its usefulness."

But professionalism is a tidy way to look at complex problems, she suggests, and complex problems are not solved neatly. "For instance, if we are going to tackle issues of funding," she said, "those aren't easy."

Densmore goes so far to suggest that pursuing the professionalization of teaching may separate teachers according to their financial resources. In California, for instance, student teachers are encouraged to gain admission into teacher education programs that prepare them for a new type of teaching certificate that greatly increases their marketability to public schools in the state. The certificate communicates to districts that the candidate has had special preparation in teaching students who do not have English as a first language and in teaching students who are diverse: racially, ethnically, or racially. Yet this new option—outwardly admirable—has created a situation where students in teacher education are pitted against one another.

"This credential," Densmore commented, "means the students have to stay in the teacher education program for at least one extra semester, maybe two additional semesters, so the teacher education program becomes more expensive.

"This is a concrete example of what happens when we talk about professionalization. Usually people talk about increasing the educational requirements of teachers, but that excludes a lot of people. In particular, it leaves out low-income people and people of color." It is already difficult for beginning teachers of color to "break into the ranks," as Densmore put it.

"Many teachers hold out hope that if they are granted professional status their working conditions will improve," she pointed out. "They believe their workplaces will become less bureaucratic. But if one looks at what has happened in medicine and law, we see the reverse, and I can't think of any reason why teaching would be an exception to that."

Admission, for example, to the national exam proposed by the National Board of Teacher Certification, does not come without a price tag. "The exam fee," Densmore reported, is "$975.[3] Some states are considering waiving the fee for teachers who pass the exam, but we do have to consider the teachers who cannot afford that exam fee. Right away there is a division."

Although Densmore said she does not believe in "the old community control concept, where everyone raises his hand and votes on what should be taught," she still urges participatory decision-making onto educators. "I don't want a situation where just the 'professionals' are making the decisions about what gets taught, for example. If we don't figure out mechanisms to involve community representatives and parents more, many decisions are going to be isolated from public debate and put strictly in the hands of experts. Because many educational issues are political and social, that can be dangerous."

Relating the dangers to the state of California, she indicated the strong charge given to teachers to be more effective in dealing with language minority students because of the numbers of immigrants in the state. "We have students in kindergarten through twelfth grade who are all at different stages of English acquisition. There is considerable contemporary research that shows that teachers need to understand students' cultural backgrounds in order to teach them effectively."[4]

But she is distressed by teacher educators at the college and university level who do not believe it is necessary to teach prospective teachers about culture and language. "There is a lot going on behind those arguments," she said. "The parents of many of the second language students could tell teachers many useful things about their attitudes, about their children, that would help teachers work with them. We need mechanisms to make that kind of participation happen; making sure that parents have a voice that really counts, not just a voice for the sake of public relations."

Yet she realizes the pitfalls inherent in total community control of schools, and noted: "I have dedicated a big part of my life to learning about teaching, and when I have equal say with someone who hasn't devoted any time to these issues at all, I can't think it is fair—not in the interest of student learning. So there isn't an easy formula in terms of setting up little boards of certain numbers and compositions, like three teachers, one principal, and one parent."

If the word "professional" is so laden with confused and conflicting meanings, I asked Densmore what word she would substitute when referring to the issues surrounding better working conditions for teachers, greater teacher collaboration, and increased work on lessening achievement gaps between student groups.

"What professional teachers are doing," she said carefully, "is what good or competent teachers are doing. If we talk about what it means to be a competent teacher, we see that we need to be more precise and more specific about what good teaching is. But one danger is that we end up emphasizing the technical aspects of teaching too much."

There is a body of technical knowledge about teaching, Densmore quickly inserted, "and I don't want to suggest teaching is a hocus-pocus magical art. We do know useful teaching strategies and techniques for use with language minority students that are effective teaching strategies for all students. But if we say: 'This is good teaching,' we might standardize teaching even more, which is ironic considering that part of being a professional is having autonomy and discretion on the job over what to do."

It is clear that Densmore sees the issues related to professionalism as democratic issues that would be furthered if parents, especially low-income parents and parents of color, could engage in a genuine debate and dialogue with teachers. It is a point she returns to again and again. "Latino parents, for instance, often view the teacher as a parent. When their child is with the teacher in school, that teacher is taking their place. When they have an opportunity to talk with the teacher and the teacher doesn't have the detailed knowledge about their child that they expect her to have, they think: 'The teacher doesn't care.' If there were a dialogue, they could understand where the teacher's energies have to go, or the reasons why the teacher doesn't have detailed information on their child."

She concluded: "It's the way a democracy works. Over time, the citizenry becomes more informed. One thing to be gained from the cumbersome, energy-consuming dialogue is that is how teachers can earn the respect of parents and community representatives. We, as educators, *do* have to earn it. With the ideology of professionalism, sometimes people assume it."

Notes

1. Boyer 1983; Carnegie Forum on Education 1986; Holmes Group 1986; National Commission for Excellence in Teacher Education 1985; National Commission on Excellence in Education 1983.

2. See, for example, Larson 1977; Oppenheimer, O'Donnell, & Johnson 1982.

3. Richardson 1995.

4. Chavkin 1993; Scarella 1990.

Wayne J. Urban: Teacher Unions, History, and Professionalization

Wayne J. Urban is Regent's Professor at Georgia State University in Atlanta, where he teaches in the Department of Educational Policy Studies and in the Department of History. He is a long-time student of the history of teacher unions and the author of Why Teachers Organized *(Wayne State University Press, 1982). In addition to his academic research and teaching, he also has maintained close ties with teacher organizations He also has written* Black Scholar: Horace Mann Bond, 1904–1972 *(University of Georgia Press, 1992) and has edited the* American Educational Research Journal *(1990–92) and* Educational Studies *(1982–1987). He is a past President of the History of Education Society and currently serves as President of the American Educational Studies Association. In 1992, he prepared, under contract, a history of the research division of the National Education Association.*

Although a careful scrutiny of the history of teachers' unions and organizations reveals they did not push the movement of teaching from an occupation to a profession, nonetheless there was nothing innately "unprofessional" in their agenda, Wayne Urban believes. Instead, a myriad of reasons—some complicated, some straightforward—explain why teaching did not assume professional status.

What was the agenda of teachers' organizations and unions, if not to professionalize the occupation?, I asked. What factors mitigated against teaching becoming a profession? Are those factors constant today?

Clearly, Urban has thought carefully about all of these factors and their interaction with each other. "Some reasons that unions did not push teaching to professionalize are obvious," he said. "For instance, teaching is a gendered occupation. Women entered the occupation differently than men did. Men ran the associations; women were the troops. That was one of the problems when the associations began—and it remains a problem today."

But structural factors also influenced the occupational course of teaching. Emphasizing the separateness of elementary and secondary teaching, Urban points out that the two are almost completely different occupations. "There is a kind of fracture within the occupation that has an impact in all kinds of ways."

One way in which this rupture continues to have an impact is the long-standing belief held by elementary and secondary teachers that they have little in common, he maintains. "They talk *to* each other in a certain way, but they really talk *past* one another. With the advent of middle schools, it is not clear what will happen. Will we have three tiers instead of two?"

High school teachers are much more traditional than elementary teachers, he says. "Larry Cuban documented this well.[1] If you try to get teachers to act together, you are trying to get groups to work together that are almost independent of one another."

Structurally, the work of elementary and secondary school teachers continues to differ profoundly. "High school teachers work in five or six periods per day where they see thirty different kids in each period," he pointed out. "Elementary teachers tend to work with the same children for the entire day. They are less specialized, less broken down than high schools are."

Historically, the training that elementary and secondary school teachers received encouraged a status differential between the two. Secondary teachers received university training, were highly content-oriented, predominantly male; elementary teachers, by and large, went to normal schools and were predominantly female.

Does this fragmentation, I asked, explain why teaching has not really become a profession?

"It explains why teachers don't all pull together," Urban replied. "But there are many other reasons why teaching is not a profession. Administrators professionalized early and maintained their professionalism in the sense that they controlled the rest of the occupation. They did not allow the control that they maintained to trickle down, so it remained a kind of inhibitor on teaching becoming a profession."

The Evolving Agendas of Teacher Unions

Have teachers' unions, historically, contributed to the fact that teaching has not professionalized in the same sense as professions such as law and medicine?, I asked.

In his reply, Urban meticulously draws an evolving picture of unions, their agendas over time, and their attitudes toward the teaching occupation. "In the beginning, unions *reacted* to professionalization," he explained. "Administrators took over the NEA (National Education Association), incorporated the teachers into it, but maintained control of the union. But the early unions, in the progressive era, were reacting to the centralization of schools and the corporate model that was coming into the schools.

"While they may not have been completely anti-professional, it would be fair to say they were backward-looking in the way that most trade unions were in that period. That is, the craft unions tried to get together to stop industrialization. Obviously, they weren't successful. In teaching unions, we find the same thing. They were looking back to the earlier era, when, despite everything, they were parts of communities.

"Early on, they contributed to teaching not professionalizing. In fact, they stood against the professionalization of education. But as we advance through the history of teachers' unions, things become muddier."

Urban illustrates how attitudes toward professionalization became mixed by relating the tale of the leaders of the early New York Union, who were strongly in favor of the stratification of schools and increased levels among and between school staff. "High school teachers dominated the AFT (American Federation of Teachers). Probably you could claim that they dominated the AFT from its inception, including all the way to Shanker, who came out of the New York City junior highs."

The philosophical course of the AFT in the 1940s and 1950s is unclear since they were decades of unrest and change, he says. The NEA, however, remained the administrators' organization. "Teachers did belong to the NEA. That is, there was a department of classroom teachers, but they belonged in a very limited way. They were in the organization on the administrators' terms. Neither school administrators nor high school teachers were interested particularly in the elementary teachers. In that sense, the unions and organizations certainly contributed to teaching not professionalizing because they refused to acknowledge that there was more than one occupation within the profession."

Women teachers belonged to other organizations apart from teachers' unions, Urban explains. "They belonged to clubs, to subject matter associations, to elementary teachers' groups. These groups had a very different agenda than the unions—a kind of club agenda that might have an educational reform aspect to it, but more in a women's club sense than in a trade union or occupational organization sense."

The concerns of female teachers and the concerns of teachers' unions were divergent, Urban says, although women frequently were highly progressive— often the most progressive—in their actions.

"Us Against Them": Administrators vs. Teachers

What about the traditionally adversarial relationships between administrators and teachers? "The adversarial quality of the relationships will probably always be there in a subtle way," Urban said thoughtfully, "but once administrators and teachers enter collective bargaining, it is institutionalized."

Collective bargaining is institutionalized symbolically by the physical arrangements in the room where negotiations are conducted and by an "us against them" mentality, he continues. "To start with, the parties don't sit at a round table. They sit at a rectangular table, with two sides to it. One side is management; the other is the union. I wouldn't say that collective bargaining caused the adversarial relationship but it did bring it to the surface and institutionalized it. That is what collective bargaining is all about: two sides negotiating with each other. Collective bargaining does vary from state to state, and it is important to realize that some states don't have it at all."

For instance, currently approximately 75–80 percent of teachers nationally work under a contract, Urban says, but the South does not have collective bargaining. "The South is still anti-union," he pointed out, "and more conservative in general. Florida is the only southern state that has collective bargaining."

Did the stratification of administrators and teachers that began in the 1920s also contribute to adversarial relationships? I asked.

"It distanced teachers from administrators," Urban replied. "Having a central office distances the superintendent from the schools. Prior to the existence of the central office for the superintendent, if he wasn't located in the high school, he was very likely close to it physically. Now there are separate locations for the central office. Insofar as familiarity breeds contempt, distance breeds a kind of estrangement. Although this doesn't exist just in urban systems, it is always strongest in urban systems. As things get larger and larger, the jobs get harder and harder and further removed from the classroom."

As the distancing of superintendents from teachers evolved, so did the distancing of principals from teachers, as their roles developed from the principal/teacher to the principal as administrator and overseer of the school—almost a corporate CEO. "This is something that can be documented, in Atlanta for instance, through personnel directories," Urban pointed out. "In the 1890s, women principals are very common. By 1920, they are almost gone. I make the inferential leap that the qualifications to become a principal changed and became more formal, academic, and less experiential.

"Obviously, this made it very hard on women. Most of the city women teachers came up through the normal schools, not through the university channel."

Urban points to Ella Flag Young, who was the first female superintendent of a major city school system (Chicago: 1905–15). Young was the first woman president of the NEA and was associated with several progressive reforms.

"Ella Flag Young had to qualify for a bachelor's degree before she could get her Ph.D. She had never been through a university, and instead received her schooling at a normal school. She had to qualify for a bachelor's degree through examinations.

"That was common. Ella Flag Young was able to do this for a variety of reasons, but most people, when confronted with an obstacle that large, throw up their hands in despair. There doesn't appear to be any way for them to surmount the odds. It doesn't matter if these obstacles were intentional or not," he reflected, "because the result was stark. The number of women principals declined dramatically.

"In some systems, when you become a principal, you can go from an elementary school to a secondary school, back and forth. Often you are running a school about which you have little knowledge. That is, your knowledge is book knowledge of school administration that you received in the university along with your knowledge of the system. Although I wouldn't discount either one of those, I would simply say that sometimes the principal has little direct knowledge of pedagogy or the life of what goes on in the institution that he or she runs."

Why did this increased stratification of roles among school staff and a more technical/scientific role for school administrators evolve?, I asked.

"Superintendents raised the qualifications so that the administrators below them had to conform," he said. "The universities were part of that. Early on, the universities became involved in education but they were primarily involved in secondary education and school administration. They left elementary education alone because that was the province of the normal schools. All the normal schools are now colleges and universities, of course."

It sounds like this probably contributed to the stigma traditionally borne by elementary education as lightweight, not a serious academic pursuit, I suggested.

"I see vestiges of it currently," Urban said. "In my university, I am in a big department called Policy Studies, which is a melding of educational administration and curriculum people and history and philosophy people. The area the educational administration people and curriculum people struggle over is the area of supervision of instruction.

"Teachers have always had a broader strong autonomy," he continued. "They have had their classrooms, and they have controlled their classrooms. As long as you have had control of your classroom—at least until the last decade or so—you pretty much could do what you wanted."

Bargains were made between teachers and administrators, implicit ones, Urban believes, that delineated territory and turf as well as parameters of control. "In other words, if you take care of your classroom you can do what you want."

Preoccupation with Salaries and Pensions

What about the fact that early teacher organizations focused almost exclusively on salaries and pensions as their primary goals? Was there any sentiment that once they resolved those basic issues they would take up the aspects of teaching that would push it to professional status?, I asked.

"The focus wasn't on salaries and pensions to the exclusion of other concerns, but I think people felt other concerns could be taken up in other arenas. They saw their teacher associations as a place where they took up their economic quest. They discussed other concerns in small classroom organizations and informal meetings," Urban replied. "People misunderstood badly what the early organizations were about, so when I wrote about them in *Why Teachers Organized*, I admit to overstating the emphasis on salaries and pensions in order to make a point. Now I'm making a moderate retreat on that.

"In the 1940s there was a big push for a single salary scale. In the South, the single salary scale meant putting the black teachers on the same scale as the white teachers. In the South and elsewhere, it meant putting the elementary teachers on the same scale as the secondary teachers. There was a tremendous fight over this among the teachers.

"The NEA—interestingly enough, since it was dominated by administrators and males—took a very large role in pushing for the single salary scale. In my work on the research division in the NEA, I discovered they had a woman in their research division who went around the country in the forties, working with all the local associations to try to get the single salary scale. It was very much a feminist issue, although it wasn't stated as such. The women were trying to get equal pay with the men—equal pay for different work. That is a case where the NEA was quite strong. The AFT, on the other hand, being strongly high school oriented, didn't play a very big role in that movement."

To Urban, this piece of history shows that the pursuit of salaries and salary-oriented issues is certainly not an unprofessional endeavor. "To have a salary scale was an enormous relief to teachers," he noted. "If you had a salary scale, you had some predictability in your life at the very least. The school boards were quite willing to retaliate against teacher leaders and the salary scale offered some protection."

The Genesis of Teacher Organizations

To gain an idea of how teacher organizations began, Urban offers the genesis of the Chicago teachers union as an example.

"Margaret Haley's Chicago group was the prototype of a teacher organization. It started as a benefit society for the sick. Some teachers got together and put money in a pot, the purpose of which was to pay women who were ill. So there was a strong mutual aid aspect to the beginnings of teacher unions—which, although limited—doesn't strike me as unprofessional.

"I want to take the organizations off the hook," he added. "Teachers didn't fret—and still don't—about whether they are professionalized or not professionalized. It's an academic overlay on the occupation. If the organizations weren't doing things that you and I think were professionalizing behaviors, maybe that's more our problem than theirs. They had a clear and substantial agenda, and they worked at it. We, on the other hand, come in after the fact and decide whether their agenda was professional, anti-professional, or non-professional."

But they did use the word "professional," he says. "The NEA used the word all the time when they would argue against the AFT. What they seemed to mean by it, most of the time, was that anything other than 'professional' was blue collar."

The word "professional" was used, Urban believes, as a slogan. "Generally, it means: 'I don't like what you're doing. It's not 'professional.'"

How did the NEA and the AFT go from their days of conflict to current talk of merging?, I inquired.

"In the beginning, the early AFT actually met at the NEA meetings. In the 1920s, a very strong anti-union decade because of the Red scare and post–World War I, AFT membership plummeted. The NEA used that, and grew substantially in the twenties. In Edgar Wesley's history of the NEA it is easy to see how its membership exploded in the twenties.

"So there was a kind of adversarialism by the twenties, but it was more opportunistic and strategic than anything else. Meanwhile, the AFT was fighting for its life in the twenties. In the thirties, the AFT has a whole era of Communist influence, trying to fight the Communists." He added dryly, "Whatever position one took on that, it certainly livened up the organization."

The story of the Communist struggle in the 1930s within the AFT is colorful. "The AFT, or the Communists, basically took over the New York local and the Philadelphia local in the thirties. They took them over fair and square. They worked hard and won the elections. There was a lot of concern about Communist domination, but what happened is that the Loyalist group—the anti-Communist group—dropped out of the AFT local and started their own local. They then got the national AFT to throw out the Communist local and to give them the charter. All of this took six or seven years to play out.

"In the late 1930s, the AFT president was elected on an anti-Communist platform. The membership rose, not for ideological reasons but for economic reasons. The Depression was tough for a lot of people, and one way teachers dealt with it was to join the union."

Collective bargaining came first to New York City and then spread around the country. "In 1973, the NEA passed a new constitution and became a kind of independent union at that point. They totally revamped their Washington office, giving much more power to the executive secretary. They increased their staff and made it their business that they would compete with the AFT to become the recognized bargaining unit for teachers."

While this was happening, although their membership did not dwindle, their clout diminished. "Acrimony increased from the seventies on, the period of 'I can't stand you and you can't stand me,'" Urban observed. "The logic all along, though, has been toward a merger. That is, if you spend an enormous amount of your resources fighting this other organization in representational elections, that is that much less money you can use to service your members."

The AFT is still the strongest teacher union in big cities, he says, and the NEA strongest in suburban areas, medium-sized and small towns. "The NEA still has approximately 2 million members and the AFT still has 500,000 to 750,000. Both of those memberships are fairly stable. When the unions were at the height of their opposition to each other, the NEA would say, 'We'll never join organized labor.' NEA has always had a secret ballot in their elections, and the AFT has always elected their president from the floor—a common trade union practice, by the way.

"Once someone becomes a union president, that person is there if not for life, for a very long time, until there is a scandal or something moves them out. It requires more of a political campaign to oust a president who has been elected from the floor than it does when you know you're electing a new president regularly by secret ballot."

The fact that the NEA president has increased national visibility has aided those who want to see the two unions merge, Urban believes. "The first really visible NEA president was Mary Hatwood Futrell. Part of her visibility was that she was black; another part was that she had a chance to become visible in the office and known as the NEA president. When a journalist needed a quote, they no longer automatically went to Shanker, because there was now another person at the national level with an identity."

Mergers at the local level also fueled the push to merge at the national level, he says. "At the local level, they pay the dues. They're the people who actively gear up to fight with each other at the next election, depending on their contracts. There were many mergers at the local level—San Francisco and Los Angeles, for instance, are merged. The latest push for a merger has come from the bottom up and also from the top. This change at both levels of the organizations has brought the unions to the point where they are amicable as much or more than they are adversarial."

Teachers' Choice of Unions

How do teachers choose between the two unions?, I asked. What considerations enter into their choice of membership?

"When a state passes a collective bargaining law," Urban responded, "the law usually includes a procedure for representation election. An election is held among the unit. The AFT comes in and says, 'Vote for us for the following reasons,' and the NEA does the same thing. Possibly a group of teachers gets together and says, 'Vote for no agent for the following reasons.' Depending on the law, if one of those three options gets priority, they are elected as the bargaining agent, or there is a runoff. If AFT were to receive 40 percent of the vote, NEA 35 percent, and no agent 25 percent, then there would be a runoff between the NEA and the AFT. One of these groups is elected by the members of the bargaining unit to negotiate a contract. The initial election process takes one to two years. The law usually allows for the rival group to petition at the time of the next contract and have a second election. This does vary from state to state, depending on the law, but it is similar."

This elaborate election process not only drains the resources of the unions, but maintains a competitive climate between them. "It's debilitating," Urban summarized.

Teacher Organizations and Merit Pay

Have both the NEA and AFT been opposed to merit pay historically?, I asked.

"Yes," Urban said, "although lately the AFT has been more pliable on that issue. The initial opposition to merit pay was based on the fear of arbitrariness. Teachers had experienced inequities, and expected merit pay to be a continuation of them. The first thing that unions maintain is that merit pay won't work. The second point they make is that it's unfair; it would result in favoritism. They fear that administrators will choose their favorites and reward them. That latter point actually has a fairly strong basis in fact. It is difficult to have truly objective teacher evaluations."

Urban explains the relative pliancy of the AFT on merit pay in political terms dating from the Reagan administration. "During the Reagan years, the NEA was the enemy; the AFT managed not to be the enemy. One way not to be the enemy was to appear not to oppose merit pay. It fits into Shanker's general position in the last decade which has been for school reform and increasing standards. The AFT wants to be reasonable about merit pay; they want to look at the plans and see if they are worth anything. So rather than being flat-footedly against it, they are willing to take it on a case-by-case basis."

The real root of opposition to merit pay by teachers' unions, he believes, is that merit pay is inherently anti-organizational. "Organizations are founded for mutual benefit," he noted. "Or they are founded for other collective purposes. To ask an organization to sanction a process like merit pay is so American. We have to believe that some individuals are better than others."

Merit pay is part of the cycle of education reform, he says—one minute it is a topic receiving national attention and scrutiny and the next it is a dead issue.

Since school boards determine teacher salaries, I asked, why does there continue to be high distrust focused on administrators among teachers? "School board members come and go," Urban said, "while school administrators are always there. Although school boards do determine salaries and legally nego-tiate the contract with the teachers, usually it's the superintendent's represen-tative who does the actual negotiating. My sense is that the adversary is much more the administration than the board."

In *Why Teachers Organized*, Urban discussed an incident in Florida in 1968 when teachers went on strike for professional issues, not salary/pension issues, and this was used against them by the community. I asked him to elab-orate on this incident and any effect it may have had on other, more recent efforts of teacher unions to use their power to professionalize teaching.

"The Florida Education Association [FEA] sold this action to the teachers by saying, 'We're doing this for the kids. They're taking money out of our schools and away from our kids.' FEA took 35,000 teachers out of the class-rooms statewide on that basis.

"The problem with that rationale is that anti-strikers can clearly make the point: 'How can you say you're doing this for the kids when what you're doing is harming the kids?' So that is where the teachers really lost."

They walked out for altruistic reasons and their strike failed?, I asked. "That was the stated purpose," Urban said. "But this was not a collective bar-gaining state, nor was this a union. This was the Florida Education Association, trying to do something unprecedented—have a statewide strike. The AFT, for instance, would never have had a statewide strike. They would have realized they couldn't pull it off."

Although approximately 35,000 teachers out of a total of less than 100,000 went out on strike, no schools closed, Urban says. "They were caught because if they claimed that despite the fact that the schools were open good instruction wasn't occurring because the substitutes weren't qualified—which in many cases was true—then the response was: 'Why aren't you working? If you were working, there would be qualified teachers!'"

In the short term, the strike failed, Urban says, but in the long view, it was a victory. "Not long after that, a collective bargaining law was passed in Florida. The AFT moved in; college professors organized. So the cause of teacher organizations benefited in the long run from that walkout, but at the time it looked like a crushing defeat."

Is there hope that teaching will become a profession like law and medicine?, I asked.

"No," Urban said without hesitation. "Instead, I see law and medicine becoming more like teaching. The traditional professions are becoming less autonomous."

Note

1. Cuban 1993.

Kent D. Peterson:
The Real World of School Leaders

*Kent D. Peterson is a Professor in the Department of Educational Adminis-
tration and was a Principal Investigator for the Center on Organization and
Restructuring of Schools at the University of Wisconsin–Madison from 1990 to
1995. Over the past decade he has studied school principals and worked closely
with dozens of districts and leadership academies across the country to develop
effective programs to nurture successful, visionary leaders. His research
focuses on the realities of principals' work, school improvement, leadership,
and culture building. This work is used in a variety of leadership academies in
the United States, Canada, and Europe. His work has appeared in* The Public
Interest, Educational Administration Quarterly, *and* Educational Leadership. *He
is the co-author with Terrence Deal of both* The Principal's Role in Shaping
School Culture, *and, more recently,* The Leadership Paradox: Balancing Leadership and Artistry in Schools.*

Kent D. Peterson's view of leadership negates the conventional wisdom that
leaders are born, not made: Leaders, he believes, can learn to lead.

Is leadership innate or acquired?, I asked. If it can be learned, what facilitates it? What hinders it? Can anyone learn to be a leader?

"If we look at almost any human organization," Peterson replied, "whether
it is kids on a playground or a school or a corporation, we see people who are
leading others. There are people who are motivating others, encouraging them
to do things, and helping coordinate what is going on—all over the organization, not only at one level. To think someone has to be Joan of Arc to be a
leader is wrong."

While Peterson admits that certain people have particular abilities that fall
in the leadership arena, he emphasizes that "good, basic, solid leadership can be
learned."

In his work for a variety of leadership academies, Peterson has developed
a combination of training activities for leaders that include simulations, case
studies, and analyses of leaders in novels, biographies, and film. "When I work

156

with leaders or potential leaders, we talk through what they do to motivate people, to keep the focus on the mission, to articulate the vision for the organization. Even people who aren't good interpersonally can improve their ability to lead."

He refers to the early writing on leadership, which centered on trait theory, the belief that individuals were born with certain traits and characteristics that enabled them to lead. "Many of the beliefs expressed in these early writings have been debunked," he noted. "Today we view leadership as a set of skills that, for many people, are developed early. They learn these skills in school, at camp, and on athletic teams. They learn how to interact with people, how to set some informal goals, and how to have a mission that they work to accomplish."

Gender and Leadership

What differences, I asked, does he see in terms of gender where leadership skills are concerned?

"The research on school principal leadership is quite clear," Peterson said, "that on average women have been found to be better instructional leaders than men. This is not to say some men aren't excellent instructional leaders. Yet even when controlling for background, experience, educational level, and the number of years in a classroom, a whole series of studies still found that gender makes a difference. No one knows why exactly."

Women, Peterson suggests, do tend to be more collaborative and facilitative in their leadership styles than do men. "Some of the recent research finds that women are more able to work on teams and tend to be more focused on problem-solving and inquiry versus argumentation and advocating for their own position."

Collaborative leadership, he pointed out, which is the type of leadership advocated by most educational reformers, is not territorial or obsessed with power, but encourages the development of leadership skills in others. "Men can lead in a collaborative manner," he observed, "but on average, there appear to be differences between men and women."

Style and Substance

Personal style influences the tone of leadership set in an organization, Peterson says, ranging from the more casual to the more formal—and can have a profound impact on the quality of work and morale in the organization. "One's personal style encourages the same style in others," he noted. "If a person's style always is to be thinking and talking about work—whether eating pizza or having popcorn or drinking a cup of coffee—that will affect others' actions. As a colleague, you either buffer yourself from it or it becomes part of the culture.

"The style of good modern leaders and the structures that they build tend to merge and connect. Their managerial style ultimately merges with their values and their interpersonal style. For instance, not sharing any information about the school's budget with anybody on the staff immediately sends a message, a symbolic message about control, secrecy, privacy, and power."

People underestimate how all-encompassing it is to be a leader, Peterson maintains. "Leadership is actually a statement of your values and how you will make decisions. It's important to realize that in schools, principals are really powerful. Principals and the teacher leaders that they nurture shape what goes on in the school, whether people stay or leave, whether it is all right to talk about an innovative program or not."

The right leadership style, he says, can determine whether ongoing assessment of school improvement initiatives occurs or is tacitly forbidden. "With the right leader, school staff will say: How is our whole language program working? Do we need to focus on more phonics? They are not dogmatic; they are able to change. In schools, the leadership style of the principal shapes the culture by actions such as hiring and excommunication."

Different Leadership Styles and their Effects

One powerful, although not particularly positive, leadership style identified first by James McGregor Burns is what is termed "transactional." Peterson describes it as: "You support me; I'll support you. If I get money to hire you, then you will turn around and hire me. This style is characterized by figures such as Lyndon Johnson—an expert at political bargaining."

Its converse is transformational leadership, which he explains as "identifying a set of values that transform the organization, values that are more deeply and widely held than at the individual level. In schools, these are probably community-wide values. What transformational leaders do is articulate a vision for the organization that touches on those deeper values that are held by a large group of people, with the effect of energizing people.

"Doing this touches people's hearts rather than just their heads," he continued. "It makes people want to accomplish some valued ends because it is important to them, not just because they were told to do it. The transformational leader builds a culture of shared values, beliefs, rituals, and traditions."

How, I inquired, does the transformational leader arrive at the values that are correct for the organization which he or she leads?

"One way," Peterson answered, "is to go into a school, pick up on those deep values that teachers and the community hold that perhaps have never been articulated or voiced, and start to articulate them. Sometimes there is an existing culture that is strong and principals work to identify the deeper values that both community and staff hold."

At the extreme, a negative example of an effective transformational leader, he points out, is Hitler. "He articulated a set of fears and racist views that others held, and established rituals and traditions around those views and fears. He established an integrated worldview that was horrible, and effectively used symbols and traditions to make people connect to it."

A more positive example, he says, is Gandhi. "He also tapped into a whole set of beliefs and hopes of the Indian people in a way that hadn't been done before. As a well-educated Indian who could have moved into the bureaucracy and been supportive of the British Crown, instead he wore the clothes of a very poor person. Because the British taxed salt, at one point in his leadership he walked many miles to the ocean and made salt. He started to sell salt and did not pay the tax. The symbolism of this was liberty, independence from England, and also a way to demonstrate that the British control of the Indians economically could end."

Gandhi also connected the people in India, Peterson points out. On a smaller scale, this is a significant activity and priority for school leaders at all levels of the organization. "Leaders help people feel they are part of a shared community. At one school that I studied, they have what they call a 'Super Saturday,' which is a conference that brings between 500 to 600 people from across the region. The entire staff participates; each person runs a seminar on some new teaching technique or participates in the design of the brochures or the advertising for the event. This is just one example of a powerful way to pull people together."

Leaders also possess the ability to analyze a situation and arrive at solutions if problems exist. "To be a good leader, one has to be a good manager as well. You have to deal with the budget, with discipline, and with coordinating teachers. If you don't do that well, talk about values and hopes and dreams is not going to succeed. You will not be successful, because the basic things that teachers need are not being done."

Leaders as Managers

In the schools that Peterson and his colleagues studied in the research conducted by the Center on Organization and Restructuring of Schools, they interviewed some principals with strong values and beliefs—who had difficulty with the more prosaic part of their jobs. "They couldn't get anything done," Peterson observed. "The symbolic message that they send is that the routines that make it possible to teach are not important. The principal does not value those things because he or she is not putting any time into them."

Attention to routines is doubly important in schools, he believes, because of the power of chaos. "Even the best schools can fall apart," he said. "If you, as a leader, don't take seriously the routines, you can have all the traditions and rituals that you want—but people will perceive you as phony."

How do leaders do both?, I asked. How are they able to attend to the more mundane aspects of managing an complicated organization as well as providing leadership on values and goals?

In his reply, Peterson pointed first to the fragmented, hectic quality of typical school life. "All the research on principals shows that they are interrupted constantly," he replied. "An elementary school principal averages about two minutes per interaction in inner cities. They could spend all their time just dealing with crises.

"If principals have a vision and also have a lot of problems to solve in their schools, they have to be a problem selector. If they don't have a vision, they become fire fighters. If they do have an educational vision for their schools, they are able to focus on those areas. They deal with immediate, pressing issues like a gang fight, but they also work in areas they consider important, like new ways of approaching math instruction. Principals must have an idea of what intellectual quality is and what kids ought to be able to accomplish."

Even in schools that have few problems, principals run the risk of becoming what Peterson calls "caretakers."

"They wander around the building and talk to people," he said. "But if a principal is able to become a problem selector, he or she looks for something new to do every year, whether it is some new program to examine, some new tradition to establish, some new group of students to focus on. You could work twenty-four hours a day as a school principal and not finish everything."

Structural Inhibitors and Leadership

In what ways, I asked, does the present structure of schools affect leaders? What structural changes seem especially promising in offering new directions for leaders?

Many constraints on schools, Peterson emphasized in his response, end up having the effect of shackling leaders. "One major constraint is the lack of autonomy," he said, "to make choices about what is important. The lack of school autonomy gets translated into the lack of individual autonomy at the classroom level. In many schools, they rigidly follow the state or district mandates on how many minutes of reading, of art, and of science to have each day even when these are not producing learning.

"Another problem is that the community often wants the schools to provide an education like the ones it received, rather than an education that their kids actually need in today's society."

As an example, he mentions that the use of calculators has been very controversial in many schools. "It has taken a decade or more for schools to start using calculators regularly. They are still spending lots of time on old math like long division rather than use of data and probability. The reason is that the community wants things to be taught the way they learned them."

Learning, Peterson noted, "is painful enough—whether the content is taught in a new way or not. Many communities also are fighting computers in the classroom. This goes back and forth, and has for many years. There was the new math movement, and then we went back to basic skills. Now we are moving toward authentic instruction or some form of it. We may swing back to basic skills because of political or community pressure."

This pressure is not inconsequential to leaders, he insists, because in many organizations the customer rules. "The customer is powerful, and many decisions are made with a lot of customer input. When corporations started to restructure themselves, they did two things: First, they listened to what customers had to say about what they wanted, and second, they realized that sometimes they had to convince the customer that something new would be better for them.

"Third, in corporations, they involved the customer in figuring out how to serve them, but they didn't ask the customer: How do we build this? Right now in education, the community wants to tell the organization how to produce the outcomes. In a corporation—as long as you are law-abiding and don't ruin the environment—you can work in teams or you can work individually. The customer isn't concerned with how the outcomes are produced, only that they *are* produced."

Because teachers and administrators do have special training, skills, and knowledge, if the community tells them how to do their jobs, doesn't it have a demoralizing effect on their performance?, I asked.

"Often," Peterson said, "it means that leaders have to spend a lot of time convincing the public that what they are doing and how they are doing it is going to work. This is important, but it is time that could be spent directly on improving the quality of teaching and learning."

The increase in lawsuits and the increasingly litigious nature of the American public have made it necessary for schools to be increasingly cautious, even wary about new undertakings, he points out. "All these conditions make it very difficult for leaders to focus on producing quality learning. Another ongoing problem is the lack of high-quality staff development provided by districts and states. Schools need ongoing, state-of-the-art staff development to keep them current. The state of California has one of the only comprehensive non-university-based programs for school leaders."

The lack of autonomy at the school level and at the individual classroom level make it difficult for schools to effect real change, Peterson believes. "First, they frequently—too frequently—exist in communities that are not ready for change. Second, the professional development system is not up to speed; it is not developed to bring new ideas into schools.

"In contrast, the most effective leaders I have seen have been those who were highly connected to networks of information. In addition to their own interest in new information, they played a key role in encouraging teachers to bring in and work with new ideas."

Another area that restricts leaders from concentrating their primary attention on teaching and learning are the restrictions posed by teachers' contracts, he points out. "Many contracts don't provide time for professional development for teachers. They don't always provide incentives for participation in professional development."

Site-Based Management: Solution or Problem?

Site-based management seemed to be one of the answers to restructuring schools for shared leadership, I commented. How, I inquired, do you assess it after researching it for five years at the Center on the Organization and Restructuring of Schools?

"Almost all the research on site-based management," Peterson said, "finds no positive correlation between it and student learning. Nonetheless, we found it is probably a necessary, but not sufficient, condition. Many people believed that structural changes would solve all the problems with schools, and they maintained that if you provided people with the autonomy to make their own decisions about how resources would be allocated, improvements would blossom and schools would boil over with new ideas. It didn't happen.

"The metaphor that I use," he continued, "is if you want someone to improve the quality of his or her writing, you don't buy them the latest computer with the latest word-processing program and put it on their desk. That isn't sufficient. You say, 'Here is how you use it to improve your writing.'

"What happened with site-based management is that it was a tool that was placed in a school without a purpose. It is a little surprising that schools didn't view it as a tool with which to make decisions about how to improve student learning. Instead, they frequently became sidetracked and focused on administrative and management issues. In schools where leaders have focused on using it to improve student learning, it has had an impact that is related to a sense of empowerment.

"School staff may not need formal decentralization, but there ought to be what is sometimes called participatory management—people involved in decisions about budget and staffing issues. I believe that you cannot have a powerful professional culture that focuses on student learning without some form of shared decision-making."

In your work with school leaders, what have been the most important lessons that need to be shared with other leaders and potential leaders?, I asked.

"The most important thing is being able to articulate a set of goals that everyone works on together," Peterson replied promptly, "to be able to talk about how everyone's contribution is valuable. One of the things that happens with a mix of people with varied backgrounds and training is that people are divided into the so-called professional and the so-called nonprofessional staff. This is unfortunate, because organizations don't function without everybody working together toward some valued ends.

"Second, leaders need to be able to work with people to make everyone's work flow smoothly. The leader helps facilitate the relationships and connections between staff, units, and activities and then ensures that these work toward shared ends.

"Finally, the most difficult piece is making tough decisions about staffing," he concluded with some empathy. "There are some whose values or skills or motivation are counterproductive to a unit or to a school. The leader has to find ways to either buffer others from those individuals or to help those individuals find work elsewhere.

"If there are so-called free riders in a school or people who do not pull their own weight, they can exert a very negative pull on a school. Colleagues are not going to tell other colleagues, 'I don't think you should work here.' Leaders have to do that, and it is difficult. Where everyone works together toward shared ends, the creative energy increases and spreads."

Patricia K. Anderson:
Reflections on Professionalism and Leadership

Patricia K. Anderson has been the principal of Sullivan High School in Chicago, Illinois for two years and, before that, an assistant principal for six years. She has held a variety of positions in schools, including those of high school English teacher, high school and elementary school counselor, and department head. She also worked for the Illinois State Board of Education as a state coordinator for the Illinois Alliance of Essential Schools. Anderson has worked extensively on school reform through the Coalition of Essential Schools and has presented numerous workshops on the Socratic seminar, on creating change in urban schools through personalizing instruction, and on exhibitions of mastery. She is a member of the Chicago Annenberg School Reform Collaborative which was responsible for obtaining an Annenberg grant for Chicago. Anderson received her Ph.D. in Administration and Policy Studies from Northwestern University. She has participated in a U.S. Department of Education video on Goals 2000; has been a panelist for an NEA, AFT, and Coalition of Essential Schools co-sponsored symposium; has appeared in "Restructuring America's Schools," a videotape produced by ASCD; and has been a frequent conference presenter.

Being a progressive, forward-thinking school leader pushing for reform is far from easy, as Patricia K. Anderson will attest. In our conversation, she carefully separated her own definition of professionalism from initiatives targeted toward the professionalization of teaching—and pointed out that principals need to see their own occupation professionalized in order to attract and retain the best school leaders.

Professionalism appears to have a uniform meaning, yet most people invest it with a personal meaning as well. What does it mean to you, I asked, to be a professional?

Anderson thought for a minute and then responded, "First of all, being a professional means that I hold myself to a personal standard. That personal standard is one that usually supersedes the parameter set by my school system or my superiors. Any job that I would take on, I would perform according to my personal standard.

"Second, being a professional means that I meet the requirements devised by my school system and my superiors. Third, it means that I am a model for my faculty and my students, which means that the way in which I do my job is very important."

Is your personal standard relentlessly self-critical, or kinder?, I asked. At what point does this standard spill over to standards you set for others in your work environment? Can this create problems in working relationships?

"I'm extremely critical about what I do and how I do it," she responded. "I want to make sure that the job I do is one that I can be proud of, which usually means that I don't strike a good balance between the personal and the professional. Usually the professional side of my life takes over because there is always something to be done at a high school. Whatever doesn't get done in a day is taken home and many hours are spent there.

"The fact that I'm critical of myself sets a standard for my faculty. I don't expect them to work any harder than I do."

Yet this high standard for herself and others, she admits, can create difficulties. "There are people at the school who may not understand that standard or think that perhaps the system demands less," Anderson said candidly. "Or they think that their friends at other schools don't have to work that hard, so why should they? Of course, I try to talk about the mission of the school and why it's necessary to do things to conform to it in an attempt to get everyone to understand why we doing things."

But ultimately she believes that professionalism for principals has a harder edge, requiring a certain degree of willingness to impose a "bottom line" upon staff. "Basically, certain things need to be done. If they are directives from the central office, for instance, I try to take as much of that work load from teachers so that they can teach. If we do have a disagreement, we discuss it and perhaps there is a change."

Since Anderson also has been a classroom teacher, I asked: Is there any difference in your attitude toward professionalism now that you are a principal? If so, how does it differ from the attitudes you held as a teacher?

"There is a difference," she said thoughtfully. "It is much harder now to get everything accomplished because the parameters of the principalship are so broad, and seem to have broadened in the last couple of years. I understand from principals who have been in a principalship for many years that the position requires so much more in recent years. We seem to be responsible for so many problems, things that are not our fault, but that do exist. We are expected to deal with issues such as violence in schools. It can be difficult because the system may not have in place people or policies that easily support what we do."

She added, "Maintaining a high standard in dealing with these issues is more difficult because schools have so many more demands placed on them by parents and communities. Our role as jugglers is very difficult, and keeping a high standard in place as we deal with those demands is probably more difficult currently than it used to be."

In The Middle: Principals as Buffers

In what ways has the principalship changed?, I asked Anderson. Is there a perception that the principal is caught in the middle between the demands of the central office, the school board, state mandates, and the desires of parents? Are external and internal mandates overwhelming?

"We used to deal with school matters," she noted. "Now many, many things funnel through the schools because schools are a viable organization through which things can get done. Immunizations, for example, go through the schools. We have to exclude students whose shots aren't up-to-date or whose physical examinations are not current. That is just one example of extra things the school is asked to do. In the past, schools had a less comprehensive role."

Where do salary and status enter the picture of professionalism?, I inquired. Aren't they important as well?

"I agree with the movement to professionalize the teaching occupation," Anderson said. "This would be positive for teachers, and it also would be positive for principals if we could professionalize the principalship. This year, for the first time in many years, principals in Chicago received a raise. The cost of living has gone up; other organizations have had their bargaining units work for their raises. Principals have not had that type of advocacy and yet their work load and responsibility continues to increase tremendously."

The benefits of professionalizing the occupations of teaching and school administration she sees as manifold: attracting the best people to positions and providing the nudge needed to keep people current. "Too often, someone gets into a position and twenty years later updates herself through participation in a professional group or through reading journals. Clearly, that isn't enough, particularly when one thinks of the kinds of changes occurring in education. Professionalizing these occupations would mean that the best people are attracted to the positions but also that they must stay current to keep the positions."

While increased pay and improved working conditions may improve the lot of teachers and principals, will they result in a rise in public respect for school staff?, I questioned.

"Physicians have managed to achieve this type of status and respect," Anderson replied, "although of course respect cannot be mandated. In this country, if someone is a parent, in some cases that person automatically becomes an expert on the educational system. Professionalization would be positive for teachers because it would create standards that teachers would have to live up to. If society offers high standards and high status for teachers, teachers will act accordingly."

Higher societal status for teachers, she believes, would also result in perhaps less profound changes for teachers that are nonetheless important: subtle shifts in behavior, dress, and level of preparation. "Part of higher standards and increased status for teachers means that their behavior would change to become more professional, their dress would change accordingly, and their continued preparation for their classes would mean they would become updated scholars in their classrooms."

The benefit would accrue to students, she believes. "Students can only benefit from continually updated scholars in their classrooms."

If teachers could attain the same societal status as physicians and lawyers, she believes students would regard them with increased respect. "The tone of decency that we want in schools would be recaptured," she noted.

"Teachers would be taken more seriously. Parents might approach us differently as well, more as collaborators, realizing what we're trying to do for their children, rather than as people who make unrealistic demands on them."

One common argument against increased teacher and administrator pay suggests that their salaries be divided into an hourly wage with summer vacations and holidays factored in—a formula guaranteed to give the impression that teachers and administrators make considerable more money than their actual salaries would reflect. This argument annoys Anderson, who said: "If people only understood what the school day is like, they would not talk in that way. I wish I could be shadowed by someone all day for a series of days. My days last 12 and 15 hours, not 6 hours. There are meetings on Saturdays; there are meetings at night. This is not compensated time."

A typical day, Anderson said, consists of early preparation at home for whatever meetings are scheduled for the day. After a preliminary glance at her calendar and messages, she walks into the halls to greet students or help staff with identification checks at the front doors. "I am in the halls so that the teachers and students can see me, and I greet them at the door as well. Then I return to the office to try to answer calls and do paperwork.

"Along the way," she added, "there are calls from parents and teachers who need to see me about certain issues or there are meetings with my administrative staff, with teachers who are working on special projects. The rest of the day includes time in the halls, working from the first floor of the building to the third floor, so that I am visible, so that my staff knows that I support what they do. My presence has another side as well: sometimes I help clear the halls or quiet students down."

Much time goes into preparation for meetings, which usually occur during the evening or on weekends. "I'm often taken off my agenda," Anderson said, referring to the fragmented day principals usually report.

The Meaning of Leadership

What, I asked Anderson, does it mean to you to be a school leader? How do you reconcile being a leader with your concept of professionalism?

"It means," she replied without hesitation, "having a vision and pulling together the human and financial resources to reach that vision. That vision is created by incorporating what teachers, parents, students, and communities define as that vision for the school—it is not an independent vision. Whatever the vision is, it must take into account what the system wants to include.

"Being professional as a leader also means that the leader must stay abreast of all the movements in education and also remain very watchful of the needs in the building. She must talk to people constantly, maintain an open-door policy for teachers, and keep dialogue flowing. I know that in my position I must be able to maintain an evolving dialogue and, at the same time, pull all the threads together so we can all be on the same page."

Apart from vision, what about managerial tasks that the principal must complete? How does a school leader keep this part of the job from over-whelming the visionary and philosophical aspects? In her response, Anderson pointed to the importance of having high-quality staff.

"That function means that the leader makes sure that systems are in place that work well and then continues to monitor them," she said. "The only way that can occur is to place excellent people into positions where they can become monitors of quality."

Anderson also believes that principals benefit from a wide range of previous positions within schools, ranging from teaching to counseling to coaching. "I've been lucky," she added. "I've been a counselor, a coach, a curriculum writer, a principal, a classroom teacher. This helps me a great deal. Since I know what so many jobs entail, I don't assign work that is unrealistic to departments or people."

Keeping a Vision Alive

What about specific actions that a principal must take in order to keep the school's vision paramount and lively?, I asked. Since the school's vision may be somewhat philosophical or even spiritual, how does that flourish while business and daily crises are attended to?

"At Sullivan High School, we had to resurrect our vision last year," Anderson responded. "When we became a Coalition school, we recreated a vision and we worked hard on it. Otherwise, it can easily take a back seat to other things.

"Our faculty broke itself into four small groups in which each discussed the vision, arriving at consensus. Now, when we take any kind of step or movement, we look at what is proposed to see if it fits our vision. We also look at every proposed change to see if it will affect the type of graduate we want to produce. We then review it when we write our school improvement plans. Teachers, along with community members and parents, look at the vision continuously to see if the school improvement plan reflects accurately what we say we are going to do in the vision."

Principals and Unions

How can school principals work to break down traditionally adversarial relationships—which some believe have been heightened with the advent of collective bargaining?, I asked Anderson. In what ways can principals effect collaborative relationships with teachers?

"Sometimes the union *doesn't* advance the school vision," Anderson commented, "even if teachers are identifiably invested in the vision. Or sometimes teachers like the vision but can't think of a way to accomplish it, or are not willing to go along with it because they feel they have some rights and their rights do not accommodate that kind of work. Occasionally they are not willing to take even a year to try it. From that standpoint, I believe that the union has not been a positive force from my point of view as an administrator."

Did her view of unions change when she became an administrator?, I asked.

"Only in the sense that I knew more about the demands that needed to be addressed," Anderson said. "As a classroom teacher, I didn't worry about it. My circle of friends and I got things done; we didn't feel we were taken advantage of. If there was a legitimate concern, I would talk to the administration about it.

"Now, I think a great deal about how something is viewed, what teachers might think of it. I absolutely am a teacher advocate and wouldn't go against any action of the union, but I don't look at it as a positive force in our school. I keep telling teachers: 'I'll protect you more than that contract will protect you because there are certain things that shouldn't be done and I know that.' It's a process of getting them to trust that you won't step on their toes. For instance, if one more student is placed in a class, there's a reason for it."

Al Shanker, I noted, has written that "professionalism" can be used against teachers to exhort them to greater effort. What is her view?

"Yes, it can be used against them," Anderson said, "because so much more, in general, is demanded of principals and teachers. There has to be a place where the line is drawn. And yet, the opposite side of that coin is the attitude that says: 'My day ends at 2:45 and therefore I'm done.'

What about the lack of protection afforded principals?, I asked. Teachers have union representation, whereas principals do not. Does that create an additional uneasiness? How do principals safeguard themselves against unrealistic demands on their time?

"We're sitting ducks," Anderson replied bluntly, "because there is no safeguard that I can see. Whatever it is, we would be named in the suit, even though we may not be aware of the circumstances that preceded it.

"I end up negotiating with myself. Some things can wait until the next day; others can't. The bottom line is that this is my school. If and when anything happens, it's my responsibility. It can be hard to cut things off: I frequently find myself involved or taking a little too much responsibility for things that should go to the engineer or the lunch room manager, because it is my school."

Effective Relationships with Teachers

What specifically is difficult about establishing collegial working relationships with teachers?, I asked. Does your perspective on collegiality differ now that you are a principal? What was it when you were a teacher?

"It is difficult to be shoulder to shoulder with teachers, working on a project in the same capacity with them once you are a principal," Anderson reflected. "It is difficult for them, because they have to become accustomed to your presence and also to the fact that sometimes you have an equal vote and other times you can override them because you have the authority to do so as principal. My work with the Steering Committee for the Coalition of Essential Schools has shown this to me the most. There is the question of being accepted into the circle and being allowed to give my ideas and also allow them to disagree or contradict me.

"The more you do it, the easier it becomes," she added. "Teachers become accustomed to seeing you function alongside them. Collegiality means that you, the principal, will be out of your office and with teachers regularly. However, trying to balance the other parts of your job with that is difficult."

As a teacher, what were Anderson's attitudes toward collegiality with her peers?

"I grew up with the people in my teaching career," she responded. "We created a type of collegiality with each other. I don't think the school created it. The hard conditions under which we worked brought an accord to that group of people. I have thought about my experience often because I wanted to recreate it here at Sullivan.

"One way we have tried to do that is to offer events or settings in which our teachers can get together where they are free to talk about school but they don't have to. That certainly helps the climate as well. Many people don't know one another in a high school because their schedules don't coincide, and it is only beneficial when we can overcome that."

How does the personal vision that teachers and principals hold individually meld into a collective vision that isn't imposed from some external source and therefore devoid of meaning?, I asked.

"Each teacher," Anderson said thoughtfully, "has to be given the opportunity for personal goals that are professional. One way we do it at Sullivan is to write it into the discretionary fund so that I can release a teacher to pursue professional development that has something to do with his or her own department, with the expectation it will be shared with the remainder of the staff. That teacher chooses what he wants to do. He forms his impressions. From there, the school works with the information and reactions of that teacher to form the collective vision.

"This is not the same as designing a staff development activity and requiring attendance at the activity," she emphasized. "We have a common planning time every week for teachers, which allows teams or our special education teachers time to talk to each other while all the teachers are in the building but without students and other obligations."

What about the difficulty of transcending the negativity that frequently permeates settings where teachers gather?, I asked.

"That's why it is important to have shared time, accepting the fact that it may or may not be effective on every occasion," she replied. "If the time isn't well-utilized by some people, I have to make sure that it has been utilized well by the bulk of people. In that way, the school wins and so do I."

She points to their "critical friends" group as an example. "It is a group of approximately ten: seven teachers, a counselor, a person who is an administrative aide, and the school's assistant principal. They are released from class once a month to view each other's classes. They have time to provide feedback to each other, and that time is covered by an outside grant. They debrief after school about the process of teaching and what can be improved. The Nine Common Principles of the Coalition of Essential Schools lays a foundation for that. Are we doing what we say we're doing? Is the teacher a coach? How did you start your lesson? How did you sustain it? How do you evaluate it?

"Once this process gets off the ground, maybe we can broaden it. This is the type of action that will change people for the better. People will review what they're doing in the classroom and really pick it apart. But the important part is that there is a protocol for the discussion so that people are not left vulnerable. It results in changing the conversation from that of typical lounge talk to academic talk, which I view as more conversation about the teacher's craft."

Challenges and Obstacles for Leaders

What do you see as the biggest challenges facing school leaders today?, I asked. Personally, what do you see as your greatest challenge as a principal?

"One of the biggest challenges," Anderson responded, "is making sure that through all we have to do, student achievement remains a major factor and that we manage to raise it despite all of the obstacles. I emphasize this, because often we look at the reasons our students aren't achieving and provide demographics, statistics, attendance and dropout rates to explain the problem rather than confront it with specific actions that will make a difference.

"But we have to figure out how to raise achievement to grade level at minimum. Another paramount challenge for school leaders today is maintaining commitment to our school visions."

How about working successfully with a student population that is increasingly diverse?, I suggested.

"Certainly multiculturalism is alive and well at Sullivan," she said, "with over thirty different dialects spoken in our building. Multiculturalism is at the forefront with us."

As far as personal challenges, Anderson sees her own as communicating adequately with teachers so that trust is developed and they see her role as one who clears their path so they can do their jobs. "I hope they understand there is logic behind my actions," she mused. "However, we all fall into bad habits; we all make assumptions. I believe that if people know who you are and what you stand for, everyone is much more likely to succeed."

Part IV

Change and Constancy: Commentaries on Educational Reform

When you get there, there is no there there.

—Gertrude Stein

Overview of Part IV

Under what conditions can educational reform succeed? What are common mistakes made by educational reformers and those who are eager to see improved student achievement, authentic pedagogy and curriculum that lifts student learning to a powerful level, and configured schools that include a strong teacher voice in decisionmaking and governance? To what extent are there lessons to be gleaned from the history of educational reform efforts in this country? In this part, I sought answers to these and other questions and elicited comments on the current national standards movement and the impetus to privatize schools.

Herbert M. Kliebard begins by providing a context for the history of reform in the United States, laying out the conditions under which reform falters and flourishes. Next, Michael W. Apple critiques the push to privatize schools and the national standards movement by discussing the rise of the neoconservatives and neoliberals—and the vast influence he believes that they wield on the market and on education. Thomas A. Romberg, an early and ongoing leader in the national standards movement, presents the rationale that dominated the *Standards* developed by the National Council of Teachers of Mathematics, and turns a watchful eye to the future of education in the United States. Fred M. Newmann discusses the research he and his colleagues at the Center on the Organization and Restructuring of Schools conducted from 1990 to 1995, specifically the structural conditions that enable authentic pedagogy and powerful intellectual student learning—along with the limitations of those same structural conditions. Theodore R. Sizer critiques the reform with which he has been the most closely associated for over a decade: the Coalition of Essential Schools. At the same time, he looks at the large picture of reform and reports that he is heartened by what Americans have managed to achieve. I conclude this part with the experience of one school leader, Dennis R. Williams, who worked with the School Development Program of James Comer at West Mecklenburg High School in Charlotte, North Carolina. Williams candidly discusses the difficulties and rewards of one school's initiative to boost student achievement and teacher engagement—and his own views as the leader of that reform.

Herbert M. Kliebard:
The Supreme Context of Reform

Herbert M. Kliebard is currently a Professor in the Departments of Curriculum and Instruction and Educational Policy Studies at the University of Wisconsin–Madison. He was born and raised in the Bronx, New York. After receiving his baccalaureate and master's degrees from City College of New York, Kliebard taught in public schools for eight years. He holds a doctorate from Teachers College, Columbia University. Since 1963, when he came to the University of Wisconsin–Madison, he has specialized in curriculum studies, particularly in the history of the American curriculum and in policy issues related to secondary education. His first book (with Arno Bellack), The Language of the Classroom, *was published in 1966. His most recent book is* Forging the American Curriculum *(1993), and the second edition of his* The Struggle for the American Curriculum *(1995) has just been released.*

To an observer of the terrain of educational reform, its landscape could appear bleak: schools and the people who inhabit them appear remarkably resistant to change. In fact, most reforms and school improvement programs seem to enjoy temporary success at best and then vanish—or reappear several years later cloaked in new rhetoric. What does a reform need to be even partially successful?, I asked Kliebard.

"More than an idea," he began, "a reform needs a school structure that can support it. Many reforms fail because they are inserted into a system that cannot quite digest the ideas. These ideas are then found to be unworkable or not as effective as what previously was done. In some cases they are simply found not to be as effective as the proponents of the reform had promised. As a result, they are disgorged. But in those cases where structural change supports a reform, they have a better chance of success."

What would a structure that is supportive of reform look like?, I asked.

"If you are addressing the question of integration of school subjects in reform, for example, a common complaint—particularly in the high school curriculum—is that the subjects are taught as isolated entities," Kliebard pointed out. "Something needs to connect them. As long as the structure of the school is built around separate, individual departments, as long as schedules are rigidly set so that flexible time is virtually impossible, then you will not meet with success when you try to integrate the curriculum."

He added, "This is typical of the type of thing that happens when a reform is attempted without structural changes to accompany it."

Since the structure of elementary schools typically is much more fluid than that of secondary schools, does it explain why reforms appear to flourish in elementary schools but perish in high schools?, I inquired.

"In elementary schools, you have much more flexible time and the structure is much more flexible than that of secondary schools," Kliebard said. "Just imagine if a teacher decided to take her high school class on a field trip. The rest of the teachers would be up in arms because those students would be missing their classes, whereas in the case of an elementary school, it wouldn't create such a stir."

Reforms as Slogan Systems

In his writings, Kliebard has commented on the ways in which many reforms have disintegrated into mere slogan systems used to prod people into action—and the type of action advocated by the "reform" can vary widely. In what ways, I asked, can reforms dwindle to a collection of slogans?

"Much reform currently is tied up with careerism and professionalism," he observed. "This type of reform is sometimes referred to as feckless reform. It might sound good, but in actuality, it doesn't change much. Slogan systems, as I interpret them, exist mainly for the purpose of enlisting support. A slogan's purpose is to attract allegiance. In the case of slogan systems in education, that's exactly what they do: They attract allegiance, but they don't succeed in accomplishing any kind of change."

As an example, Kliebard points to an assignment he gave in a university class—an assignment designed to pinpoint the ideas behind a slogan. "We tried to pin down what 'Tech Prep' means exactly.

"We were not successful," he added. "Although we interviewed various people in leadership positions with respect to Tech Prep, each person who came back to the class had totally different versions of what it was supposed to mean. No matter how hard we tried, we could not figure out what specifically Tech Prep is supposed to be doing. That is part of the frustration in dealing with initiatives started by slogans."

Reforms as slogans have an escape clause as far as delivering on their promises: they are difficult to critique. "At the level of a slogan system, they are very difficult to attack," Kliebard noted. "The more concrete and specific the proposal, the more vulnerable it becomes to criticism. But if a so-called reform can exist on a general level, it can remain relatively immune from criticism."

Does that explain, I asked, why some of the most superficial, "canned" staff development programs enjoy tremendous popularity for brief periods of time, although they may pass from the educational landscape without any appreciable positive change in their wake?

"This is speculation on my part," Kliebard responded, "but my sense is that doing otherwise is a big undertaking. It entails a careful and time-consuming analysis of an educational context. Instead, a school can summon some external guru for a three-day workshop. It appears to the school board that the school is working hard to improve instruction. But actually, it doesn't mean a thing. It's easy to do—it just takes money.

"Actually to initiate reform in the context of a particular school or school system is a big undertaking, the type of undertaking in which most school administrators are not willing to invest. I don't mean investment in terms of money, but in terms of time and commitment. It is much easier to call in an external 'expert' and bathe in that individual's glory."

To initiate any reform, Kliebard insists, requires a prerequisite many might not consider: sophistication. "I can't condemn unsophisticated people in education," he added, "because there is a natural tendency for people to believe that if only they follow a particular list of things to do, all will be well. If these things are followed in a particular order, then change will occur."

The popularity of lists—tremendously oversimplified "to-dos" for school improvement—is especially prevalent and persistent among many school administrators, Kliebard believes, because their training typically lacks grounding in curriculum and instruction. "Part of the problem is the way school administrators are trained," he pointed out. "They are trained in aspects of their job that by and large do not require the kind of creativity and sophistication that school improvement needs. Instead, they are trained in the technical side of the job: finance, law, and things of that nature. They are not asked to step outside that narrow training very often."

This training not only narrows their perspective on school change, it makes administrators especially uncomfortable when they must deal with the fulcrum of change: what goes on in the classroom. "Many school administrators," Kliebard added, "feel inadequate when they step into a classroom and are reluctant to give even a novice teacher suggestions on his or her teaching. Many administrators in this situation will confess openly their feelings of inadequacy.

"But the more common response, in my experience, is the statement that they don't have the time," he said. "Instead of dealing with what goes on in the classroom, they are too committed to matters of discipline, community relations, and public relations."

How has the administrator's role changed over the years, I asked, to the point where instruction is the least part of the position? "At one time," Kliebard reflected, "a school principal was actually considered to be an educator, in much the same way one thinks of an English schoolmaster. The term principal comes from principal teacher, that is, the foremost teacher among the teachers in the school.

"But in the twentieth century, school administrators—for various reasons—began to pattern themselves after the captains of industry, the CEOs. With certain exceptions, they don't see their responsibility as actually addressing the process of education, which is unfortunate."

Why such respect for and modeling of corporate chief executives?, I inquired.

"In our society, CEOs seem to be the role models for everybody. Everybody wants to listen to the opinions of business leaders, even with respect to schools, " he said with some disapproval. "There is a growing reluctance on the part of school administrators—and obviously there are many exceptions to this—to engage in thinking about the educational process as opposed to sitting on top of a bureaucracy and delegating tasks."

He added dryly, "Many people see the CEO as a kind of culture hero, although obviously I'm not sure we ought to."

Many current reforms are headed by leaders who are prominent on the national educational scene, who take an active role in disseminating word of the program, and who serve as a lightning rod for the movement. Certainly, most educators would think of Theodore Sizer, James Comer, and Robert Slavin as examples of such leaders of reform. Do reforms need an identifiable leader?, I asked.

"They don't," Kliebard replied emphatically. "In the case of age grading, that reform was probably dictated by a number of social factors that included a huge growth in the school population that made it necessary that the reform be instituted. I don't dismiss the role of the leader, providing the leader understands and appreciates that education is supremely contextual and that very few reforms can succeed without paying very careful attention to the particular context in which the reform is taking place.

"The particular context means the very particular institutional culture that exists in every school in the school system. It does not mean that it is safe to assume that a generalized reform can be successfully implemented regardless of the context."

The template of a generalized reform, although it has mass appeal because of its simplicity, will not fit every school?, I suggested.

"Exactly," Kliebard said. "For example, we have seen the relatively recent school improvement movement, with its rules or lists of what needs to be done to improve schools. The items on such lists can be almost as trivial and meaningless as stating that if schools have better bulletin boards, they will succeed in transforming a bad school to a good school."

From Lists to Standards

Given his dislike of lists for school improvement, I was curious about how Kliebard assesses the current national standards movement: Do the national standards in different content areas provide specific guidance that will improve the quality of curriculum and instruction, or do they fall in the category of lists of unrelated content that students must learn?

To explain his perspective on the national standards movement, Kliebard steps back into educational history. "An early belief was that not everybody can profit from algebra, literature, foreign languages, and so on," he said. "Instead, the belief was that we need to provide a range of other subjects for the 'incapables.' However, that approach to curriculum seems not to have worked.

"The alternative would be to proceed from the assumption that perhaps all children can learn certain types of academic content. They won't learn the same amount or to the same degree or in the same pattern, but it is possible that they may all profit from the study of history, literature, science, and mathematics. The national standards movement seems to be moving in that direction."

What, I asked, are major obstacles to a sensible application of national standards?

"The principal obstacle," Kliebard emphasized, "is the assumption that the standard academic subjects are present to be simply digested. If we're going to move in the direction of a common curriculum, we then have to reconstruct those subjects in such a way that they are more relevant to the modern world and the way people think today.

"We can't just assume," he continued, "that the curriculum of 1895 would be appropriate for the 1995 student just because it was, for the most part, an academic curriculum. We can have an academic curriculum and at the same time address modern concerns, giving children the opportunity to come to a better understanding of what the world is like and what their position is in that world. So although on the one hand the standards seem to be an effort to provide more rigor, they don't necessarily reconstruct the academic subjects so that they mean something to children, which can be a grave mistake."

How do schools proceed, I asked him, considering that the number of standards are great in number and overlap, especially in content areas such as history, social studies, civics, and economics?

"That is a mistake," Kliebard observed. "I'm not a fan of lists, or of listing topics that should be covered in history or in other subjects. Merely listing the specific knowledge and understanding that students have to display it as a result of a given period of study is not my idea of providing appropriate direction. Instead, I would do it in ordinary prose—ordinary prose that addresses itself to why we want to change a subject like history and in what direction.

What kind of insights and understandings does history provide? If we can't do that, let's throw it out and forget about it.

"If we really examine why history is taught," he added, "we may come up with a different way of looking at it and valuing it. In some versions, the standards don't approach curriculum from quite that point of view. Instead, they seem to try to isolate exactly what content in the various subjects is the most important."

Sheer quantity and specificity of items that students need to learn are not just misguided educationally, he maintains, but volatile politically. "Once we start listing everything that people should know about history, some people will say: "How about this? Why isn't this included? They're studying this and not that?' So even from a political point of view, I think these sorts of standards are unwise."

Relations between Universities and Schools: Mutual Distrust

University researchers persistently try to change schools, and school staff frequently express resentment about what they perceive as a lack of understanding about schooling on the part of universities. University professors and researchers appear convinced that if only schools would follow their recommendations for change, significant accomplishments in boosting student achievement would ensue. What explains what appears to be profound mutual distrust between schools and universities?, I asked Kliebard. Why does it persist? How long-standing is it? What are its roots?

"The roots," he said thoughtfully, "lie in the respective cultures of those two institutions. University culture, particularly as it is reflected in a school of education, is very different from the culture of an elementary or secondary school. By that, I mean there are different norms, values, and a different sense of what is important and unimportant.

"University people don't appreciate sufficiently the lives of teachers. What does a teacher really think is important and valuable? Teachers, for example, will speak about classes in which students are enthusiastic, in which students show interest in what they are doing, in which lively discussions occur. Improved achievement, while paramount to university types, lies somewhere in the background.

"But in the university culture, researchers put achievement first and foremost," he added. "Researchers come up with proposals to raise achievement, and teachers resist."

Is there hope, I asked, that this negative relationship can change?

"Unfortunately," Kliebard said, "I don't see any particular signs that we are moving in that direction. The ones who talk about a change tend to be university researchers. If you attend an AERA [American Educational Research Association] meeting and are a teacher, I doubt you will find much of relevance or interest."

Lessons From Past Reforms

Are there lessons we can learn from the broad historical picture of reforms within the last 100 years, I asked, and are there more current lessons to be found from the most recent wave of reform?

"The main historical lesson—although I'm always hesitant to use the word 'lesson,'" Kliebard said carefully, "revolves around the disparity we just talked about. That is, reforms instituted strictly from above may elicit compliance for a while, but they won't have staying power. There were times when reforms emerged at the local level, and they tended to be more successful. The other view, of course, is that reform fails when it does not take into account structural issues."

Is it possible, I asked, to compare the most current wave of reform—reform since the mid-1980s—to any other particular era of reform? Does it resemble any other era?

"At the present time, we need to insure that there is academic rigor in academic subjects, which is reminiscent of the movement initiated by the National Education Act of 1958," he commented. "But this is not that era. There is no Cold War any more; much of the thinking of that period reflected Cold War thinking. Nevertheless, there are some similarities. If we think about the present era and look at the context for thinking, we see that currently business plays a much larger role in defining what is good and important."

The movement initiated by the National Education Act "ended in a whimper," Kliebard says. "It is one of the great misfortunes that we don't understand why. It may have had something to do with the Vietnam War. At the time, there was an enormous expenditure of money devoted to the creation of textbooks, teacher training, and the like."

Is this an example of the type of pendulum shifts that seem common to education?, I asked. Why do they occur? What explains them?

"I'm not sure that the metaphor of a pendulum shift quite captures exactly what happens," Kliebard responded. "If we look at the present, with the business community playing a much larger role in defining what is good and important in education, we see some similarities to other times, but it's not really the same. The context, or some of it, is different."

Rather than pendulum shifts, Kliebard prefers to think about events in education as a continuum with ebb and flow. "Depending on the conditions, one thing may be more prominent and powerful than another," he pointed out.

"The conditions right now—almost like weather conditions—are conducive towards paying attention to rigorous academic standards. But at the same time, there are policies that mitigate against that."

Using the example of a public resistant to the use of calculators in the teaching of mathematics, he says, "The public perception of true mathematics is that one is able to do calculations as opposed to the views of researchers who advocate the use of calculators. Again, this is a reflection of two different cultures at work. The academic culture believes certain things about mathematics; the popular culture looks at mathematics differently. There is a lesson in the clash of the cultures, I believe, because if there is such a public and massive lack of perception, then there is significant danger that a proposal will not succeed."

Kliebard then volunteers what he considers the most pressing problem facing American education today. "It is the growing alienation and disaffection that our students feel with respect to what they study in school," he said. "Attendance and dropout figures don't tell the full story. Even many 'good' students who score well on tests and stay in school do not really feel that what they study makes any sense.

"In many cases, they put up with school because they have been convinced by educators and/or parents that if they stick it out they will get into a good college or that their life will somehow be better in the great hereafter. The task before educators," he concluded, "is to develop a curriculum that meets the demands of modern living in a way that is visible to students. This does not mean a 'dumbing down.' Quite the contrary, it means reconstructing the academic subjects in such a way as to preserve their intellectual dignity."

Michael W. Apple:
Privatization and the
Common Good

Michael W. Apple is the John Bascom Professor of Curriculum and Instruction and Educational Policy Studies at the University of Wisconsin–Madison. A former elementary and secondary school teacher and past president of a teachers' union, Apple has worked with institutions and groups of people throughout the world to democratize educational research, policy, and practice. He has written extensively on the relationship between education and differential power. Among his more recent books are Official Knowledge: Democratic Education in a Conservative Age *(Routledge, 1993),* Democratic Schools, *coedited with James A. Beane (Association for Supervision and Curriculum Development, 1995), and* Cultural Politics and Education *(Teachers College Press, 1996).*

The push to privatize public schools through a panoply of means such as school choice, vouchers, and the spread of charter schools clearly alarms Michael W. Apple, who warns of multiple and complicated factors about which the public should be cognizant before enlisting into the troops that are marching in the privatization movement.

Why, I asked him, despite the research that shows the destructive effects of school choice on low-income students and students of color—those who may lack advocates to sponsor them into an appropriate school—does the push to privatize schooling continue to gather momentum?

"The reasons are complicated," Apple began, "and they are multiple. We live in a society where, for the past twelve years, we have been told through highly funded and widely publicized media that what is public is necessarily bad and what is private is necessarily good."

This message, he believes, has helped convince the public that public servants are inefficient, even lazy, while the private sector functions as a paragon of efficiency and clear thinking. "But people do not agree, fundamentally, that everything that is private is good and everything that is public is bad. There

185

must be an element of good sense in the argument for people to agree that private is best. People *do* understand that schools have become highly bureaucratized, that there are many instances where people are not listened to—or perceive they are not listened to—and people share a perception that this bureaucratization is immensely expensive."

These two conditions—a constant message that something is gravely wrong with public schools coupled with a growing sense that something truly is misguided about public education—create the climate that spawns the urge to privatize public schooling, Apple believes.

He also indicts what he calls "a loss of memory" about the beginnings of public schooling. "People have forgotten what an experiment public schools were, how valuable they are. They have forgotten that the public schools are one of the last places where people of different classes and ethnic groups do come together in a society that is increasingly polarized, especially polarized by class and race. This loss of memory about the public schools is ahistorical and quite damaging.

"An example is the current attack on Affirmative Action. Some of us apparently have the notion that the private sector, without any regulations, will provide opportunities for everybody. To reach that notion, we have a loss of memory about the fact that until only forty years ago, segregation was legally sanctioned in the United States."

Nostalgia for a Romanticized Past

Along with amnesia about the recent past, Apple also maintains that a collective nostalgia about a romanticized past has contributed to the public malaise that has fed directly into the urge to privatize schools. "There is a romantic belief that somehow the private sector fixes itself and that degradations of various types do not occur. We know from places that have totally privatized under the aegis of the discourse of choice that what has happened is that class, racial, and gender distinctions have been revivified, strengthened, and rebuilt—all in ways that are very destructive.

"There is a sense," he continued, "that it was so good in the past. What actually has happened has been a very real change in the ways we think about not just schools, but larger issues like democracy. Democracy used to be a political concept. People got together, built their institutions, and participated in them. Democracy wasn't simply voting; it was actually acting. But under the leadership of a coalition of forces centered on conservative beliefs, we have changed the very meaning of democracy in this society so that democracy now equates consumption practices. If I can guarantee that the world is a supermarket and you have choices, then everything is fine. Choice isn't a political concept; it's an economic concept. There again is the loss of memory. No longer are people members of any groups. They are declassed, deraced, and degendered so that we are all individuals pursuing our own profit and our own gains."

The problem with a view of the world as a supermarket full of choices, Apple contends, is that everyone is not able to partake of the choices. "There are people who can go into a supermarket and make purchases, and there are others who have to stand outside and consume with their eyes," he noted. "That is what we are going to get in the larger society, not just in education."

The Roots of Romanticism about Education

What, I asked, is the source of what appears to be the current respect—even reverence—for the private sector, for what is corporate, for the entire business community? In his reply, Apple turned to an historical overview.

"The United States is the only country of its size and type in the world that has never had a labor party," he pointed out. "We have a tradition of individualization, of people creating wealth, and of leaving people alone to create wealth. Another part of our history has been formed by dissidents, by people pointing out that there have been robber barons and other abuses. That part of our history has been lost or forgotten. Finally, there is a sense on the part of many that the state has taken over everything and that the corporate sector is efficient. This is part of a lot of lies that have been told."

A deliberate deception?, I asked.

"Let me give you an example," Apple replied. "We can take a city in the state of Wisconsin and leave it nameless. This city used to have automobile manufacturing, and its schools were basically all right. There was some mobility: kids from the working class were able to go to college if they wanted to because there was enough financial wherewithal in their families. Their parents worked in the auto plants making enough money so that if the child did well in school, he or she could go to college.

"These automobile plants wrested twenty years of things from the state, including no taxes and 'free' infrastructure development that included roads and sewers that were built for nothing. Ultimately, those plants left and went south to Mexico. From that time on, we have had communities that are totally fractured. Mental health problems are incredibly high—as are suicide rates. Moreover, many people have no sense of a future for themselves."

It is not a coincidence that student test scores plummeted under the economic circumstances that engulfed the public schools in that city, Apple believes, and he emphasizes the corporate role in carefully distancing itself from responsibility and instead placing blame on the public schools. "Corporations then say:

Why would we build new factories in those places where the school system looks very bad? These people are not well-trained; they seem not to care about work. That rhetoric cuts off the history of massive profits on the part of corporations—the whole reason they have moved south. Profits are higher if they move south, even though in the process they destroy entire communities."

The well-focused and deliberate message, Apple maintains, promulgated by corporate leaders who control the media is: Our schools are falling apart, there is no stability in the communities. "What we don't hear," he added, "is the precursor to that, which is: 'We left. Therefore the schools fell apart.'

"Part of this great faith in privatization occurs because only part of the story is being told. The destruction of community is never costed out. The cost that the state, the government, the community, and the people of these communities have to bear is never costed out and made public."

The Uneasy Coalition

A tense alliance of political groups that normally would not be allied currently huddle under the same umbrella, Apple emphasizes. "Four groups are deeply involved in the push to privatize public schools," he said. "The first are folks who are neoliberals, who really do believe that privatization is important. These are people who want education to work. The role of the school, as far they're concerned, is to produce human capital. They see kids as future workers. In order to be workers, this group wants them flexible, competitive, changeable, creative at the same time, manipulable in some ways, and moveable. This is a competitive economy, they argue, and we need people doing new things."

Apple points to the logic underpinning the neoliberal investment in education for work. "Some really believe that we can solve the unemployment rate by having people become skilled. They believe that one of the things schools should do is teach these skills. Many of them also believe that the root cause of a lack of competition is the school system."

Scanning the ten fastest-growing occupations in the U.S. would confirm their beliefs, he noted. However, this is deceptive. "If one adds up all ten of the fastest-growing occupations in the United States, the total number doesn't equal the number of janitors that are needed at the same time. The *real* labor market, not the fictitious labor market that the neoliberals are telling us about, is a labor market geared for fast food work, health care orderlies, and other service jobs."

Does he see the neoliberal views as well-intentioned? I asked.

"I don't see this as a conspiracy," he said carefully, "but I do think people don't understand what is going on. What is going on is a lie. Unfortunately, the huge number of jobs that will require high-tech skills just don't exist."

Within the neoliberals, Apple points to a subgroup that he calls "ideologues, people who are strong believers that everything must be privatized. They would say: 'Let's get the state off people's backs. Let's get them out of the business of education.'"

These ideologues see the state as an accountant, he maintains, that hands out checks to people with which they can make and pay for their choices.

Although neoliberals might sound conservative, they have taken liberal ideas about individual rights and liberties and changed them to fit into what is essentially a conservative agenda, Apple says. "Neoliberals believe that the only good state is the state that is invisible, so they have taken the old liberal ideas about individual rights and liberties and applied them to corporations. That is why they are called neoliberals. They are conservative, by and large, but they want to set loose the free market, either to control schools so that everything is done with the intent of producing workers or so that schools themselves have no control whatsoever."

Just as there are neoliberals who have taken liberal ideas and adopted them to their own devices, there are neoconservatives, he adds. "They are in favor of the market, but they don't like its chaos. In particular, they want strong government control over values and knowledge. These are people who believe that one of the reasons we are not competitive is that we have lost a sense of the Western tradition—not that people lack work skills and discipline.

"Of course," Apple continued, "the Western tradition is a fiction. There never was one standard culture in the United States. Our country always has been made up of diverse groups. Whatever connected us certainly doesn't look like this bag of virtues that the neoconservatives want everybody to know."

While the neoliberals want a very weak state, the neoconservatives want a very strong government that controls morals and values but that is weak in the market. Apple terms it "a puzzling compromise. There is tension between the two groups, but both want the market. One wants it with no-holds-barred. The other believes that a no-holds-barred approach to the market will be a disaster because people will not then learn 'appropriate' values and we can't allow that to happen."

A third group, what he terms "authoritarian populists," have assumed an increasingly important role. "These are religious fundamentalists who have to be convinced that privatization is good. These folks are very worried about their economic future. They realize that the gap between the rich and the poor in the United States is growing at a massively rapid rate."

He added, "Authoritarian populists are often middle-class folks or working-class people who see their lives genuinely falling apart."

In what ways are they populists?, I asked. "They genuinely want things for the people, they feel connected to community, and they see that their families are falling apart," Apple replied.

Authoritarian populists often are opposed—almost instinctively—to big business. "They feel that big business does not look out for the little people, and they feel like little people," he explained. "It takes hard work to get them to believe that privatization—that is, big business and setting the economy loose—will help them. For that reason, neoliberals and neoconservatives in this alliance have used very creative talk to get these people to believe that they ought to come under this big umbrella that is quite conservative.

"The way they have been convinced has been through the message that women are taking their jobs, that African-Americans, Latinos/Latinas are taking their jobs, that feminism is destroying the family—all because government is intervening."

Authoritarian populists will thus support privatization for other reasons than the neoliberals and neoconservatives, which makes for an especially tense alliance of factions. "There is no guarantee that this umbrella held over three very different groups is going to succeed in keeping people together," Apple warned.

Why has privatization become so popular at this juncture, so popular that three groups with differing agendas have joined forces to promote it?, I probed. Apple points to three major reasons.

"In order for these three very different groups to form an alliance, one group must be in leadership," he replied. "Somebody has to hold the handle of the umbrella, and it is the neoliberals, the people who really do believe that the economy will solve all problems. They are in control of much of the alliance."

It would seem, I commented, that given the alliance Apple outlines, the times are ripe for demagoguery.

"That is exactly what we're witnessing," he said. "One of the things that we're seeing is a cynical manipulation of the language of standards and a cynical manipulation of the idea that if we just fix schools, everything else will be fine. There is also a cynical manipulation of the idea of teenage pregnancy.

"There is a huge amount of duplicity as well. People know that if you put your finger to the wind you will find out what will turn people to follow you. It isn't necessarily conservative versus liberal versus moderate versus radical, either. Instead, the country has lost its way politically, so it has become cynically manipulative at the level of politics. Demagoguery becomes politics. It is impossible to win an election without engaging in duplicitous, cynical rhetoric. We see it at state government levels, where governors throughout the country talk about education but know that the crisis is not simply in schools. But, if they want to be elected, they can't blame their own policies and they can't blame economic policies, so they blame the schools. That's very cynical."

Exporting the Blame

Are the schools actually as bad as the claims that stem from a multitude of sources, including blue ribbon panels, researchers, and politicians? Do you see the schools as actually faltering in a profound way, I asked Apple, or is the message of the schools' failure part of the manipulation that he sees?

"There *has* been a process of exporting the blame," he responded. "Economically dominant groups make decisions about de-industrializing the United States, which is what has happened in many inner cities across the country. We exported millions of jobs outside the boundaries of the United States and destroyed large portions of stable communities. In that way, the crisis was exported downward. Large corporations exported the crisis onto government, saying: It's government's fault; it's too regulatory. The government can't say: Mea culpa, so it exports the crisis onto schools, welfare agencies, legal assistance, and health care, among others."

The effects on schools are profound and lasting, he maintains. "Schools in these communities are in crisis. Objectively, they have less to work with than they did before. For instance, in the farm regions of northern Wisconsin, people were getting by until the massive downturn of farm economy and globalization of markets. With the destruction of the family farm, schools now are counseling centers, suicide prevention centers, all sorts of things. The conditions in those communities are bad, and the kids bring those conditions with them when they come to school.

"It is *not* just an issue of poor black kids, as the stereotype would have it," he emphasized.

The same bleak scenario has unfolded in cities across the country as well. "There is no doubt that some schools are difficult places. I don't want to romanticize what it's like to teach in inner-city schools—I spent many years teaching in inner-city schools—although it is tremendously powerful when you succeed."

Exporting the blame quickly turns into blaming the victim, he points out. "We always hear about children at risk. To call a child at risk is one of the worst stereotypes you can put on a child. Once a kid gets a label it's very difficult to get rid of it."

Just as the public does not hear about the difficulties of losing a label once it has been applied, Apple says it does not hear about much of the creative work currently underway in public schools. "In the book I edited with James Beane, *Democratic Schools*, we told the stories of four successful, largely inner-city schools, where teachers in the face of declining economies and tense, polarized communities have made an immense impact on kids' lives. There are thousands of these kinds of schools.

"Instead, we hear that all schools are failing unless they are run by private corporations like Educational Alternatives, Inc., or Christopher Whittle. There *are* public schools that work. Yes, many schools exist under very difficult circumstances, but we need to hear the powerful stories of teachers, administrators, and community workers throughout this country who do very interesting work under extremely trying circumstances."

A Progressive Critique of Schooling Stands Interrupted

Educators who come out of the progressive tradition are caught in an odd place, Apple believes, because the conservative alliance, he says, has interrupted a more progressive critique of schooling. "Many progressive educators who critiqued schools for not always doing what their rhetoric said they were doing are now defending schools, which is a paradox. Schools are no less linked to class dynamics than they were before. They are even more racially polarized; they are more segregated than they have been in forty years in the United States. Black communities actually have less power now than they did under segregated school systems.

"We could dismantle the public schools altogether—which is what the conservative coalition would like—but the task now is in part to defend the gains that were made. Even though there is a real crisis, it would be a disaster to destroy the last public institution in this society, the last chance for people to get together."

What hope is there, I asked, that public schools will survive and even flourish in the face of the pressures visited upon them—economic and political, real or imagined?

"The only hope for the actual transformation of public schools in difficult situations," Apple responded, "is to link them much more deeply to communities and to transformations going on outside. Admittedly, it is a tightrope. In the schools that I work with, the reason that they last and make a difference is not just because of the transformation going on inside them but that they are remarkably interesting in the way they deal with communities and the risk they take with those communities. They refuse to become so popular that they create a Levittown image.

"What often happens with educational reforms," he continued, "is that one school is successful. It is seen as a house, perhaps a choice of four houses, that can be replicated across the national landscape. Schools are much too complicated for a tract-house mentality of schooling to succeed."

The Future of National Standards

Although national standards efforts have multiplied from the original content and performance standards set for mathematics, they appear to have faltered in the current political climate. Why?, I inquired.

"The only standards that had a real impact were those in math," Apple noted, "and as with any standards that are set, we have to ask: Whose knowledge is this?

"National standards were seen as important; we didn't want to lose the talent and know-how that would be required for international competition. The reasons behind national standards never were about the improvement of the general population. By and large, the reason funding went into the national standards and the reason they were seen as a warranted reform at the national level had very little to do with education, and a lot to do with the economy."

The conservative alliance that Apple spoke of earlier is responsible both for the success and current tenuous future of the national standards movement, he believes. "National standards required the idea of a strong government, that the government would establish tests, and that the standards would not be just suggested, but institutionalized within a more national system of education. In order to keep the conservative coalition together, of course the group with the most power dominates. That coalition currently is less neoconservative than it is authoritarian populist. The authoritarian populists don't want standards. They want a guarantee that the basics are taught but they don't want big government intervention."

Whether national standards are voluntary or mandated is a moot point, Apple pointed out. "The United States is the only country of its size and type that does not have a Ministry of Education. The reality of American schools, though, is that they have central control without anybody really knowing it. The central control is guaranteed by the market in textbooks."

Textbook adoption policies control schools quite effectively, he maintains. "The states of Texas, California, and Florida control the curriculum in the United States. Whatever is accepted there is accepted in the rest of the country. While there is no mandate to use textbooks, our teachers stick to textbooks and those textbooks are written with Texas and California in mind, because they control 30 percent of the textbook market.

"So we really have national standards already—hidden national standards—which are decided by the pressure groups, the alliances, the conservative politics of those two states. We are more democratic than other countries because technically we don't have central control, but we do have central control, and our central control is not carried out very democratically. Up until a few years ago, you could not speak in favor of a text in Texas. You could only speak against it at a hearing. How that counts as democratic I'm not certain."

A Common Culture: Is it Possible?

Given the increased polarization of American culture by race, class, and gender, I asked: Is it possible to attain a common culture in the United States that will respect every individual's ethnic, racial, and gender identity?

In his answer, Apple pointed to the Los Angeles Public Schools, where approximately 110 different languages are spoken by students. "The English-only movement, this fiction that believes that if we all spoke English we would have a national identity, is such a misreading of the American past that it is really quite remarkable. In Milwaukee and in New York City, for example, there were so many languages spoken and so many languages used in instruction that it's very misleading to think we all spoke the same language.

"A common culture is not something that everybody shares. It is not whether or not we all know that George Washington did or did not chop down a fictitious cherry tree. A common culture denotes the *process* by which we discover who we are. In other words, a common culture is the democratic process by which we decide what binds us together. It doesn't refer," he said with some heat, "to some imposition that an elite group somewhere imposes on these unwashed and unclean immigrants that are supposedly washing over our shore. That is the history of the United States."

So what is the solution?, I asked. Can we all live together?

"Many say we are all a nation of immigrants," Apple replied, "that we are all the same. But some of us came here in chains. That isn't being an immigrant, and we are still living the results. The only reason for a common culture is that it would put into place the process through which we could ask: Who are we? What divides us? What brings us together? Such a process would provide a context for a democratic deliberation about which knowledge we share.

"After all," he concluded, "that is the process that makes a democracy. The common culture must be temporary, because we are constantly remaking ourselves. Anything that standardizes us is un-American, because this nation is still being remade. To stop that process is to assume that once there was this 'Thing' that we all shared. It is a total misreading of history; the worst way to think about what a common culture really means. This is one of the major reasons why we must reject the manipulative politics of the conservative restoration."

Thomas A. Romberg:
Mathematics for All

Thomas A. Romberg is one of the world's foremost experts in the field of mathematics curriculum reform, and is especially well-known for his work as chair of the Curriculum and Evaluation Standards for School Mathematics *and the* Assessment Standards for School Mathematics *of the National Council of Teachers of Mathematics. For this work, the American Educational Research Association gave him both its Interpretive Scholarship and Professional Service awards in 1991. He is the Sears Roebuck Foundation–Bascom Professor in Education at the University of Wisconsin–Madison, where he directed the National Center for Research in Mathematical Sciences Education for the U.S. Department of Education from 1990–1996, and currently directs the School Mathematics and Science Achievement Center, also for the U.S. Department of Education. He is internationally well known for his study and involvement with mathematics curriculum efforts. He has had fellowships to both Australia and the USSR; has examined current work in England, Australia, the Netherlands, Russia, Sweden, Norway, Germany, Spain, and Venezuela; and collaborated with scholars at the University of Utrecht on "Mathematics in Context," a grades 5–8 realistic mathematics program.*

The development of national standards for content and performance in mathematics was long overdue, Thomas A. Romberg maintains, bolstering his argument by pointing to the curious lack of standards in American schooling—a deficit that sets the United States apart from many other countries. Although national standards in many content areas have been contested hotly on a number of fronts—from the national political arena to local school board meetings—the logic behind them, as Romberg presents it, appears solid, even immutable.

"For a variety of reasons, we had no set of content and performance standards prior to the last few years," Romberg observed. "For a set of social agencies like schools not to have sets of such standards seems rather strange. The lack of standards doesn't mean there haven't been criteria, but the criteria have been licensing criteria or criteria associated with the size or shape of buildings or electrical codes or safety criteria."

Why, if standards for content and performance are so important, have American schools neglected them?, I asked. What criteria have been used to measure student and teacher performance? What has been the alternative to a set of standards?

To Romberg, these questions are best viewed from a historical perspective. He first points out how the United States shifted from an industrial to a technological society—without a corresponding change in public schooling. "At the turn of the nineteenth to the twentieth century," he explained, "a kind of industrial model became the central feature of American educational practice, much like the assembly line notion of Henry Ford in which a given number of cars were built per day by breaking down complex tasks into individual small pieces, putting them into some order, and then doing them in that order."

This assembly-line notion of learning became the way schools were organized, Romberg points out—and may have made as little sense 100 years ago as it does currently. "Children come to school and do certain things in the first grade. In the second grade they do other things. Everything is done in a specific order. Chapters are arranged in a corresponding order in textbooks, and within chapters are the two-page spreads that delineate what will be done today and then tomorrow."

Scope and sequence became the content criteria, Romberg says, by which the curriculum was assessed as "reasonable"—as was the pace at which students could progress through it. Performance criteria became how well they achieved in contrast to other students. In that way, coverage—rather than learning—became the criterion that propelled American schools and, in fact, remains a dominant force today. "This scientific-industrial model became the central focal point of how materials were organized, the way in which content should be taught, what the level of performance should be, the pacing, and the sequencing."

He added, "But content and performance standards were not part of this."

Romberg indicts this approach as "patently absurd. It is ridiculous to hear a first-grade teacher say that she isn't supposed to deal with numbers over 99 because those are dealt with in second grade."

Part of the whole rationale behind the standards movement in mathematics, he says, was motivated by "the utter nonsense" of the tradition of American schooling. "For instance, you have to be able to do three kinds of percentage problems in seventh or eighth grade, otherwise you can't do algebra. If you aren't good at algebra, you can't do geometry. Why would those decisions be made? There certainly isn't anything empirical that indicates students have to do this. It is purely the layout of the sequence that dictates it."

The Revolution in Mathematics

In mathematics, Romberg says, the change from an industrial society to a technological society became glaringly apparent in the last twenty years—necessitating dramatic changes in the way in which mathematics is taught and learned. "At the turn of the century, mathematics was basically shopkeeper arithmetic," he noted, "with paper and pencil calculation skills as the focal point. Today, no one makes a living doing shopkeeper arithmetic.

"Instead, we need for students to understand a lot about calculation—not necessarily to be good at calculation—and be able to use the technology to do more complex calculations than could ever be done by paper and pencil. Nobody would do most of the statistics that are done today in most occupations, such as quality control or building statistical models for prediction, because it would be impossible without the availability of electronic technology."

The starting point for the revolution in mathematics, he says, was a fundamental change in the ideas that underpin the traditional mathematics curriculum. "The starting point of the NCTM (National Council of Teachers of Mathematics) *Standards* was to ask: What do we really expect students to do if they are going to be productive in the twenty-first century? Our notion was to rethink the mathematics, so we needed to rethink the important concepts in mathematics and the way in which they ought to be approached.

"Secondly, business and industry was asking for students with other kinds of mathematical background. They wanted students who knew how to build math models, for instance, to use the technology to help them solve more complex problems. They needed students who had much more statistics, a lot more experience with probability, and much more of what is called discrete mathematics."

Other factors came into play as the mathematics community began to develop their standards, Romberg says. "One was our awareness that the traditional school model holds that the mind is a muscle and it needs lots of exercise—you have students practice skills. The typical math lesson becomes the presentation of a problem, a demonstration of how to work it, and then lots of practice on many similar problems. The next day, a slight variation might be undertaken. With this approach, there is little opportunity for students to think about why they are doing what they are doing.

"There was also a prevalent assumption that mathematics could be broken into little pieces and students could be trained to become proficient in all those little pieces with the result that somehow—magically—they would be able to put the pieces together to solve problems at some future date, perhaps in college. There was no sense that what students were learning was useful for anything else; instead, it was a rite of passage."

A third influence on the standards was knowing how youth construct knowledge. "Part of the past problems with teaching math," he continued, "is the prevailing assumption that students don't know anything so you have to start by treating them as blank slates and feed them one piece after another. That isn't true. Almost all kindergartners know how to add and subtract. They may not use the symbols we use, but they certainly understand the process of taking away or adding on or comparing who is bigger or smaller. Their language is filled with comparative notions and adjectives."

Clearly, Romberg believes that educational experiences that build upon students' existing knowledge, experiences that are not isolated from one another, help construct a deeper understanding of mathematics. "The best way to get students to acquire new knowledge is to build upon the informal knowledge that they have, negotiating with them the use of common words, symbols, and rules. The language of mathematics, after all, was invented by people to represent things, just as any language was invented.

"If you can do that, the shift in psychology turns to thinking of things in wholes rather than in pieces," he added.

Learning should be viewed as the acquisition of a set of processes one can use to solve problems, Romberg believes. "The acquisition of a language for mathematics will help us solve those problems, and the best way for students to learn this language is to pose problems that give rise to the need for a symbol or a sign."

The Current Status of Standards

After the initial recognition that the mathematics standards were a massive accomplishment, I said, how have they played out? How well are educators succeeding in implementing them?

Romberg answered, "Many things happened in very positive ways. First of all, the *Standards* are a statement of the vision of where we *want* to be—how the curriculum ought to be organized, how it ought to be taught, and how it ought to be assessed."

The developers of the *Standards* for mathematics were cautious about whether the document would enjoy a warm reception from practitioners. "The history of American education being what it is, we hoped the *Standards* document would not be one of those documents that graduate students would read but that would have little impact beyond the intellectual group talking about teaching and learning—and about what things ought to be like instead of what is really going on in schools."

He added, "The intellectual history in education is filled with lots of documents that talked about the way things ought to be."

The impact of the *Standards* has been substantially larger than the mathematics community believed it would be, Romberg says. "Basically I see action at three levels. First, we see states writing state frameworks based on the *Standards*, state systemic initiatives, and urban systemic initiatives.

"Second, over forty states are developing new state assessment procedures based on the *Standards*."

Third, the local level has not lagged behind, Romberg notes. "Approximately 85 to 90 percent of the secondary teachers in this country are familiar with the *Standards*, and about half of the elementary teachers, which is remarkable. Eisenhower funds from the federal government have helped school districts do work around the *Standards*."

The extent of awareness about the *Standards*, coupled with efforts to change curriculum and pedagogy to conform to their approach to teaching and learning mathematics, amazed the developers of the *Standards*, Romberg says. "We expected it would take to the turn of the century—at least—and probably longer, before the changes could be seen completely."

But events of the last year have cast a shadow over the previously rosy picture of the mathematics standards as one reform initiative that seemed slated for success. Romberg sees the political events of the year in a larger context, as part of an ongoing dialectic within American education. "Everything in American education," he said, "has this kind of positive versus negative interaction at some point.

"At the federal level, there is the push to dismantle the Department of Education and federal involvement in education generally. Education is not the central part of that argument, but it is part of it. The initiative to dismantle federal involvement in education has a good deal to do with getting the federal government out of the states' responsibility for education. The Constitution does say that education is a state responsibility."

But Romberg sees the push to dismantle the federal role in education as not aimed at mathematics reform, per se, but at the cost of education and what he calls "philosophical views."

"Although it may not have to do specifically with the *Standards*," he added, "this push to dismantle federal involvement in education certainly is having an impact on some things that are happening in relationship to the *Standards* and to the curriculum and tests that are being developed. Part of what is going on is a conservative statement that says: Why do the schools need to be different? There are," he emphasized, "a *lot* of people out there who believe if it was good enough for me it should be good enough for my children. One colleague describes this attitude in terms of what would happen if Rip Van Winkle fell asleep in 1950 and awoke today. He would have a hard time in most businesses and industries—but he would feel comfortable in schools."

What about the fact that many people had negative experiences with math?, I asked. Wouldn't that make them desire a different experience for their children?

Romberg laughed. "I received many letters after the *Standards* came out," he said, "from people asking why we were trying to make math fun or interesting. I have one that actually says that life is full of hard work, drudgery, tragedy, and failure and the one place to learn it in school is in math class. It is absurd."

This hearkening back to a past now perceived as better than the imperfect present is a wave of misplaced nostalgia that has a stultifying effect on nascent reforms, he observed. "Many people don't realize that in 1951 less than 60 percent of American students finished high school. Instead they think: Weren't those wonderful days?

"Furthermore, the math curriculum has been geared for one track, the college-preparatory math-science student. Historically there has never been another track, other than the expectation that by the end of the eighth grade one ought to be good at shopkeeper arithmetic. That combination—everybody is going to be good at arithmetic coupled with the high school expectations that say there is only one track—creates no alternatives."

Observing what other countries do in mathematics heightens the discrepancy, he added. "Other countries have never organized math the way that we do. Very often, particularly since World War II, they have developed programs for students who are not necessarily college-bound math-science students. These are programs that do something with these students. Only recently have we begun to think about alternatives to the college-preparatory program in this country."

Is the parental criticism coming from any particular end of the political spectrum?, I inquired.

"It's everywhere," Romberg said, "but it comes primarily from two groups. One group are upper middle-class parents who expect their kids to go to college and want to make sure that they get high SAT scores. They are not as concerned that the child learns anything as they are worried about will he or she score high enough to get into Harvard, Yale, or Brown. They are concerned about their child's test scores as early as the second grade. They fail to understand that the tests are changing too.

"In one sense they're absolutely right. The *Standards* were developed as a basis for talking about mathematics for all, and if the student truly is very talented in math, he or she ought to go considerably beyond what is listed in the *Standards*."

So the *Standards* do not speak to the elite?, I asked.

"They don't," he said, "and one of the criticisms that people in university math departments have advanced has been that the *Standards* are all right, but what about the students who are going to be math majors? They complain about the students in the rest of the university who have to take a math course and struggle with it, but they do want the best students for their honors courses in math."

The second camp of criticisms stem from parents of students who have been labeled as low achievers. "These are the students who have been sorted out and put into remedial courses. For example, some people in the African-American community are criticizing the *Standards*, arguing that we just now have begun to figure out how to deal with getting kids to meet the old criteria, improving their test scores—and now you're changing the rules on us."

As an example, he points to one group that argues that algebra is "a social right. They don't want us to remove algebra courses as they have been taught in high school now that they have their kids ready to take them."

He noted, "Actually, algebra ought to begin in 4th or 5th grade because all one is dealing with are variables. Students understand that they differ in height, for instance. We can use the letter 'h' for height and plug in any value we want, depending on whose height we are talking about. In that way, we can begin to deal with ideas that lead to algebra very early. Most of the algebra we teach in a 9th-grade course typically can be covered in an informal, intuitive way in 5th, 6th, and 7th grade."

Another criticism of the *Standards* is that parents see them as diverting attention from the goal of improving test scores. "No one is against improving test scores," Romberg observed, "except we would like the test to measure what is important. If the items on the test aren't about important mathematics, I don't care about improving student performance on those items. Why include things like some of the word problems? Nobody does those problems, except in math classes. Instead, there are real problems they can figure out."

The Future of Mathematics Reform

What does the future hold?, I asked.

"It will be interesting to see what will happen when the new curriculum funded by NSF (the National Science Foundation) based on the *Standards* start becoming available for use and teachers start using them on a wide scale. Overall, the math profession is committed to this reform. I don't see the profession backing away from it. I see much more effort going into teacher training, into professional development, and into states changing a lot of their policies on assessment.

"The reform effort will continue," he added evenly. "It will experience problems. There will be negotiation back and forth. As an example, look at the use of the calculator. Many people assume that we are never going to teach kids anything about calculation other than how to grab this device and operate it. But nowhere in the *Standards* did we argue that the ideas of estimation and mental calculation aren't important. All we *are* arguing is that if society has a tool like a calculator that people use regularly, kids ought to have the same tool. They ought not be denied the opportunity to have the tool.

"On the other hand," he continued, "they ought to understand what it means to add and subtract. They ought to understand what a reasonable answer is when they do use this tool. Calculators can be wrong! It's absolutely critical that we put more emphasis on ways to approximate and estimate answers. I would be disappointed if someone couldn't shift a decimal point and figure out the cost of something times ten. Or if something is 10 percent off, one should be able to figure out how much that is. We want students to have a variety of calculation skills."

Overall, Romberg remains upbeat about the future. "The impetus for reform is going ahead faster and stronger than I would have guessed five years ago," he said. "There is a tendency to assume we have solved everything in three to four years, but we argued when we wrote the *Standards* that it would take twenty years or so. We have made very good progress.

"But many stupid things have been done. The portrayals that we no longer teach mathematics, that it's fun and games, are misguided, as is the assumption that we're advocating grade inflation so that everybody passes. Instead, we're trying to set higher standards for all students," he concluded, "we're trying to push a lot of ideas that have not been taught before and that are so important in today's world."

Fred M. Newmann:
Restructuring for Authenticity

Fred M. Newmann, Professor of Curriculum and Instruction, University of Wisconsin–Madison, directed the National Center on Effective Secondary Schools and the Center on Organization and Restructuring of Schools, both funded by the U.S. Department of Education's Office of Educational Research and Improvement. With thirty years experience in school-reform research, curriculum development, and teacher education, he has contributed new curriculum in the analysis of public controversy and community-based learning and innovative ways of conceptualizing and scoring authentic instruction, assessment tasks, and student work. In addition to these topics, his publications deal with curriculum for citizenship, higher-order thinking in social studies, education and the building of community, and student engagement in secondary schools. His recent research, focusing on the subjects of mathematics and social studies, asks how restructuring in schools nationwide affects student achievement and what must be done to help schools advance excellence and equity in student achievement.

Fred M. Newmann's perspective on educational reform is fortified by ten years of intricate, federally funded research: first, as director of the National Center on Effective Secondary Schools he oversaw and participated in a complicated five-year program of research on secondary schools; second, as director and a key researcher at the Center on the Organization and Restructuring of Schools, he played a similar role in an even more elaborate program of research that sought to discover key structural levers that can boost student achievement. Permeating the research agenda in which he has been involved for the past decade has been the belief that the high quality of students' intellectual learning must remain front and center of any reform or school improvement effort.

After such a substantive program of research that has included observations of restructured schools nationwide, what have been the key lessons you have learned?, I asked. Have there been any surprises? What findings have the power to inform the progress of educational reform?

Lessons from Restructured Schools

In his reply, Newmann pointed first to an overemphasis on structural variables in current reform efforts—an emphasis that can leave the intellectual rigor and power of student learning virtually untouched.

"The main lesson that I have learned," he began, "is that as we attempt educational reform, educational change, and educational improvement, we often become more preoccupied with the specific techniques, structures, and administrative arrangements. The problem with implementation of the 'hot-button' reforms is that we have become so preoccupied with the problem of implementing their techniques and procedures that we lose sight of the basic issue: deciding what we mean by high-level intellectual learning for kids."

As an example, Newmann pointed to a typical scenario one might encounter with a school that has decided to restructure its schedule, first by lengthening its class periods from 45 minutes to 90 minutes. "Initially, the intent of that type of reform was to give teachers more opportunity to study topics in depth with their students instead of rushing off to another class—something especially needed in lab classes, but applicable to other classes as well," he said.

In such a school, it is likely that a number of teachers do not have any particular vision of intellectual learning for their students, he points out. Instead, they may be committed to what he terms "survey knowledge, rather than a philosophy of depth in the curriculum."

As these teachers begin to implement a schedule change that necessitates a whole new way of conceptualizing their instruction and curriculum, managing the innovation can distract them further from a careful examination of the intellectual quality of what students learn. "They become preoccupied with how to cope with the kids for 90 minutes instead of 45 minutes; how to manage this innovation becomes their major concern. Their attention is deflected from the reason for the change, which is to enhance the intellectual quality of the kids' experience in school."

Political tension develops as teachers polarize around their positions, still not engaged in consideration of kids' learning, but worried about how a change in their structural arrangements will affect them personally. "Who is in favor of the 90-minute period?," Newmann asked. "Who is against the 90-minute period? Those in favor of the 90-minute period spend a lot of their energy trying to win support for that particular innovation, trying to win over their colleagues. Those who are against the innovation end up thinking of good reasons why they shouldn't adopt the innovation.

"As a result," he continued," the innovation itself becomes the major focus for discussion, conflict, and energy. A number of innovations, whether they are site-based management, more flexible scheduling, moving to heterogeneous grouping or team teaching, moving to portfolios, begin to take on a life of their own. Almost any innovation acquires its own life in terms of political issues, management issues, and implementation issues."

As those interested in reform and change begin to enact these reforms, Newmann believes that the main reason for the reforms can be abandoned. "We end up making technique and the mechanics of reform more important than the intellectual quality of kids' learning," he added.

The Intellectual Quality of Students' Learning

Awareness of this too-frequent phenomenon in schools led Newmann and his colleagues in the Center on Organization and Restructuring of Schools (CORS) to articulate a vision for the intellectual quality of students' learning, followed by suggested conditions that schools need in order to promote that vision. "We found that a number of structural innovations, like site-based management and team teaching, can be helpful. They can keep people focused on the quality of student learning, but they are helpful only when the school itself has a human commitment to a vision of student learning. They are helpful only when that vision," he added, "drives the use of these innovations. Too often the innovations are adopted because that's the fashionable thing to do in the current reform."

How can commitment to a vision of student learning be discerned?, I asked. Aren't there school staff who might voice a commitment that they don't possess or only feel at the most superficial level?

Newmann explained the research design carried out by CORS researchers, which included team visits to schools for a two-week period. "During our visits, we asked teachers what their goals were; why they were doing what they were doing; and we asked them about the major issues in the school. We observed teachers meeting in teams and in faculty meetings."

What he and his colleagues found, he says, varied: in some schools most of the debate and discussion among teachers centered on issues related to the intellectual quality of students' learning—and in other schools, staff were preoccupied with completely different issues. "For example, in some schools," Newmann noted, "we found that most faculty dialogue, staff development, and basic concerns centered around a vision for students' intellectual learning, for the quality of that learning. In other schools, staff would focus on issues such as parental support given kids at home. The latter problem is not insignificant, but it is an example of issues that detract from curricular and structural problems."

Articulating the Vision

As Newmann's team of researchers began to articulate their own vision of intellectual quality of student learning, they mapped backwards, first analyzing significant adult intellectual accomplishment. "We asked ourselves: What are some of the characteristics of significant adult accomplishments that involve serious intellectual work? We came up with three major characteristics.

"First, adults with a record of accomplishment are generally involved in constructing knowledge rather than reproducing specific bits of knowledge already developed by other people. If we think about the work that attorneys, journalists, or interior designers do, we see that they have to employ some novel kinds of thinking and organization of information—rather than regurgitation or reproduction of the work of others."

The second characteristic, he says, involves building a bridge from prior knowledge to something new. "We call it disciplined inquiry, which means that there is a systematic type of inquiry that is built on prior knowledge. Problems are usually approached in some depth and in some complexity rather than in a way that suggests superficial familiarity with a lot of isolated knowledge. These adults also have some kind of elaborate form of communication, a symbol system or a complex language system that they use when learning more about the problem that they are studying. This language system is used to communicate their findings."

Finally, the product of their work—whether it is a newspaper article or an argument in front of a judge—has some value to others. "In short, their intellectual products have value beyond demonstrating success in school," Newmann observed. "These three characteristics constitute a vision for high-quality intellectual experiences that we should strive to achieve for all kids."

Translating the Vision into Practice

How can this vision—which is clearly a complicated one—be translated into the everyday school lives of students?, I asked.

"We were very interested in whether restructuring initiatives actually improved the quality of instruction for students of all ages," Newmann said, "but we needed some vision of what we meant by the quality of instruction. We translated this general vision of achievement into specific standards that we used to examine what was going on in classes. To what extent were kids constructing knowledge in their lessons? Were they using disciplined inquiry? Were they applying this knowledge to issues in the real world?"

The researchers created a measurement scheme that they used to look at the quality of instruction provided by teachers and the types of assessment they used to measure student learning. "Using that scheme," Newmann added, "we tried to determine if restructuring innovations such as site-based management and cooperative learning helped schools in practicing what we call 'authentic pedagogy.'"

The key finding, he reports, was that authentic instruction in a class or school boosts achievement for students. This result was confirmed through systematic study of over 130 elementary, middle, and high school classes—half in math, half in social studies—in 24 restructured schools nationwide and it also held up in 800 high schools that were part of the National Education Longitudinal Study of 1988.[1]

He quickly added, "If that is true, what are the conditions in the school that tend to support authentic pedagogy? That was the next part of our research."

To begin with, schools need a united staff with a clear sense of purpose about what kids need to learn, he emphasizes. "Schools need a sense of professional community," he said. "Authentic pedagogy is very difficult and very complex. It is not a recipe that can be used in a formulaic way to teach every class in the same way. Teachers have to spend a lot of time thinking, planning, revising their plans—and they need help from one another to do it well."

In order to achieve professional community, genuine collaboration between administrators and teachers needs to occur. A third hallmark of the conditions in the school that support authentic pedagogy is a teacher-held sense of collective responsibility for all students in the school.

"In other words," Newmann pointed out, "everybody has to work together for the benefit of the school. We call that collective responsibility."

Achieving Professional Community

The CORS researchers found that schools with higher levels of professional community among staff were more likely to offer authentic pedagogy; correspondingly, students in those schools had higher levels of achievement.

How did the more successful schools achieve professional community?, I asked. What particular blend of human resources and structural variables was key to improved intellectual quality of student learning? Is this a mixture that is difficult to realize in conventionally structured schools?

"There are certain structural conditions that seem particularly important," Newmann replied. "If the school had autonomy and authority to hire the staff that it wanted, that was one. Another was that interdependent structures were in place in the school to promote collaboration, such as teachers working in teams. The school did not rely on isolated individual teachers; it assumed that teachers and administrators had to work in groups. A third condition we found is that smaller schools, in general, made it more possible for teachers to work together.

But again, these structural attributes alone were no formula for success."

Staff who are committed to working with students and who are willing to resolve conflicts that arise in the course of school life are critical, he emphasizes. "You have to start with a certain minimal level of individual commitment, talent, and resources," Newmann commented. "Leadership can help to enhance these resources and build the trust that's needed for collaboration. Finally, when you add some of these structural conditions on to that, this really helps build professional community."

The Role of External Agencies

The leadership of the principal plays an important role in coalescing all these disparate elements, but so do external agencies, Newmann points out. "We know that schools are nested in a whole array of influences, whether they are district policies, parents, and reform efforts all over the country. Schools receive all kinds of external signals about what they ought to do or ought not to do. For this reason, we were interested in what kinds of actions external agencies might undertake to help schools promote professional community."

Four basic actions on the part of external agencies, the researchers discovered, had helpful impact on schools. "The first was setting intellectual standards for student achievement," Newmann noted. "There are a variety of efforts by states and professional associations to try to define higher standards for what students should know and be able to do. Schools are not blindly adopting prescriptions from these external sources, but we found that a number of these efforts appeared to enhance dialogue within the school about expectations for students."

Continuous staff development that aided schools in implementing some type of innovation was also helpful, he noted. "This type of staff development wasn't a one-time only workshop, but was built on some type of continuous program that focused on curriculum or assessment and went on for a period of years."

Deregulation of schools—or autonomy from external demands—was a third helpful factor in furthering professional community. "Freedom from regulations gives schools the autonomy to develop their own vision," he added.

Finally, parental involvement that was organized to be helpful to the goals of the school was another assisting factor. "We found parental involvement to be mixed," Newmann acknowledged. "In some schools, parents were united and highly supportive. They assisted the school in a variety of ways, from giving helpful feedback to raising money to fighting political battles on the school's part if the school was in jeopardy because of district cutbacks or other actions.

"There were other cases where parents were in conflict over the school's goals. For example, in one school there was a big fight over the merits of phonics instruction versus whole language instruction. This sort of conflict among parents can also polarize the faculty and create a lot of problems."

In short, an intellectual vision for learning, standards for pedagogy consistent with the vision, professional community, and external support are central to the CORS findings of how schools might restructure to provide powerful intellectual learning experiences to children.

Restructuring and Diversity

I asked Newmann if he and his colleagues observed any appreciable differences in student achievement that could be attributed to their diversity. Was authentic pedagogy sufficient to raise the achievement of all students, or where there gaps that corresponded to student diversity or social class?, I inquired.

"With our various studies combined, we were looking at approximately 1,500 schools nationwide," he replied, "with a tremendous variety of social composition. We wanted to find out if authentic pedagogy was restricted to affluent, high-achieving students or if it is possible to deliver authentic pedagogy to students of all races and socioeconomic classes.

"We found," he said, "that it is possible. In the school restructuring study where we chose schools deliberately because they were restructured, the degree of authentic pedagogy was not related to the social origins of the students. This was encouraging.

"Another question is whether the benefits of authentic pedagogy are equal for all students regardless of race and social class. Is it possible even if authentic pedagogy is delivered equally, that whites will learn more than African-Americans? We found in the school restructuring study that authentic pedagogy has equitable benefits, which are about equal, once you control for students' initial level of achievement. Authentic pedagogy does not discriminate in favor of white, affluent kids."

Did you find that authentic instruction, just by its very nature, would adjust to students to become "culturally relevant," to use Gloria Ladson-Billings' term?, I asked.

"We didn't study that explicitly," he responded, "but I believe it does. If teachers are providing authentic instruction, they have to take kids seriously. They have to listen to them, they have to respond, they have to give students feedback that is meaningful to them. A number of the schools we studied were explicitly concerned with trying to be culturally responsive. One could infer from our findings that because students from different cultural groups benefit equally, their teachers are more culturally sensitive."

Best Practices in Staff Development

Although Newmann points to continuous staff development as especially helpful to encourage professional community and authentic pedagogy, what specific experiences provided by staff development are most helpful?, I inquired. Second, what explains the temporary success of some of the worst types of staff development—programs designed as templates to place over any school without attention to its context?

"There was no single approach to staff development in the schools that we studied," Newmann explained. "In one school district, for example, they had external professional development called Applied Learning. All teachers were required to participate in summer institutes and follow-up work during the year. Teachers also worked a good deal developing their own materials and talking about their vision.

"In another school, there was little external influence on staff development. Much of it occurred during their weekly team meetings when they met to work on developing interdisciplinary curriculum. There was no external guru working with them, but they had the time and the kind of work structure that permitted their own professional development activities to flourish."

Overall, Newmann selects two characteristics as hallmarks of useful staff development. "Teachers need a lot of time to share their practice with one another," he observed, "and they need to stick with the problem that they are working on for a long period of time. An approach where one month they work on portfolio assessment and the next on communication skills is not what they need. Schools varied considerably in whether professional growth was stimulated mainly by an external agency or a home-grown effort in the school."

The fleeting success of superficial, external staff development programs, Newmann believes, can probably be attributed to the fact that they momentarily provide a common vocabulary for school staff. "Sometimes a common language helps bring people together in a school and helps them acquire new ideas," he said thoughtfully.

Is it necessary, I asked, to have one person or a small group of people who function as catalysts to keep people moving, to keep the impetus growing? What mitigates against a group of teachers working together and not making progress?

"Research literature," Newmann observed, "suggests that most groups are productive because there is leadership in the group that keeps the group on track. In any group, there is a need for leadership that keeps people on task, whether it is a teacher within a group or an external facilitator."

Authentic Assessment

Authentic pedagogy and heightened intellectual quality of student learning require, somewhat inexorably, forms of assessment that differ from standardized tests. While many practitioners will report that they are working with forms of authentic assessment, they may or may not be accomplishing what experts on authentic assessment believe is necessary. What exactly is authentic assessment?, I asked. What steps do school staff have to go through in order to develop assessments that are authentic? What criteria do they need to consider?

Newmann, who has done pioneering work on authentic assessment, responded, "Authentic assessment is basically making demands on students that are inherent in doing authentic intellectual work. In other words, the tests or projects you use to grade students must require construction of knowledge, disciplined inquiry, and the problems posed should connect to the real world. If a teacher says that she's using portfolios, that is not necessarily authentic assessment. We need to know what kind of work was part of the portfolio. Similarly, to know whether performance assessment is authentic we need to know more about the intellectual demands required in the performance."

He draws careful distinctions between authentic assessment and techniques that help reach it. "Authentic assessment," he continued, "has to transcend those techniques. Giving a speech is a technique; developing a portfolio is a technique. In our work, we have tried to develop standards that describe the intellectual quality of what people do. So the question becomes: In terms of the construction of knowledge, are you organizing, interpreting, and manipulating information?

"If a kid has submitted a portfolio, it may be only a scrapbook of his work. If the individual entries in the scrapbook never require him to do any thinking, the task is not authentic."

To determine whether assessment is authentic requires rigorous examination of the intellectual quality of the work, Newmann insists. "Have the kids had to organize information? Have they considered alternative points of view? Did they have to show some understanding of disciplinary content? Were they required to produce some elaborated form of communication? Did they connect their work to some problem in the real world?"

National Standards: An Assessment

The work in which Newmann has been engaged for the past five years has necessitated the development of standards. Given your work developing standards for authentic pedagogy, how do you assess the current national standards movement?, I asked. What have you learned in your own work developing standards that informs your perspective on the national standards movement?

"It is useful to have a standards movement," Newmann responded, "because it helps us think more about the intellectual quality of work. It is healthy to create serious national dialogue about it. One problem, however, is that you can't settle the issue of what kids ought to know and be able to do through empirical research. The ultimate decisions on curriculum content are choices that reflect cultural taste, politics, or some other factors. It's not as if you can have some dispassionate curriculum wizard telling you, through research, what kids ought to study."

Instead, a democratic society, he believes, should support many people participating in decisions about what youth should learn; these decisions must remain flexible—open to change and refinement. "This is especially necessary in a society with great inequalities of wealth and power," he said. "The jury is still out over whether a reasonable consensus can be reached over these standards.

"The second problem, which is somewhat related to the first problem, is that too many 'standards' have been proposed in the content areas. If you take all of these documents seriously, there is too much to learn. The standards movement has not resolved the problem of selecting what really needs to be understood in depth as opposed to just prescribing these voluminous encyclopedias of all the things that people need to learn. That is one of the reasons that a number of schools do not find the existing lists of standards helpful: They see that too much is required. The resistance is not to the principle of standard-setting, but to the results of the exercise so far: standard-setting hasn't addressed the issues of state or national consensus and quantity."

While the standards developed by CORS researchers do not specify what content students should learn, they could be applied as standards to judge the specific content standards developed by other groups, Newmann believes. "For example, some group might say that all kids need to understand the First Amendment of the Constitution. Our standards indicate how to frame these understandings as high-quality intellectual work. Otherwise, the content of the standards themselves could be interpreted in a fairly traditional way in which lots of information is transmitted and kids memorize it.

"In contrast," he continued, "our standards transcend specific content. They say, in effect: 'If you teach the First Amendment or the Fourteenth Amendment, you need to do it in a way that it promotes construction of knowledge, disciplined inquiry, and so on.'"

The Push to Privatize Schooling

Given his many years researching schools nationally, I asked Newmann for his perspective on privatization of schooling and the current push it is receiving from its many advocates. Why now?, I asked. What is so attractive about privatizing schooling? What logic suggests it will have different effects than public schooling? Why has privatization captured so many people's imaginations and so much public attention?

"The evidence that public schools have not done a great job for lots of kids has contributed to the interest in privatization," Newmann said. "There is a belief that the current system hasn't worked so we need to change it. There is also a naive notion that the market is going to solve this problem. People who believe in the market maintain that if we give people more choice and more competition, that will enhance the quality of education. Their assumption is that the customer or the whole market mechanism will produce higher quality. The combination of disillusionment with the existing system and faith in the market as an alternative system are two reasons why privatization is favored."

But he strongly disagrees, speaking again of the role of democracy in education. "Privatization is a major mistake," he concluded. "Public education has to be considered a public good, because in a democracy, we all need highly educated citizens. The major argument for education in a democracy is that an educated public is necessary in order to secure liberty and equality for all citizens in this society. To the extent that education becomes privatized, it means that education is an individual commodity to be chosen by consumers based on what they want for *themselves*, not on what all members of society need to insure equal dignity for all.

"Choice within a system that has public standards for all students' learning and is publicly financed is consistent with education for democracy. In this case, parents and citizens reflect first of all about the education of *everyone*. Within this framework they can then choose the school that seems best for their children. But when public money is used to support only the private educational aspirations of consumers, this undermines the basic reason for education in a democracy."

Note

1. National Education Longitudinal Study of 1988.

Theodore R. Sizer:
The Constancy of Change

Theodore R. Sizer, a long-time authority on educational reform, is University Professor of Education and Chairman of the Coalition of Essential Schools at Brown University. Throughout his distinguished career, Sizer has been at the forefront of issues confronting educators interested in and directly working on school reform. In addition to his positions at Brown University in the Education Department and with the Coalition of Essential Schools, Sizer became director of the Annenberg Institute for School Reform in 1994. Former Dean of the Graduate School of Education at Harvard University and also former Headmaster of Phillips Academy (Andover), Sizer has been the recipient of numerous honors, including honorary degrees from several colleges and universities, a Guggenheim Fellowship, the James Bryant Conant Award from the Education Commission of the States (1992), the Distinguished Service Award of the Council of Chief State School Officers, and citations from organizations which include the American Federation of Teachers, the National Association of Secondary School Teachers, and Phillips Exeter Academy. Sizer is well known for his books, including Horace's Compromise: The Dilemma of the American High School *(1984),* Horace's School: Redesigning the American High School *(1992), and* Horace's Hope: What Works for the American High School *(1996). In his work with the Coalition and the Annenberg Institute for School Reform, he is engaged directly in furthering school restructuring efforts nationwide.*

Theodore R. Sizer has been at the forefront of educational reform for a considerable period of time, persistently advocating for an education of depth and understanding—and seeking, with his colleagues, to bring about substantive and lasting change in American education. In his work with the Coalition of Essential Schools, what have you found to be the most profound lessons about schools and reform?, I asked him. Have there been significant surprises?

"There have been many surprises," Sizer said, "most of all, the relentless momentum of the usual ways in which schools work. This momentum continues even though those ways don't stand up to common sense. Overall," he added, "I have been surprised most by the tenacious hold of familiar practice."

Why is practice so tenacious in its habits, so resistant to change?, I inquired.

"One way of looking at it," Sizer said, "is that the familiar way of doing things is tenacious because high school is a place where rituals abound. People don't tamper with rituals easily. Rituals, almost by definition, don't follow common sense. Instead, they have independent legitimization. If you don't have grade levels, how do you know who is going to go to the junior prom? That is the kind of idiotic reaction one encounters. Or, if you say, 'How can you have an English department that deals only with language and which resolutely puts off other forms of human expression,' the response typically is: 'We always have English departments.' End of conversation."

He added with some empathy, "Part of the resistance is fear, and one cause of the fear is confusion. Schools are such complicated places, so basically understaffed. They can't afford confusion. There is a common attitude which says: 'I know what I have to do and I will do it. Don't suggest that what I'm doing doesn't make sense. And certainly, don't tell me that, because if you do, you will have to show me better ways to do it. You need to prove to me that the public wants it—and it must be convincingly successful almost instantly.'"

But Sizer welcomes confusion as the launch pad for action. In a time when the public appears to want certain things from public schools, principals and administrators specify administrative goals that may be quite different from the goals of teachers, and state policy mandates a different course of action, how does a school proceed?, I inquired.

"That confusion is a magnificent opening," he pointed out. "Confusion increases as people become clear about what they don't want and what they do want. People want to be relieved from confusion, and that urge can nudge change into place. What I hear from school people that I most admire is the following: 'Think hard about these issues. Work collectively on them, figure out the best thing to do, and then do it without apology.'"

How important is a leader in serving as a catalyst for significant change?, I asked. Necessary or not always necessary?

"Sometimes leaders can be plural," Sizer commented, "but it depends. It is very hard to start any real change with a group. Somebody has to have the initiative to gather some folks to expand and shape that, and then it becomes a group. In other words," he said pragmatically, "someone has to call the meetings."

Reforms and Leadership

Current reforms, I said, seem to have an identifiable leader—whether it is Sizer or James Comer or Robert Slavin. How necessary is it to have that kind of leader to accomplish substantive reform? Historically, have successful reforms always had an identifiable leader who urged the reform forward?

To Sizer, there is a measurable difference between a leader and a person who articulates ideas. "Dewey was never a leader," he stated. "He had a project; he had a fountain of ideas for half a century.

"I absolutely cringe," he said candidly, "when people refer to the Coalition as 'Sizer's Coalition' or 'Sizer's Project.' First of all, it's not accurate, and secondly, it sends absolutely the wrong message about me and about my intentions. The Coalition already is a collective. Debbie Meier and other principals have voices that are stronger than mine. There is a chorus of voices, not just mine, and I take enormous pleasure in that. It's exactly what should happen."

Do you reject the idea that you're the leader of the Coalition of Essential Schools?, I asked.

"I reject," Sizer replied, "the statement that I am *the* leader of it. I'm now a part of a middle-sized chorus. We play different instruments and sing in different registers. The articulate school people have a legitimacy that I don't have. I haven't run a school since 1981. They still run schools or ran them until very recently. Consequently, very skeptical people are going to be more persuaded by them saying: 'Look at the kids before the school changed and look at the kids after the school changed. Tell me, if you can, if the school doesn't work.'"

The Success of Educational Reform

Given that the history of educational reform in the United States, when taken on a case-by-case basis, is not particularly heartening, do you ever feel discouraged or downhearted about your work with the Coalition?, I asked.

"No," Sizer responded. "I think reform has been enormously successful. In the United States, people started talking about mass education at public expense in the late 1880s. They were called Communists at that time. But by World War I, they were well on the way to having the framework of a free, open-access public system. By the early 1960s, they had achieved it. The overwhelming majority of the population had access to a public free education through grade 12 after World War II. At the same time, the school population was exploding in size.

"Actually," he expanded, "what was accomplished for education is one of the most remarkable examples of social welfare reform in the history of any democracy. Now, were the schools worthy of respect? Many were not. But we Americans constantly tend to underestimate the accomplishment of providing educational access for every child, even the ones who live on the little island off Maine or in remote Montana. Even these children have access to more or less formal primary and secondary education, at no cost.

"In the sweep of time," he continued, "real accomplishment is most apparent after World War II. I look at the accomplishment of that time and can only believe that if the people want to do something, they can do it. That history gives me hope. If you look at history on a shorter-term basis, you get too quickly depressed. But people tend to say: 'They've been working at this for five years. Can you show the results?'"

Such a short-sighted view clearly does not please Sizer, who says: "I understand the politics behind that but I resent the substance. It trivializes what a serious education is. What we really care about in this country is intellectual habits—back to my friend Mr. Dewey for a moment—and whether the graduates of our schools habitually use their minds in thoughtful and informed ways. That's the whole ball game," he added bluntly. "People who run around with all their measurements aren't talking about, to use a familiar phrase, 'higher order thinking skills.' We're measuring the wrong things; talking about winners or losers on basically trivial measures. Is that depressing? Yes, it is."

Superficial vs. Substantive Change

How do you explain, I asked, the fleeting success or popularity of some very superficial school improvement efforts? What accounts for their moment in the sun—their fifteen minutes of fame?

"One way to get success in a short-term program," Sizer observed, "is to write the test in the beginning. If I write the test, I'll show improvement in test scores in three years. Or, if you give me a relatively straightforward test of certain kinds of thinking skills, give me the resources to drill the kids in those and I'll show you success."

But the popularity of the superficial springs from different sources, he says. "It has to do with the basic attitudes of the system itself. At the turn of the century, an era of explosive growth of high schools, scientifically managed public hierarchies relatively immune from politics were considered the highest sources of virtue. That whole system, dependent on a docile and reactive teaching force, was widely replicated and thus quite influential.

"Yet those of us who teach kids know that we make the most important decisions, as far as the success and failure of students, and thus of the system, is concerned. Yet the system is set up in such a way that we are both denied much power to control the shape of those decisions and also are barely consulted about what those decisions might be. Instead, everything is top-down. 'We have a workshop for you to attend. We picked it because you need it.'

"This is profoundly disrespectful," he said with distaste. "It also doesn't reflect the conditions of any one school, which would allow those particular teachers to maneuver on behalf of a particular group of kids and parents. The system is set up poorly. Its power rests in the wrong place. This frustrates teachers, who become angry or cynical or both."

Does the top-down approach to school reform, the prescriptive placing of a uniform template over very different schools, contribute to the common attitude of teachers that once again they must endure—and outlast—a change effort?, I inquired.

"They end up saying: 'I'll close the classroom door and do what I want,'" Sizer replied. "The constant testing and trivialization is frustrating as well. On the other hand, most people realize that when all the testing is completed, poor kids do poorly and rich kids do better. So if I teach poor kids, they won't score well anyway. It doesn't make much difference if I do anything that I learned in that workshop because most assessment systems won't reach the talent of low-income kids."

Reform as Diversion

Fred Newmann has expressed the belief that attention to reform, particularly structural variables such as class size, team teaching, or cooperative learning, can divert teachers from paying sufficient attention to the intellectual quality of student learning, I commented. Do you agree? What is your perspective on reform as a diversionary activity?

"I agree with him, based on my experience prior to starting the Coalition," Sizer said. "That is why the Coalition has emphasized exhibitions of student work. What, in fact, are kids learning and how are they performing academically? This becomes constant, on the table, and a driving force in the development of what the faculty does. It is much easier to talk about the details, such as whether or not to have Advanced Placement courses, than it is to look at a stack of randomly collected essays to determine if they are good or not. Not only the exhibitions are important, but how they are assessed is very important—how one decides what is better than another and on what basis."

How do school staff further exhibitions of student learning given the tremendous, constant pressure upon them to raise standardized test scores?, I asked Sizer.

"If the system doesn't respect the students' real work and, in its place, the tokens of that work, it puts the teachers in a terrible bind," he commented. "A lot of Coalition schools simply do not and cannot move forward for that reason.

"The majority of schools that have plunged into the work of the Coalition," he said frankly, "have not been successful. There are all kinds of reasons; this is one of them. That is, the incentive system within the district or state rewards something quite different than exhibitions of students' real work. This is the poignant reality for a very substantial portion of our schools. They are fighting a system and, at the same time, fighting their own traditions which they have inherited. They end up battling on two fronts."

Changing the Quality of School Life

In a previous interview with me (Lockwood 1994a), Sizer commented that some schools are so dysfunctional in the quality of the human relationships within the school that they can only benefit from closing down and reopening with a totally different configuration of staff. Short of such extreme measures, how do Coalition staff deal with dysfunctional human relationships within schools?, I asked.

"One way is to push very hard to get schools to work in clusters," he responded. "For example, Adams High School, Jefferson High School, Lincoln High School, and Polk High School might work together. Let's say that the school climate at Polk High School is a disaster. The collective discussions of the faculties, the parent bodies, and the student bodies of those four schools would provide the basis for the folks at Polk to take an agonizing reappraisal of what the school should be like."

He added, "It is our growing experience that multischool groupings or clusters are not the only financially realistic way that sustained outside involvement with 'critical friends' is going to take place, but are also substantially the most useful. It isn't the circuit rider from Brown dropping in and telling folks what he or she thinks of their school. It is folks in the community or in the school who say, 'We know how hard it is. The kids from Polk don't know what's going on. I wonder why they don't know what's going on?' That's because their school hasn't addressed the issues of importance.'"

Sizer says he is increasingly persuaded that the size of the scale within which the school operates is very important. "The size of the school, the size of the district, the size of the community all affect more than just the development of the school culture," he pointed out. "Therefore, size actually becomes the basis of character development—and the basis of the human alliances which are necessary to push through the kind of serious reform that is required."

That suggests, I said, that there will be some painful moments for school staff, as they are confronted with evidence of their dysfunctionality or failure.

"They know it already," Sizer said. "Pain comes from having it made public and having to deal with it. The bitterness that many people feel because they get not much more than criticism from the system is very, very deep. They feel that they are being scapegoated and they have a good deal of justification for that point of view. There is not much human kindness in the system, and it leads to the conclusion that people outside the schools are people who don't have to deal with thirty-five kids in a class and they don't give a damn."

The polarization of teachers against parents is intense, but might provoke positive change, Sizer emphasizes. "I sense this polarization around the country, and I believe it is an example of the confusion people experience when they scream at each other: 'You don't get it.' It's not that teachers have all the answers, but the confrontation may be the necessary painful precondition for something better."

I asked Sizer if he would do any things differently as he reflects over the course of the Coalition of Essential Schools. If so, what would be examples?

"In the Nine Common Principles, we talk about size, but what we said was far too limited. The size of the unit in which kids are schooled makes it possible for me to know the kids that I teach, but also makes it possible for me to know the other kids. The issue of scale includes the scale of the districts, too. I didn't get that right in the beginning," he said objectively.

"In the early days, we made a decision to stay away from policy and politics. Since you can't do everything at once, we started with pedagogy. That was naive," he continued, "because there has been a lot of movement in the policy and bureaucratic community. Some of that action has helped the reform and some of it has weakened it profoundly. You have to be a player in the larger scene if you're going to protect what goes on in the smaller setting.

"The third issue is that there is no way to predict what will happen. As recently as five years ago, I would not have predicted the extent of the possibility of the profound changes that are going on. States are shutting down their departments of education, both the Republican and Democratic parties are supporting school choice and charters. The unthinkable has become thinkable."

Collaboration: A New Direction for Reform?

In a time where it is impossible to predict the next issue to receive attention in the educational arena, can he say with any certainty that collaboration between reforms—such as the work he is engaged in with Howard Gardner, James Comer, and the Educational Development Corporation—will be a strong new direction for reform in general?

"We all learn something everyday," Sizer said. "So, in that sense, it is promising. When we meet with our collective colleagues, we are saying that we are all looking at the same elephant but we all see different sides of the elephant. For instance, Jim Comer is a physician, a psychiatrist, and has thought seriously about families with little children. Therefore, he has a different view—a very sophisticated view—of child development and human learning. Howard Gardner has done pioneering work on performance assessments and offers yet another point of view about abilities or intelligences."

However, the difficulties of collaboration must not be minimized; it is no prescription for success, Sizer wants to emphasize. "I am absolutely adamant that collaboration is very difficult," he noted. "Not that people aren't happy to do it, but if the projects have any intellectual depth, it takes more than just a few meetings and a bottle of sherry to accomplish something worthwhile. You really have to work to understand the different points of view, and then you have to try to involve carefully the meaning of those different points of view as they are woven together into something better.

"The ATLAS Project," he concluded, "has been very slow, in some people's opinion. They ask: 'Where's your design? After nine months, you don't have a design yet?' And our response is: 'We're just beginning to get a sense of what that design might be.'

"I'm all for collaboration because it deepens and enriches the work," he concluded, "but it requires a kind of scholarly commitment which a lot of us don't understand. To put it another way," he mused, "collaboration simply isn't just adding things together. It's reconceptualizing the whole basis of a different experience."

Dennis R. Williams:
An Illustration of Reform

West Mecklenburg High School is located in Charlotte, North Carolina and has a student body of approximately 1,450 students: 51 percent Caucasian, 46 percent African-American, 1.4 percent Asian, .3 percent Hispanic, and .8 percent Native American. The principal who led it through the School Development Program of James Comer, Dennis R. Williams, is now the Chief Administrative Officer for the Charlotte-Mecklenburg School System. Williams holds an Ed.D. in Educational Leadership with a concentration in Curriculum and Instruction from the University of North Carolina at Chapel Hill. Noted for his innovative spirit and interest in school restructuring, he has served on numerous task forces and consults for educational agencies and school districts throughout the nation. Recently he was presented with the Charlotte-Mecklenburg Ben Craig Outstanding Educator Award and with the Patrick Francis Daly Memorial Award for Excellence in Educational Leadership, given by the Yale University School Development Program.

When Dennis Williams went to West Mecklenburg High School as its new principal in 1992, he knew his job wasn't going to be easy. A neighboring high school, which he describes as "somewhat dysfunctional," had just closed and reopened as a magnet for science, math, and technology. As a result, approximately 400 students who previously attended the school—those with significant discipline problems—were sent to West Mecklenburg.

"Just as we were beginning the whole Comer process," Williams remembered, "these additional students entered the school. It was fairly significant, because on a scale of 1 to 10—with 1 the lowest and 10 the highest—West Mecklenburg functioned at the 2 level. Out of the eleven high schools in the district, West Mecklenburg was certainly in the bottom quartile."

The entry of new students known to have serious discipline problems further polarized an already divided school and community. "The students who joined us were angry because we had been their archrivals," he said. "Parents were skeptical about their presence, teachers were overly concerned about having them in the school, and the student body didn't want them, either."

Although the student population experienced some conflict around race relations between African-American and white students, that was not the sole problem, Williams reports. "We had a very large population with serious delays in their learning, so the academic and social challenges were tremendous."

Why the Comer model? Why not some other school reform initiative that offered hope for an improved set of school dynamics and boosted student achievement? "The Comer model is built on child development principles," Williams noted, "with a heavy emphasis on relationships. Those two factors make it quite different from other school reform efforts.

"Dr. Comer makes it perfectly clear that education is a people business," he emphasized, "and we have to be concerned about the total child if we are going to move from point A to point B. We cannot be so driven by results that we forget about relationships. That is a key difference with the Comer process. While we understand that student achievement is the bottom line, we feel that the only way we can achieve the type of results that we would like to see in schools is to pay particular attention to relationships and to developing the total child."

Williams saw the first step of the reform as dialogue: discussion that engaged as many stakeholders as possible, including students, parents, teachers, support staff—"every single staff member," he says, which uncovered long-held perceptions of the school's strengths and weaknesses.

Responsibility and Results

One key component of the Comer model is its emphasis on a no-blame philosophy that simultaneously insists that all stakeholders must take responsibility for improved outcomes. "We didn't need to waste time pointing fingers," Williams said. "Because of the tough school climate at that time, it was easy for students to point fingers at teachers, who pointed fingers at parents, who pointed fingers back. Everybody pointed at the central office for creating the situation. We knew this was wasted energy, and if we didn't stop doing it we wouldn't make progress."

Abandoning blame meant embracing responsibility for change, he says—an important distinction. Many teachers at West Mecklenburg, he reports, had given up on students altogether.

"We had many teachers who would say: 'Give us better students and we will produce better results.' We had to make it clear that we understood that the teachers' job was tough, and we were there to support them, but we had to have an attitude that we could make a difference in students' lives.

"We had to believe," he underlined, "that what is most important is not what students bring with them when they come to school but what they meet when they arrive."

Williams encountered considerable skepticism from staff, staff he describes as "traditionalists"—who had seen reforms come and go with little positive effects. As a result, he expended considerable effort demonstrating that this reform would be different. "They had seen reform after reform with no positive impact, and instead, things were getting rapidly worse," he explained. "We had to demonstrate to the faculty that this process would be different—and that the leader was serious about sharing responsibility with staff."

Although shared decision-making is an integral piece of the Comer model, Williams told staff he reserved the right to make 2 percent of the decisions but 98 percent of the decisions would be made by teachers in collaboration with parents and central office staff. "I didn't have enough faith at the time to give up total authority," he remembered. "I felt it was my duty to reserve the right to make some of the decisions. As it turned out, I made less than 2 percent of the decisions. Instead, I *influenced* the decisions of others.

"We talked a great deal about the collective wisdom of the group," Williams said. "The philosophy that we embraced was that no one person can possess wisdom that is greater than the wisdom of the entire teaching staff, the entire school community. That community, obviously, includes the principal.

"I made it perfectly clear that I didn't have all the answers, that if we were going to progress everybody had to participate. Each person, in my mind, held a piece of the puzzle. We needed everybody to bring his or her own piece to the table so we could fit the puzzle together. Teachers saw that I shared information freely with them; that influenced their decisions. Many leaders refuse to share information."

He recognized that sharing information was key to the reform's success, and a very powerful gesture on his part, as was the willingness to allow decisions to be made that personally he might not endorse. As a result, he gained credibility.

"They saw that their principal meant business, that his actions were consistent with what he said. On issues that were really sensitive to me, I would not exercise the 2 percent authority that I retained for myself. Instead, I would go along with the team decision, but if we were not successful and did not receive the results that we should have received, then I pointed out to teachers that they would have to be bold enough to bring the issue back to the table so we could discuss it again."

He shrewdly points out a characteristic of human nature that he used to further the reform. "Any time the majority of your staff wants to do something and understands it is up to them to make sure it is successful, they will do everything they can to make sure that the kids succeed with that particular strategy."

Enacting the School Development Program

Although the School Development Program is specific about the need for three "mechanisms," three "guiding principles," and three "operations," Williams tailored some of the model to fit his own leadership style and the school's needs.

Instead of allowing teachers to self-select to serve on the school's governance committee, Williams admits he interviewed teachers from different disciplines in an attempt to get what he calls "the best and the brightest" on the team. "It is a way to start," he reflected, "but I don't advise anyone to continue in that way. Over time, of course, teachers voted for the representative they wanted from their discipline on the governance team."

At the beginning, he took an active role in managing meetings—perhaps more active than the School Development Program would recommend. "I had to set the tone and show them what the process should produce over time. After two months, we selected co-chairs for the school planning and management team. These co-chairs were teachers who slowly accepted the leadership role. As they did so, others began to participate more fully.

"Of course," he added, "the process evolved over time. The immediate goal was to ensure that all strategies and day-to-day operations filtered through the school planning and management team, but what happened over time was that the team became facilitators of the decision-making process as opposed to being the decision-makers themselves."

He admits to initial hostility. "Initially, the faculty perceived the group as an elitist team of decision-makers who were favorites of the principal and held the upper hand on other staff members."

To change that perception, the teachers on the planning and management team had to show through their actions and beliefs that they were not the sole decision-makers for the school. "I had to drill into the hearts of the teachers on the team that they were *not* the decision-makers. Instead, it was their job to get out within their various disciplines, mingle with their peers, and bring back input that was reflective of the whole faculty," he said.

Did this diminish some of the perceptions that the planning and management team were the favored few? "Initially, teachers didn't believe me," Williams noted. "I was not the first administrator they had encountered who promised them power in the decision-making process.

Simultaneous with the planning and management team, West Mecklenburg began a student services management team—referred to by Comer as the mental health team—because a large number of students required a variety of support systems. Bringing all support staff together to serve on that committee broke up the previously fragmented approach to support services, with social workers, school psychologists, and counselors working in isolation from one another and from classroom teachers.

"This group mapped out an action plan to deal with the problems we knew we had in the building at that time," Williams said. "As we involved teachers in the decision-making process about the instructional program, we simultaneously tried to provide support to students and teachers so they could both be successful in the classroom.

"The third mechanism, the parent component, began the first year as a message to parents. We worked to let them know that we needed all parents—not just those who had been involved traditionally through the PTA or the Booster Club."

The strategy for reaching parents who had disconnected themselves from the educational process was proactive: Williams sent a core group of volunteer parents out into the community. "We divided our attendance areas into zones," he explained, "and held community meetings in the neighborhoods to try to interest parents in the school. Our message was: We care about your children; we need for you to be involved in the educational process.

"Initially, those parents who had not been involved with the school were the biggest critics of what we were doing. They had a lot of concerns, and they wanted to share them. Once we got through that—which is to be expected—they also became involved in the decision-making process, finding ways to support their children and the teachers. That support made an enormous difference in the school climate, almost immediately, because the sons and daughters of those parents were the biggest challenge for our teachers.

"Their parents had been disconnected from the educational process for years. We knew we had to get them involved because of the high correlation between parent involvement and student success in school. Going to the neighborhoods and their churches was a very powerful strategy. We recruited a very small nucleus of parents who were bold enough to go into their neighborhoods, knock on doors, make telephone calls, look parents eye to eye, and ask for their involvement."

Parents were represented on the planning and management team as well, but their participation grew slowly. "We began somewhat traditionally with the PTA president and the Booster Club president," he recalled, "and then recruited some other parents. Over a year or so, the parent component grew so large that we had a separate parent committee."

Parents were involved in school activities in traditional ways—such as fundraising and open houses—and newer, less traditional ways. "We told teachers to expect to see parents in and out of their classrooms, and to welcome them as partners. We tried to make our school as inviting as possible to parents, just as we tried to make it inviting to children.

"On another level, we wanted to move parents into decisionmaking for the school. We really believe that if we give parents the same information we have and guide them through the process, their input will be just as critical as anyone else's input. We needed their support for the changes we were going to make."

As an example, Williams points to a schedule change from a six-period day to a four-period day. Other changes included the institution of Tech Prep, national models for teaching civic and social responsibility, and the advent of new, strict disciplinary policies.

The Best That We Can Do

In order to move into strategies that would affect student learning and achievement directly, Williams led a schoolwide scrutiny of student achievement. "We looked at all indicators of success," he stated, "including SAT scores, scores on standardized tests, disciplinary reports, teacher performance, our dropout rate, and the number of students we had in high-level courses. Everybody was involved in the process. At the end of it, we asked: 'Is this the very best we can do?' The answer was, of course: 'No, this is not the best we can do.'

"I then asked: 'If we continue to do the same things we have done over the past ten years, do you think we can produce results other than what we see right here? Do you think it is time we consider doing things differently?' The answer to the latter question was 'Yes.' I gave them my assurance that they would be involved in the decisions about what we needed to do differently, and this assurance motivated them to engage in the process. We were able to establish something people don't talk about anymore, and this is trust.

"I believe firmly that people do not venture out into new directions unless they feel they have the trust of the administration and also that there is trust among teachers and between the school and home."

The first steps in boosting student achievement were to change from an annual assessment to assessments at the end of each quarter, which enabled staff to make curricular and instructional modifications prior to the end of the school year.

Based on the weaknesses that the assessments revealed, staff developed a comprehensive school plan—another integral feature of the School Development Program—to address areas of concern. "Our plan included more than academic goals," he said. "Teachers had concerns about discipline, so we found the teachers who were best at discipline and had them share strategies with other teachers as well as conduct a dialogue with them about what they could do differently.

"If we were dealing with cooperative learning as a strategy, we had to make sure that people understood how to work together as peers. We had teachers discuss it at faculty meetings—but we made sure the discussion was not very structured. It was informal, and everyone felt he or she could participate. Whatever strategy we addressed depended on what people felt they needed help with."

A Community of Learners

During the second year of the School Development Program's implementation, Williams believes the school truly became a community of learners. "During the first year, everything was happening so quickly that teachers didn't completely grasp all of it. They needed time to reflect, and when they came back the second year they came back as different people."

But the atmosphere of the first year was tough, Williams wants to communicate, and district support enabled him to maintain a "no excuses" policy. "We expected *everybody* to perform at high levels. My job was to support teachers and students so that could occur. If we had teachers who didn't care about students, who were ineffective, who were not receptive to the type of support system we had in place, I was very clear about the results. We would run those teachers out of the school just as fast as we could."

A number of teachers chose to leave the school the first year, he remembers. "The first day of school at the first faculty meeting, I made the following statement: 'If you do not want to be at a school where students are achieving at high levels to the point that we receive national and international recognition for our efforts to be of service to students, you are in the wrong place at the wrong time. We will support our students, we will demonstrate excellence in everything we do, and those people who do not want to do that will not be allowed to stay.'

"I also stated that we would not wait until the end of the school year to dismiss people. In October, people started to leave. The first six months were very stressful because we had some teachers in the school who should not have been teachers. They had no interest in students. Some were misplaced and we counseled them into other jobs. Others had to be pushed out. We lost one administrator who was very popular; that created a lot of tension. New rules for students weren't easy, either."

Yet the toughness that extended across the board was necessary, he believes. "The first year, I confiscated fourteen handguns. Students were not used to high expectations about discipline. A number of them were not accustomed to going to their classes. Attendance was an issue, and as a result, parent support for our school had dwindled."

Beyond Basic Skills

One of Williams' first actions to improve student learning was to eradicate all basic skills classes. "Expectations for a number of students in the school were: 'They can't do anything but the minimum.' We had students floating through the school taking courses out of sequence, taking courses in a way that wouldn't prepare them to do anything once they left the school. A smaller percentage were really focused on taking the right courses and preparing themselves for the future."

The result of eliminating the basic skills courses meant that students began to be pushed to achieve at higher levels. "It was stressful for both students and teachers. Students were not used to being in academically challenging classes, and teachers were not used to diversity in their classrooms. We had to provide simultaneous support to students and to teachers to make it work."

After six months, students began to ease into the new discipline policies and teachers relaxed as they worked with students. "Over time," Williams reported, "higher expectations were established. Both students and teachers stopped fussing about it; it was the new norm."

As he reflects about the stressful first months of change, Williams identifies the premise of his ongoing argument: "Everyone wants to be attached to a school that is doing well. High school students want to have a great school experience. Teachers want to feel that they are having an impact on student achievement. When we share an expectation of excellence, everybody benefits. The question becomes: How do we work together to make that happen?"

To show students that discipline policies had teeth, the school suspended students involved in fights for ten days and filed charges against them. "Many times they ended up in jail and parents had to get them out, which cost $125. Once students understood that it didn't matter who you were, who your parents were, which side of town you lived on, if you fought on campus you would be arrested and prosecuted—and suspended from school for ten days—that got their attention."

Even though parents had to pay to bail their children out of jail, their anger wasn't directed at the school, Williams says, because they were deeply concerned about safety on campus. "This was a small percentage of students who were holding everyone hostage in a situation where no one could learn."

Indicators of Success

The first indicator of success became students' willingness to talk to the administration and to teachers. "Students became part of the monitoring process. They began to tell us if someone had a weapon, or drugs, or contraband that they were not supposed to have on campus. Many times we were able to resolve those cases quietly." Students, he adds, reclaimed their school.

Part of the School Development Program insists that consensus must be reached on all decisions, which could be perceived as difficult and frustrating. Williams, however, is a proponent of reaching consensus. "In the long run," he observed, "if you look at the amount of time it takes to go back and clean up decisions when consensus for them wasn't reached, you see that you gain time if consensus is reached when the decision is made."

One of the most surprising—and gratifying—results of the School Development Program's implementation at West Mecklenburg is that teachers rose from a previously demoralized state to take ownership for the progress of the reform. "Teachers rose to the challenge," he said. "Initially, we had a buddy system in place. It didn't matter if you were doing what was right. Instead, everything was framed in terms of: 'Are you my friend? Do we socialize? Do I like you? How does this decision affect me?'

"When we moved to a higher level of professionalism, teachers bought into the reform. They stopped protecting ineffective teachers and started making decisions based on what was best for students as opposed to what was best for adults."

Improved Student Outcomes

Student outcomes showed dramatic gains as a result of the School Development Program, Williams reports, pointing to a 95 percent increase in the number of students with perfect attendance. There was a 75 percent increase in the number of students who made the A/B honor rolls; a 50 percent decrease in major disciplinary infractions by students. In survey results, 96 percent of teachers reported that they liked the school's new schedule; 77 percent of students reported they liked it as well. "We were able to demonstrate," Williams said with some pride, "a 25 percent increase in the number of students enrolled in higher-level courses and a 25 percent decrease in the number of dropouts."

As part of the Charlotte-Mecklenburg system's quality control, the district surveys teachers, students, and parents on an annual basis and the information is included as part of the school's evaluation along with other indicators of success. "In 1992–93," Williams reported, "73.2 percent of teachers felt that students were intimidated frequently by other students whereas the following year that number decreased to 21.4 percent. The average for the district was 31 percent. Approximately 81.3 percent of teachers saw violence as a frequent problem in 1992–93. Three years later that number was down to 21.7 percent; the average for the system for the high schools was 23 percent. In 1992–93, only 23.9 percent of teachers believed that students behaved in an orderly manner; in the 1994–95 school year that number was up to 62.2 percent, while the district average was 49 percent."

Two figures related to Williams' leadership on the survey included a statistic that reports that 93.9 percent of teachers believed that the principal was current on educational trends and innovations, while another statistic reported that, in 1994–95, 85.7 percent of teachers believed their principal gave teachers authority to make key decisions. "I really worked hard on that," Williams said carefully. "I am a quiet person, more an introvert than an extrovert. Yet I am a man of strong convictions, so sometimes people back off in a dialogue with me because I feel so strongly about my beliefs.

"What hurt me badly—and what concerned me the most—was my relationship with students," Williams admitted. "Being the principal and making the decisions I had to make at the outset precluded a warm relationship with students. I didn't have the rapport I wanted with them. They saw me as the hard-nosed principal who didn't care and was trying to make life difficult for everybody."

Toward the end of the second year, his relationship with students improved. "Going into the third year, I knew we had turned a corner, because not only did we have the support and understanding of the teachers and the community, the students—who are the most important people in the school— had established or allowed me to establish the right relationship with them."

Despite the impressive record of achievement at West Mecklenburg High School, Williams seems most proud of his trajectory from what he describes as "very humble beginnings" to his present position. In fact, he reports considerable pride in his experience as a coach, commenting that few people show interest in that part of his background—even though, as he suggests, there is a clear parallel between it and his present work. "I coached football and basketball," he concluded with some pride, "taking two teams that had long histories of losing most games into conference champions."

Afterword

As this book of conversations ends, I would like to draw a few personal conclusions. At the outset, in addition to the many questions I formed prior to my conversations with the educational leaders featured in this volume, the questions that arose spontaneously during those conversations, and the ones that occurred to me while writing this book, the main question I asked myself was: What broad themes will this new genre of conversations with selected researchers, practitioners, and reformers yield? In what follows, I sketch the themes apparent to me after writing this book.

Resistance to school change initiatives and the complexities of school improvement is even more profound than has been reported. When I began this book, I was cautiously optimistic about the likelihood of effecting significant change in schools. Years of dialogue with researchers and practitioners, as well as familiarity with the research literature on school improvement and reform, had succeeded in convincing me that measurable change or improvement would be a hard-won commodity. As I conclude this book, I am convinced that the difficulty of achieving measurable change or improvement and the complexity of resistance to change efforts has been underreported and underemphasized although there certainly are reports and testimonials about the difficulty of effecting measurable or systemic change. Schools are institutions inhabited by humans—and as such, are riddled with all the complexity human beings possess: maddening inconsistencies, clashes of politics and personalities, and occasional flashes of inspiration. As Barth's and Peterson's comments bear eloquent testimony, the life of the practitioner is not easy—one in which external, and often competing, mandates command action. As Kliebard pointed out, the well-intended agendas of university researchers often conflict with the practical, day-to-day realities of school life.

The ability of some individuals to effect change has been underestimated and perhaps unappreciated. Despite the considerable difficulties, both systemic and individual, certain individuals share the dispositions and traits that insist on school improvement. What they have in common is the ability to make difficult decisions, decisions that may make them temporarily unpopular (this is particularly evident in the stories of Patricia Anderson, Thomas R. Hoerr, and Dennis Williams). However, they acknowledge the importance of the collective, not the individual, as they work to build consensus. Although they believe and are committed to group process, they do not allow themselves or their staffs to be paralyzed if it is not readily accomplished. In short, effective school leaders are everything the school improvement literature believes they are: strong, visionary, intelligent, and able to work successfully with diverse groups.

Effective change agents, reformers, or school leaders share the ability to evaluate their efforts without defensiveness and use the results of their evaluations to progress toward their vision of an improved school or improved schooling in general. These conversations reveal the self-evaluation in which these practitioners and reformers habitually engage, without defensiveness, and their ability to learn from mistakes or well-intentioned efforts that proved not as successful as they wished. Along with the ability to evaluate reform and change efforts, these leaders—especially the reformers and practitioners—share the ability to maintain a vision of improved schooling and use their evaluative efforts to inform their change efforts. If the result of their evaluations and self-scrutiny is less than positive, they do not allow their efforts to be derailed, but instead shape and reconfigure them.

Public policy can become a straitjacket that impedes change. As Barth in particular points out, external mandates—while well-intentioned—can present yet another obstacle to change as practitioners sift and winnow through local and state mandates along with national exhortations to action issued by blue-ribbon panels and commissions. These mandates and exhortations often conflict, contradict, and confuse. As the current debate over students' access to the Internet versus censorship clearly reveals, public policy is often not helpful in guiding local decisions and frequently can impede change efforts due to the amount of time that must be expended in complying with external mandates.

Problems in schooling should be considered in context, not in isolation from one another. It is too easy, when searching for solutions to complicated educational problems, to reach global assumptions. Examples include: "If teaching became a profession, significant reform would result"; "If we have comprehensive national standards, student achievement will rise"; "If we abandon all special programming in favor of heterogeneous grouping, every student will benefit"; and "If we pursue a rigorous course of character education in our schools, student behaviors will improve and thus the broader society will benefit." As the comments of the educational leaders in this volume reveal, none of these and other assumptions about education will withstand scrutiny when placed into a broader context. For instance, if special programming is abandoned in favor of heterogeneous grouping without an investment in teacher training so that teachers are equipped to provide instruction to heterogeneous groups—and if adequate support systems are not in place—the outcome will be dubious at best.

Effective educational leaders reject the "magic bullet" approach to school improvement. Complicated problems demand intelligent and carefully crafted solutions, and these conversations reveal that, although the "magic bullet" approach to school improvement still has popular appeal, the most informed educational leaders uniformly reject it. No one program that proposes change can possibly provide all the answers to the complexity of the problems that riddle public education—and sensible programs do not attempt or claim to do so.

The specific reform is frequently not as important to school leaders as is the framework it provides to effect change. As the practitioners in this volume demonstrate through their comments, although the reforms through which they have effected school improvement are sympathetic to their own philosophy and ideas about reform, perhaps their greatest contribution is the ability to provide a structure that facilitates the school leader's efforts. This structure is not overly prescriptive, however, or a simplistic "to-do" list. In fact, school leaders who succeed in effecting demonstrable change are to be commended for their rejection of simplistic, "canned" school development programs that promise much but due to their reductionistic nature cannot deliver.

Each of the broad themes outlined above provides an interesting line of inquiry for my future work and should, in turn, yield other broad themes through the same developing genre of conversations with educational leaders.

Bibliography

Apple, M. W. (1993). *Official knowledge: Democratic education in a conservative age.* New York: Routledge.

Apple, M. W., & Beane, J. A., Eds. (1995). *Democratic schools.* Alexandria, Va.: Association for Supervision and Curriculum Development.

Banks, C. A. McGee, & Banks, J. A., Eds. (1995). *Handbook of research on multicultural education.* New York: Macmillan.

Banks, J. A., & Banks, C. A. McGee, Eds. (1993). *Multicultural education: Issues and perspectives*, 2nd edition. Boston, Mass.: Allyn and Bacon.

Barth, R. S. (1986). The principal and the profession of teaching. *The Elementary School Journal, 86*(4), 471–92.

Barth, R. S. (1988, May). Principals, teachers, and school leadership. *Phi Delta Kappan, 69*, 639–42.

Barth, R. S. (1990, March). A personal vision of a good school. *Phi Delta Kappan, 71*, 512–16.

Barth, R. S. (1991, October). Restructuring schools: Some questions for teachers and principals. *Phi Delta Kappan, 73*, 123–28.

Barth, R. S. (1990). *Improving schools from within: Teachers, parents, and principals can make the difference.* San Francisco: Jossey-Bass.

Bolman, L. G., & Deal, T. E. (1991). *Reframing organizations: Artistry, choice, and leadership.* San Francisco: Jossey-Bass.

Boyer, E. L. (1983). *High school: A report on secondary education in America / The Carnegie Foundation for the Advancement of Teaching.* New York: Harper & Row.

Brown, B. B., Mounts, N., Lamborn, S., & Steinberg, L. (1993). Parenting practices and peer group affiliations: Toward a new model of parental and peer influences in adolescence. *Child Development, 64*, 476–82.

Brown, B. B. (1988, Spring). The vital agenda for research on extracurricular influences: A reply to Holland and Andre. *Review of Educational Research, 58*, 107–11.

Brown, B. B. (1995, April). Helping students by recognizing peer crowds. *Journal of Reading, 38*, 568–69.

Brown, B. B., & Steinberg, L. D. (1990, March). Academic achievement and social acceptance. *The Education Digest, 55*, 57–60.

Burbules, N. C., & Densmore, K. (1991, March). The limits of making teaching a profession. *Educational Policy, 5*(1), 44–63.

Burbules, N. C., & Densmore, K. (1991, June). The persistence of professionalism: Breakin' up is hard to do. *Educational Policy, 5*(2), 150–57.

Chavkin, N. F., Ed. (1993). *Families and schools in a pluralistic society*. Albany, N.Y.: SUNY Press.

Cochran-Smith, M. (1995, Fall). Color blindness and basket making are not the answers: Confronting the dilemmas of race, culture, and language diversity in teacher education. *American Educational Research Journal, 32*(3), 493–522.

Colangelo, N., Kelly, K. R., & Schrepfer, R. M. (1987, October). A comparison of gifted, general, and special learning needs students on academic and social self-concept. *Journal of Counseling and Development, 66*, 73–77.

Comer, J. P. (1980). *School power*. New York: Free Press.

Comer, J. P. (1989, Spring). Child development and education. *Journal of Negro Education, 58*, 125–39.

Cuban, L. (1993). *How teachers taught: Constancy and change in American classrooms, 1890–1990* (2nd edition). New York: Teachers College Press.

Darling-Hammond, L. (1985, Winter). Valuing teachers: The making of a profession. *Teachers College Record, 87*(2), 205–18.

Darling-Hammond, L. (1989, Fall). Accountability for professional practice. *Teachers College Record, 91*(1), 59–80.

Darling-Hammond, L. (1991, November). The implications of testing policy for quality and equality. *Phi Delta Kappan, 73*(3), 220–25.

Darling-Hammond, L. (1994, August 1). National standards and assessment: Will they improve education? *American Journal of Education, 102*(4), 478.

Deal, T. E., & Peterson, K. D. (1991). *The principal's role in shaping school culture*. Washington, D.C.: U.S. Department of Education, Office of Educational Research and Improvement.

Deal, T. E., & Peterson, K. D. (1994). *The leadership paradox: Balancing logic and artistry and schools*. San Francisco: Jossey-Bass.

Dewey, J. (1915). *The school and society*. Chicago: University of Chicago Press.

Dewey, J. (1916). *Democracy and education.* New York: Macmillan.

Fagnano, C. L., & Hughes, K. N. (1993). *Making schools work: A view from the firing lines.* Boulder, Colo.: Westview Press.

Feinberg, W. (1987, Spring). The Holmes Group report and the professionalization of teaching. *Teachers College Record, 88*(3), 366–77.

Fetterman, D. M. (1986). Gifted and talented education: A national test case in Peoria. *Educational Evaluation and Policy Analysis, 8*(2), 155–66.

Fillmore, L. W. (1990). Now or later? Issues related to the early education of minority-group children. In *Early childhood and family education: Analysis and recommendations of the Council of Chief State School Officers*, pp. 122–45. New York: Harcourt, Brace, & Jovanovich.

Fillmore, L. W. (1991). When learning a second language means losing the first. *Early Childhood Research Quarterly, 6*(3), 323–46.

Firestone, W. A., & Bader, B. D. (1991, Spring). Professionalism or bureaucracy: Redesigning teaching. *Educational Evaluation and Policy Analysis, 13*(1), 67–86.

Fordham, S., & Ogbu, J. U. (1986). Black students' school success: Coping with the "burden of 'acting white.'" *The Urban Review, 18*(3), 176–206.

Gardner, H. (1983). *Frames of mind: The theory of multiple intelligences.* New York: Basic Books.

Gardner, H. (1993). *Multiple intelligences: The theory in practice.* New York: Basic Books.

Gardner, H. (1994, September 7). The need for anti-Babel standards. *Education Week*, 56.

Gardner, H., & Boix-Mansilla, V. (1994, Winter). Teaching for understanding in the disciplines—and beyond. *Teachers College Record, 96*, 198–218.

Gitlin, A. D. (1990, November). Educative research, voice, and school change. *Harvard Educational Review, 60*(4), 443–66.

Glazer, N. (1987, May). In search of excellence and equity in our nation's schools. *Harvard Educational Review, 57*(2), 196–207.

Goodman, J. (1994, Winter). External change agents and grassroots school reform: Reflections from the field. *Journal of Curriculum and Supervision, 9*, 113–35.

Goodman, J. (1995, Spring). Change without difference: School restructuring in historical perspective. *Harvard Educational Review, 65*, 1–29.

Greenberger, E., & Steinberg, L. D. (1986). *When teenagers work: The psychological and social costs of adolescent employment.* New York: Basic Books.

Harman, S. (1991, January). National tests, national standards, national curriculum. *Language Arts, 68*, 49–50.

Hartshorne, H., & May, M. (1930). *Studies in the nature of character*. New York: Macmillan.

Haynes, N., & Hamilton-Lee, M. (1988). *Ethnographic studies of the school development program at Jackie Robinson and Roberto Clemente Middle Schools*. New Haven: Yale Child Study Center.

Haynes, N. M., & Comer, J. P. (1993, July). The Yale school development program: Process, outcomes, and policy implications. *Urban Education, 28*(2), 166–99.

Hilliard, A. G. (1991–92, December/January). Why we must pluralize the curriculum. *Educational Leadership, 49*, 12–16.

Holmes Group. (1986). *Tomorrow's teachers: A report of the Holmes Group*. East Lansing, Mich.: Author.

Hopfenberg, W. S., Levin, H. M., & Associates (1993). *The accelerated schools resource guide*. San Francisco: Jossey-Bass.

Huberman, M. (1989, Fall). The professional life cycle of teachers. *Teachers College Record, 91*(1), 31–57.

Huberman, M. (1993). The model of the independent artisan in teachers' professional relations. In Little, J. W., & McLaughlin, M. (Eds.), *Teachers' work: Individuals, colleagues, and contexts.*

Johnson, W. R. (1987, Summer). Empowering practitioners: Holmes, Carnegie, and the lessons of history. *History of Education Quarterly, 27*(2), 221–40.

Kliebard, H. M. (1988, Winter). Success and failure in educational reform: Are there historical "lessons"? *Peabody Journal of Education, 65*, 144–57.

Kliebard, H. M. (1992). *Forging the American curriculum: Essays in curriculum history and theory*. New York: Routledge.

Kliebard, H. M. (1995). *The struggle for the American curriculum, 1893–1958* (2nd edition). New York: Routledge.

Kouzes, J. M., & Posner, B. Z. (1987). The leadership challenge: How to get extraordinary things done in organizations. San Francisco: Jossey-Bass.

Kozol, Jonathan. (1991). *Savage inequalities: Children in America's schools*. New York: Crown Publishers.

Ladson-Billings, G. (1995, Fall). Toward a theory of culturally relevant pedagogy. *American Educational Research Journal, 32*(3), 465–92.

Larson, M. S. (1977). *The rise of professionalism: A sociological analysis*. Berkeley: University of California Press.

Lee, V. E., Dedrick, R. F., & Smith, J. B. (1991). The effect of the social organization of schools on teachers' efficacy and satisfaction. *Sociology of Education, 64*(3), 190–208.

Lickona, T. (1991). *Educating for character: How our schools can teach respect and responsibility.* New York: Bantom Books.

Lickona, T. (1993, November). The return of character education. *Educational Leadership, 51,* 6–11.

Lickona, T. (1993, November). Where sex education went wrong. *Educational Leadership, 51,* 84–89.

Lieberman, A. (1991, November). Accountability as a reform strategy. *Phi Delta Kappan, 73*(3), 219–20.

Little, J. W. (1993, Summer). Teachers' professional development in a climate of educational reform. *Educational Evaluation and Policy Analysis, 15*(2), 129–51.

Lockwood, A. L. (1991, April/May). Character education: The ten percent solution. *Social Education, 55,* 246–48.

Lockwood, A. L. (1993, November). A letter to character educators. *Educational Leadership, 51,* 72–75.

Lockwood, A. L., & Harris, D. E. (1985). *Reasoning with democratic values: Ethical problems in United States history.* New York: Teachers College Press.

Lockwood, A. T. (1993). Multiple intelligences in action. *Research and the Classroom.* Madison, Wis.: National Center for Effective Schools.

Lockwood, A. T. (1994a). Character education. *Focus in Change.* Madison, Wis.: National Center for Effective Schools.

Lockwood, A. T. (1994b). Language, culture, and identity. *Focus in Change.* Madison, Wis.: National Center for Effective Schools.

Madden, N. A., Slavin, R. E., & Karweit, N. L. (1993, Spring). Success for All: Longitudinal effects of a restructuring program for inner-city elementary schools. *American Educational Research Journal, 30,* pp. 123–48.

Madeus, G. F. (1991, November). The effects of important tests on students: Implications for a national examination system. *Phi Delta Kappan, 73*(3), 226–31.

Meier, D. (1992, Summer). Reinventing teaching. *Teachers College Record, 93*(4), 594–609.

Meier, D. (1995). *The power of their ideas: Lessons for America from a small school in Harlem.* Boston: Beacon Press.

Metzger, W. P. (1987, August/September). A spectre is haunting American scholars: The spectre of "professionalism." *Educational Researcher, 16,* 10–21.

Muncey, D. E., & McQuillan, P. J. (1993, February). Preliminary findings from a five-year study of the Coalition of Essential Schools. *Phi Delta Kappan, 74*, 486–89.

National Commission for Excellence in Teacher Education. (1985). *A call for change in teacher education.* Washington, D.C.: National Commission for Excellence in Teacher Education.

National Commission on Excellence in Education. (1986). *A nation at risk: The imperative for educational reform.* Washington, D.C.: Author.

National Council of Teachers of Mathematics/Commission on Standards for School Mathematics. (1989). *Curriculum and evaluation standards for school mathematics.* Reston, Va.: Author.

National Council of Teachers of Mathematics/Commission on Teaching Standards for School Mathematics. (1991). *Professional standards for teaching mathematics.* Reston, Va.: Author.

National Education Longitudinal Study of 1988 [computer file]: public use. (1994 version). Washington, D.C.: National Center for Education Statistics, Office of Educational Research and Improvement, U.S. Department of Education.

Newmann, F. M., Secada, W. G., & Wehlage, G. G. (1995). *A guide to authentic instruction and assessment: Vision, standards, and scoring.* Madison, Wis.: Center on Organization and Restructuring of Schools.

Newmann, F. N., & Wehlage, G. G. (1995). *Successful school restructuring: A report to the public and educators.* Madison, Wis.: Center on Organization and Restructuring of Schools.

Newmann, F. M., Marks, H. M., & Gamoran, A. (1995). Authentic pedagogy: Standards that boost study performance. *Issues in Restructuring Schools No. 8.* Madison, Wis.: Center on Organization and Restructuring of Schools.

Noblit, G. W. (1986). What's missing from the national agenda for school reform: Teacher professionalism and local initiative. *The Urban Review, 18*(1), 40–51.

Noddings, N. (1988). An ethic of caring and its implications for instructional arrangements. *American Journal of Education, 96*, 215–30.

Noddings, N. (1992). *The challenge to care in schools: An alternative approach to education.* New York: Teachers College Press.

O'Neil, J. (1995, February). On lasting school reform: A conversation with Ted Sizer. *Educational Leadership, 52*, 4–9.

Ogbu, J. U. (1992, November). Understanding cultural diversity and learning. *Educational Researcher, 21*, 5–14+.

Ogbu, J. U. (1994, Winter). Racial stratification and education in the United States: Why inequality persists. *Teachers College Record, 96*, 264–98.

Oppenheimer, M., O'Donnell, C., & Johnson, D. (1982). Professions and the middle class: Professionalization/deprofessionalization. In D. L. Johnson (Ed.), *Class and social development: A new theory of the middle class* (pp. 245–57). Beverly Hills, Calif.: Sage.

Payne, C. (1991, April). The Comer intervention model and school reform in Chicago: Implications of two models of change. *Urban Education, 26*(1), 8–24.

Phelan, R., & Davidson, A. L. (1993). *Renegotiating cultural diversity in American schools.* New York: Teachers College Press.

Porter, A. C. (1989, Winter). External standards and good teaching: The pros and cons of telling teachers what to do. *Educational Evaluation and Policy Analysis, 11*(4), 343–56.

Porter, A. C., Archbald, D. A., & Tyree, A. K., Jr. (1990). Reforming the curriculum: Will empowerment policies replace control? *Politics of Education Association Yearbook,* 11–36.

Pratte, R., & Rury, J. L. (1991, Fall). Teachers, professionalism, and craft. *Teachers College Record, 93*(1), 59–72.

Prestine, N. A., & Bowen, C. (1993, Fall). Benchmarks of change: Assessing essential school restructuring efforts. *Educational Evaluation and Policy Analysis, 15*(3), 298–319.

Quantz, R. A. (1985, Winter). The complex visions of female teachers and the failure of unionization in the 1930s: An oral history. *History of Education Quarterly, 25,* 439–58.

Raelin, J. A. (1989). Unionization and deprofessionalization: Which comes first? *Journal of Organizational Behavior, 10,* 101–15.

Renzulli, J. S. (1994). *Schools for talent development: A practical plan for total school improvement.* Mansfield Center, Conn.: Creative Learning Press, Inc.

Roemer, M. G. (1991, November). What we talk about when we talk about school reform. *Harvard Educational Review, 61*(4), 434–48.

Rogers, C. R. (1987, Winter). On the shoulders of giants. *The Educational Forum, 51*(2), 115–22.

Rogers, K. B., & Kimpson, R. D. (1992, October). Acceleration: What we do vs. what we know. *Educational Leadership, 50,* 58–61.

Rosenblatt, R. (1995, April 30). Teaching Johnny to be good. *The New York Times Magazine,* 36–41+.

Rosenholtz, S. J. (1989). Workplace conditions that affect teacher quality and commitment: Implications for teacher induction programs. *The Elementary School Journal, 89*(4), 421–39.

Rousmaniere, K. (1994, Spring). Losing patience and staying professional: Women teachers and the problem of classroom discipline in New York City schools in the 1920s. *History of Education Quarterly, 34*, 49–68.

Rury, J. L. (1993, Summer). *Education and women's work: Female schooling and the division of labor in urban America, 1870–1930*. Albany, N.Y.: SUNY Press.

Ryan, K. (1995, June). Character first. *The American School Board Journal, 182*, 25–26.

Ryan, K. (1995, May 17). Character and coffee mugs. *Education Week*, 48+.

Sapon-Shevin, M. (1994). *Playing favorites: Gifted education and the disruption of community*. Albany, N.Y.: SUNY Press.

Scarcella, R. C. (1990). *Teaching language minority students in the multicultural classroom*. Englewood Cliffs, N.J.: Prentice Hall Regents.

Sergiovanni, T. J., & Corbally, J. E. (1984). *Leadership and organizational culture: New perspectives on administrative theory and practice*. Urbana, Ill.: University of Illinois Press.

Sizer, T. R. (1984). *Horace's compromise: The dilemma of the American high school*. Boston: Houghton Mifflin Company.

Sizer, T. R. (1992). *Horace's school: Redesigning the American high school*. Boston: Houghton Mifflin Company.

Sizer, T. R. (1996). *Horace's hope: What works for the American high school*. Boston: Houghton Mifflin Company.

Slavin, R. E. (1991, April). Chapter 1: A vision for the next quarter century. *Phi Delta Kappan, 72*, 586–90.

Slavin, R. E., Madden, N. A., Karweit, N. L., Livermon, B. J., & Dolan, L. (1990, Summer). Success for all: First-year outcomes of a comprehensive plan reforming urban education. *American Educational Research Journal, 27*(2), 255–78.

Sleeter, C. E., & Grant, C. A. (1987). An analysis of multicultural education in the United States. *Harvard Educational Review, 57*(4), 421–44.

Sleeter, C. E., & McLaren, P. L. (1995). *Multicultural education, critical pedagogy, and the politics of difference*. Albany, N.Y.: SUNY Press.

Sleeter, Christine E. (1992). *Keepers of the American dream: A study of staff development and multicultural education*. London: Falmer Press.

Smith, M. S., Fuhrman, S. H., O'Day, J.A. (1994). National curriculum standards: Are they desirable and feasible? *Yearbook of the Association for Supervision and Curriculum Development 1994*, 12–29.

Smith, M. S., O'Day, J. A., Fuhrman, S. H. (1992). State policy and systemic school reform. *Educational Technology, 32*(92), 31–36.

Smith, M. S., O'Day, J., & Cohen, D. K. (1991, September). A national curriculum in the United States? *Educational Leadership, 49*, 74–81.

Soder, R. (1988, December). Studying the education of educators: What we can learn from the other professions. *Phi Delta Kappan, 70*, 299–305.

Spindler, G., & Spindler, L. S., with Trueba, H. T., & Williams, M. D. (1990). *The American cultural dialogue and its transmission*. London, England: The Falmer Press.

Steinberg, L., Dornbusch, S. M., & Brown, B. B. (1992, June). Ethnic differences in adolescent achievement. *American Psychologist, 47*, 723–29.

Tabakin, G., & Densmore, K. (1986, Winter). Teacher professionalization and gender analysis. *Teachers College Record, 88*(2), 257–279.

Task Force on Teaching as a Profession, Carnegie Forum on Education and the Economy. (1986). *A nation prepared: Teachers for the 21st century*. Washington, D.C.: The Forum.

Trueba, H. T. (1990). The role of culture in literacy acquisition: An interdisciplinary approach to qualitative research. *Qualitative Studies in Education, 3*(1), 1–13.

Trueba, H. T. (1993, Winter). Race and ethnicity: The role of universities in healing multicultural America. *Educational Theory, 43*(1), 41–54.

Trueba, H. T. (1988). Instructional effectiveness: English-only for speakers of other languages? *Education and Urban Society, 20*(4), 341–62.

Urban, W. J. (1982). *Why teachers organized*. Detroit: Wayne State University Press.

Urban, W. J. (1991, Summer). Is there a new teacher unionism? *Educational Theory, 41*(3), 331–38.

Whalen, S., & Csikszentmihalyi, M. (1989). A comparison of the self-image of talented teenagers with a normal adolescent population. *Journal of Youth and Adolescence, 18*(2), 131–46.

Witte, J. F., & Walsh, D. J. (1990, Summer). A systematic test of the effective schools model. *Educational Evaluation and Policy Analysis, 12*, 188–212.

Wynne, E. A. (1986, January). The great tradition in education: Transmitting moral values. *Educational Leadership, 43*, 4–9.

Zeichner, K. M. (1991, Spring). Contradictions and tensions in the professionalization of teaching and the democratization of schools. *Teachers College Record, 92*(3), 363–79.

Author Note

Anne Turnbaugh Lockwood is an Honorary Fellow in the Department of Curriculum and Instruction at the University of Wisconsin–Madison. Her work, which focuses on diminishing the barriers between educational research and practice, has been recognized by the American Educational Research Association Interpretive Scholarship Award (1993) and the Distinguished Achievement Award of the University of Wisconsin's School of Education (1993). She produced two nationally respected programs of publications targeted to educational researchers and practitioners: first, for the U.S. Department of Education's National Center on Effective Secondary Schools (1986–90) and second, for the National Center for Effective Schools (1990–94), both at the University of Wisconsin–Madison. She consults as a senior writer and policy analyst for the U.S. Department of Education's North Central Regional Educational Laboratory (Oak Brook, Illinois) and is the author of a series of papers commissioned by the U.S. Department of Education's Hispanic Dropout Project. Lockwood holds a Ph.D. in Educational Psychology from the University of Illinois at Urbana-Champaign.

Index

SUNY Series: Frontiers in Education

Philip G. Altbach, editor

List of Titles

Class, Race, and Gender in American Education—Lois Weis (ed.)

Excellence and Equality: A Qualitatively Different Perspective on Gifted and Talented Education—David M. Fetterman

Change and Effectiveness in Schools: A Cultural Perspective—Gretchen B. Rossman, H. Dickson Corbett, and William A. Firestone

The Curriculum: Problems, Politics, and Possibilities—Landon E. Beyer and Michael W. Apple (eds.)

The Character of American Higher Education and Intercollegiate Sport—Donald Chu

Crisis in Teaching: Perspectives on Current Reforms—Lois Weis, Philip G. Altbach, Gail P. Kelly, Hugh G. Petrie, and Sheila Slaughter (eds.)

The High Status Track: Studies of Elite Schools and Stratification—Paul William Kingston and Lionel S. Lewis (eds.)

The Economics of American Universities: Management, Operations, and Fiscal Environment—Stephen A. Hoenack and Eileen L. Collins (eds.)

The Higher Learning and High Technology: Dynamics of Higher Education and Policy Formation—Sheila Slaughter

Dropouts from Schools: Issues, Dilemmas and Solutions—Lois Weis, Eleanor Farrar, and Hugh G. Petrie (eds.)

Religious Fundamentalism and American Education: The Battle for the Public Schools—Eugene F. Provenzo, Jr.

Going to School: The African-American Experience—Kofi Lomotey (ed.)

Curriculum Differentiation: Interpretive Studies in U.S. Secondary Schools—Reba Page and Linda Valli (eds.)

The Racial Crisis in American Higher Education—Philip G. Altbach and Kofi Lomotey (eds.)

The Great Transformation in Higher Education, 1960–1980—Clark Kerr

College in Black and White: African-American Students in Predominantly White and in Historically Black Public Universities—Walter R. Allen, Edgar G. Epps, and Nesha Z. Haniff (eds.)

Textbooks in American Society: Politics, Policy, and Pedagogy—Philip G. Altbach, Gail P. Kelly, Hugh G. Petrie, and Lois Weis (eds.)

Critical Perspectives on Early Childhood Education—Lois Weis, Philip G. Altbach, Gail P. Kelly, and Hugh G. Petrie (eds.)

Black Resistance in High School: Forging a Separatist Culture—R. Patrick Solomon

Emergent Issues in Education: Comparative Perspectives—Robert F. Arnove, Philip G. Altbach, and Gail P. Kelly (eds.)

Creating Community on College Campuses—Irving J. Spitzberg and Virginia V. Thorndike

Teacher Education Policy: Narratives, Stories, and Cases—Hendrick D. Gideonse (ed.)

Beyond Silenced Voices: Class, Race, and Gender in United States Schools—Lois Weis and Michelle Fine (eds.)

Troubled Times for American Higher Education: The 1990s and Beyond—Clark Kerr (ed.)

Higher Education Cannot Escape History: Issues for the Twenty-first Century—Clark Kerr (ed.)

The Cold War and Academic Governance: The Lattimore Case at Johns Hopkins—Lionel S. Lewis (ed.)

Multiculturalism and Education: Diversity and Its Impact on Schools and Society—Thomas J. LaBelle and Christopher R. Ward (eds.)

The Contradictory College: The Conflicting Origins, Impacts, and Futures of the Community College—Kevin J. Dougherty (ed.)

Race and Educational Reform in the American Metropolis: A Study of School Decentralization—Dan A. Lewis (ed.)

Professionalization, Partnership, and Power: Building Professional Development Schools—Hugh Petrie (ed.)

Ethnic Studies and Multiculturalism—Thomas J. LaBelle and Christopher R. Ward

Promotion and Tenure: Community and Socialization in Academe—William G. Tierney and Estela Mara Bensimon (eds.)

Sailing Against the Wind: African Americans and Women in U.S. Education—Kofi Lomotey (ed.)

The Challenge of Eastern Asian Education: Implications for America—William K. Cummings and Philip G. Altbach (eds.)

Please remember that this is a library book, and that it belongs only temporarily to each person who uses it. Be considerate. Do not write in this, or any, library book.

Date Due

17 Apr '00			
AG 20 '00			
AG 28 '01			
AP 8 '03			
AP 8 '04			
OC 23 '04			
APR 0 8 2009			